Crem.
2o-23, 93,
178-93, 179, 191
32, 41, 49-50
124, 5, 15

FUNERALS

D0696821

Also by Tony Walter

Basic Income: Freedom From Poverty, Freedom to Work (London: Marion Boyars, 1988)

All You Love is Need (London: SPCK, 1985)

Hope on the Dole (London: SPCK, 1985)

Fair Shares: An Ethical Guide to Tax and Social Security Reform (Edinburgh: Handsel, 1985)

The Human Home: The Myth of the Sacred Environment (Tring: Lion Publishing, 1982)

A Long Way From Home: A Sociological Exploration of Contemporary Idolatry (Exeter: Paternoster Press, 1979)

Sent Away: A Study of Young Offenders in Care (Aldershot: Gower, 1978)

Other C. S. Lewis Centre Books (all published by Hodder & Stoughton)

William Abraham, *The Logic of Evangelism*

Geoffrey Ahern and Grace Davie, *Inner City God*

Michael Christensen, *C. S. Lewis on Scripture*

Basil Mitchell, *How to Play Theological Ping Pong*

Andrew Walker (ed.), *Different Gospels*

Andrew Walker, *Enemy Territory*

Andrew Walker and James Patrick (eds), *A Christian for All Christians: Essays in Honour of C. S. Lewis*

FUNERALS

And How to Improve Them

Tony Walter

Hodder & Stoughton

LONDON SYDNEY AUCKLAND

British Library Cataloguing in Publication Data
Walter, J. A. (Julian Anthony) *1948–*
   Funerals and how to improve them.
   1. Death customs
   I. Title
   393
   ISBN 0-340-53125-8

First published in Great Britain 1990
Third impression 1994

Published by Hodder and Stoughton
a division of Hodder and Stoughton Ltd,
Mill Road, Dunton Green, Sevenoaks, Kent TN13 2YA
Editorial Office: 47 Bedford Square, London, WC1B 3DP
Photoset by Hewer Text Composition Services, Edinburgh
Printed and bound in Great Britain by Cox & Wyman Ltd, Reading, Berks.

For Felix and Rosalind:
the living and the dead

Acknowledgements

Grateful acknowledgement is made to the Ewan McColl Estate for permission to reproduce 'The Joy of Living', from the album *Items of News* (Blackthorne BR 1067).

Cartoons reproduced by permission of *Punch*.

Cover concept: Kathy Keay.

FOREWORD

To the rational man funerals are illogical. They will not do the dead any good and will only upset the living. It is best to get them over with as quickly as possible with no music, no flowers, no fuss and no tears.

How often do people who know themselves to be dying misguidedly seek to protect their loved ones from grief by requesting a simple funeral for family only? How often do those who have rejected God along with Santa Claus ask to be spared 'religious clap-trap'? How often does the hygienic generation choose sanitised cremation in preference to the organic resonances of burial in the earth?

Fortunately for us, 'The heart has its reasons which reason knows nothing of' (Pascal, *Pensées* IV.277) and the funeral persists in defiance of all reason. In fact many people who have rejected other forms of religious observance and who would probably disagree with many of the ideas embodied in the funeral service insist on going to funerals and find them deeply moving.

The rites of passage which attend bereavement have a remarkable vitality and there is no society known to anthropologists which has abandoned them altogether. The Maoris of New Zealand, for instance, tactfully adopted the forms of worship of the white settlers, but they retained the 'pagan' ritual of the Tangi, laying out the body in their meeting house where family and friends will stay and cry and laugh and mourn and chant extempore prayers or poems to the dead for three days and two nights, until they have had enough. Only then are the dead buried with a Christian funeral in a Christian cemetery fenced with posts depicting pagan gods.

So what is a funeral for? What strange atavisms force us all to preserve traditions that make so little sense? Are these traditions fixed for all time or can they change, and if they can change, should they? Is it time for the 'pop' funeral, the 'do-it-yourself' funeral, the humanist funeral? What should we preserve and what toss onto the scrap-heap of archaic customs?

In this book Tony Walter, a sociologist and a Christian, attempts to answer these questions. In doing so he helps us to think clearly about a very confusing topic. He is not concerned to proselytise or to recommend a particular form of worship, but by examining the nature and purposes of the funeral he sets us free to choose whether to follow established traditions or to do something different.

More important is the light which this book throws on the nature of the society in which we live, on the stultifying repression of emotion, on the dangers of professionalising 'care' to the point where community is lost, on the devaluation of the old and idealisation of the new and on the automation of ritual to the point where it becomes meaningless.

But Tony Walter is no prophet of doom. He also recognises that a reaction is setting in. This is to be found in various settings, the hospices, the women's movement, the gay community, and in some branches of the church. The funeral is a dramatic symbol of the fact that, despite all the advances of modern science, 100% of people still die. It gives us an opportunity to make real this simple fact and to respond emotionally and by our behaviour to the life and death of another person; it helps to initiate the process of grieving; it reminds us that, both as individuals and as members of the social units to which they belong, people matter; it brings home the thought that we too are mortal and causes us to question a thousand habits of thought and behaviour which deny that fact; it also opens up the possibility that by facing our own limitations we may transcend them.

For the essential message of the funeral is that in every ending there is a beginning. However we choose to conceive this idea, whether in terms of orthodox or unorthodox religious faith or even in that angry protest that is another kind of faith, the funeral gives us hope.

Colin Murray Parkes
Senior Lecturer in Psychiatry
The London Hospital Medical College
Chairman, Cruse-Bereavement Care

Contents

List of Tables and Figures

Fifteen Modern Heresies

Like many heresies, some of the following are half-truths –
taking a bit of the truth and promoting it into the only truth,
with disastrous consequences.

1 You should not cry at a funeral.
2 The purpose of the funeral is to help the grief process.
3 The 'stiff upper lip' is silly, old-fashioned, and psychologically harmful.
4 The aim of the funeral is to comfort the bereaved.
5 The main problem with funerals is that they cost too much.
6 Little or nothing can be done about funerals.
7 The funeral exists for the sake of the next of kin.
8 To be penny-pinching about the funeral is to show disrespect to the dead.
9 Never speak ill of the dead.
10 The main reasons for cremation are hygiene and lack of space for burial.
11 Death is the greatest taboo of the twentieth century.
12 Doing without an undertaker or a priest is impossible and undesirable.
13 Ritual is old-fashioned and hypocritical.
14 Victorian rituals helped people mourn effectively.
15 If only we went back to the good old days, funerals would be much better.

If you believe any of these heresies, read this book!

AUTHOR'S PREFACE

A few years ago, at the grand old age of ninety, my father died. Wanting to do something useful, and possibly also to save us the bother of arranging a funeral, he donated his body to the local medical school. He didn't want any fuss at his passing. We, however, wanted publicly to mark the passing of a life which we had cherished, so we arranged a memorial service, to which an encouraging number of people came.

This got me thinking about funerals. Is it that the funeral is not for the dead but for the living, and therefore the living are more concerned about it than was the one who has just died? Or is there a change in attitude between the generations – between an earlier generation's desire to avoid any fuss and a younger generation's desire to express feelings more? Are attitudes to death changing?

I began to read, and noticed that death has been proclaimed so many times over the past thirty-five years as the taboo of the twentieth century that it could be no ordinary taboo – if indeed it is one at all. At dinner parties, fellow guests were intrigued to find out I was thinking of writing a book on the subject, and would spend the entire meal recounting heartily, comically, and sensitively the funerals they had been to. Strange behaviour for a subject that is taboo!

I looked too on the shelves of the bookshops. There are plenty of books on bereavement and bereavement counselling, on hospices and dying, but not a single one on funerals. Death is being revolutionised – but only in the private grief of the mourner, in the privacy of bereavement counselling, around the hospice bed. Somehow the *public* ritual of the funeral has got left out of the revolution, or certainly left out of the torrent of writing. And as I went to funerals, it indeed seemed as though they had got stuck in a time warp, even as care of the dying and attitudes to bereavement are moving on.

Yet I was heartened by the experience of dad's memorial service. The eulogy – by a black African friend who is an adopted brother in our family – enabled the congregation to focus their memories. He highlighted our ongoing community one with another, rejecting the common idea that the basic unit of existence is the individual. The all-white Cotswold congregation found this comforting, even though the address was based on an African psychology, very different from individualistic Western psychology. This made me wonder: Is modern Western psychology actually up to the job of laying a basis for the modern funeral? Clearly, if I was to get to the heart of what funerals are about, I would have to read anthropology and history, theology and literature, as well as psychology.

We had been exercised also by one other aspect of the memorial service. My father was quite clear about having no religious faith, yet within his family there is a complete spectrum of belief, half-belief, and non-belief. How were we all to commemorate my father's life with integrity? Can a religious person organise a secular funeral? Can a secular person, with integrity, be given a religious send-off? How do you respect the departed, yet comfort the living?

It was with such questions that I set out to research this book. I talked with friends, with bereaved people, with clergy, with funeral directors; I visited crematoria, funeral parlours, and hospices. Whenever I was abroad I would ask my surprised hosts about local funeral customs, and they would unfailingly go out of their way to help. Death and funerals actually helped me understand the various cultures I visited; not only did this enhance my enjoyment as a tourist, but it also confirmed that, far from being obsessed with an oddball subject, I was on to something near the very heart of what it is to be human.

Other sources of information arrived unbidden. Too many of my own friends and neighbours have died over the past three years; too many major disasters have dominated the headlines. This is the only book I have written where, on occasion, tears have trickled down my face as I typed out the text on the word processor.

I soon discovered there are no easy answers. Death is a riddle which neither science nor religious faith resolves. Science helps us explore the riddle, religious faith gives us courage and hope in the face of it. If there is anything wrong with the modern funeral – and I believe there is much wrong – we cannot place the blame on clergy or funeral directors, who generally are conscientious people working in a difficult situation. You do not resolve the mystery of death by finding a cheaper funeral director – though you may get nearer the heart of things by dispensing with one altogether.

I found funerals that did succeed in marking the passing of a loved human being with great integrity. But when those attending are few in number, knowledge of such satisfying funerals is not spread easily or quickly. I therefore decided that one aim of this book must be to spread the good news that is not being spread by word of mouth.

In my search, old familiar themes from my earlier books reappeared time and again: people's almost religious worship of the family and of personal relationships; the relation of humankind to the natural world (including our own, all too mortal, bodies); and the unexpected discovery of hope among the very people pitied or despised by respectable society.

I have written this book for a wide readership. This has meant resisting the temptation to include footnotes or to mention every possible academic criticism of my position; for those who want to read further, or to trace my sources, I have included an appendix on further reading. (Index references to this appendix are in italics.)

I am a practising member of the Church of England who believes that the task of the church is to serve all who live and die locally – not least those who only half believe. But I am also a sociologist who knows that ours is a society that is thoroughly modern, diverse, and in many ways secular. Though most funerals in the United Kingdom are conducted by clergy of the established church, there are half as many practising Muslims as there are members of the Anglican church; active Anglicans are outnumbered by active Roman Catholics; and many, many more people belong to no religion at all. Though a majority of the population still believes in God, active church members are outnumbered by those who do not believe in God at all.

I write as one who deeply respects – and enjoys – the views of his many friends who have either different religious beliefs or none at all; a respect never more deep than when those friends are confronting death. Too many Christians try to preach to the bereaved, thereby losing all integrity, while many more have themselves become secular in their attitude to death. In this book I seek both to hold to what I believe and to say much that will be of value even within world-views I do not share – precisely what anyone who conducts a funeral has to do. This may offend some Christian readers, but our calling to articulate with and for the dying and bereaved their half-hopes and half-beliefs does not entitle us to force on to them our own faith.

For those not inducted into the mysteries of modern death-speak, a note about terminology. Over time, the term *undertaker* is giving way to *funeral director*. Where the context is modern, urban and formal, I use the modern term; where it is rural, colloquial, or pre-twentieth century, I use the older one. *Crematory* is North American for *crematorium*, the building in which cremation takes place (although the buildings are very different on the two continents); the actual furnace is called a *cremator*, of which there are usually several in a crematorium. A *columbarium* is a set of niches for storing ashes.

To name all those who have gone out of their way to help me with information and ideas would not be practical, for you are many. I can only say, to all of you, whether in Holland or Belgium, Australia or Zimbabwe, Hong Kong or Thailand, the United States or the United Kingdom, thank you. Thank you to funeral directors, crematoria managers, hospice workers and others who have taken time to show me around; thank you to academics who have stimulated me and pointed me in the direction of some fascinating literature; and most of all, thank you to those individuals who have allowed me to write about the funerals of those you loved. And my apologies to those – few I hope – who have endured my rambling on when you have yourself, unbeknown to me, been hurting from your own bereavement.

Thank you also to the C. S. Lewis Centre, under whose auspices this book is published. The Centre, devoted to exploring the relationship between religion and the modern world, has wisely identified death and bereavement as a key area where personal faith and our technocratic, bureaucratic world meet – often with considerable friction.

One person must be named. Over the past three years I have worked closely with Ted Nash – discussing personal experiences, the disabling architecture of crematoria, society's values, and much else. Though we have not, as originally planned, literally written this book together, it has been very much a joint endeavour. There is a physicality about a rotting corpse, a spatiality about a funeral procession, that forces space and place into the discussion – and that makes working with an architect like Ted an essential complement for a sociologist like myself. Our two perspectives have bounced off one another, within a shared personal understanding of the Christian faith in a multicultural society.

Bath, March 1990

PART ONE

INTRODUCTION

1

THE FINAL CHECK-OUT

Church of England funerals are about as moving as the check-out at a supermarket.

Ken Livingstone MP, 1988

It's striking how little you have to do for people to thank you profusely—standards are so low they expect the funeral to be done badly.

Anglican vicar, 1989

Funerals today are far too often impersonal, hypocritical, and bureaucratic, replacing mystery with mistrust. The plastic surroundings of the crematorium or the decaying Gothic of the cemetery, the mumbo-jumbo of the officiating cleric, the endless forms to be filled in, the coffin's mock veneer and plastic handles, the suspicion about where the coffin goes as it slides behind the curtains, or where your money goes as you pay the funeral director for apparently so very little, all this speaks of a lack of integrity. Things are done to both the living and the dead by strangers, in strange places. The form-filling, the religious ritual, the anxious watching of the clock as you get lost driving around a strange town while trying to find the crematorium, the entertaining of awkward relatives from the other end of the country, the bonhomie of the post-funeral meal, nothing hangs together.

The funeral is the final statement about a person. Within a century, we have swung from showy funerals that went way over the top in displaying social status, to plastic funerals that say nothing, that say the person was nothing. No wonder some people would rather do without a funeral altogether. No wonder the funeral has become an ordeal to be endured.

And yet some funerals are not like this. Some mark the passing of a human life with sorrow but also with integrity. Some offer a chance to say goodbye. Some manage to say what is unsayable. These funerals mingle sorrow with joy, perplexity with faith, unique pain with support from friends. They create sharing where before there had been isolation, bring into focus what before had been blurred, resurrect feeling where before had been numbness. They allow anger to be expressed safely, they enable mutual forgiveness where before there had been resentment, they dramatise what before had been inner perplexity. These funerals mark the death that has happened, yet give hope for the future.

A funeral provides an opportunity publicly to mark the passing of a human life. All too often we waste this opportunity; and yet some funerals *are* being reclaimed. This book explains how this is coming about; and it shows how we can make it come about.

Personality and profit

A retired vicar told me what happened once when he was on duty at the public crematorium. After one of the services, he politely asked the widow, 'Did he suffer?' to which he received the dazed answer, 'Don't know – he put his head in the oven.' Nor was it until the handshaking which followed one of the day's twenty other services that he discovered that the adult-sized coffin he had just committed to the flames contained a twelve year old girl.

Ignorance of even the most basic aspects of a person's life and death is hopefully less common in the early 1990s. But how is it that a society that believes in the ultimate value of the individual could ever dispatch human beings with such anonymity? How did the English funeral ever come to be like the check-out at a supermarket?

An agnostic told me he was satisfied with neither religious nor secular funerals. He had been to a secular funeral where the speaker was obviously ill-informed about the deceased and the language lacked the dignity of the 1662 Prayer Book. He actually preferred the next funeral he went to, a Catholic one, which at least signified that something important had happened. His wife chipped in, saying how chilly she feels de-ritualised Anglican and Nonconformist funerals are – if you cannot accept the theology, there's nothing left. For this couple, the best funeral they had been to was a Quaker one.

Sheer municipality dominates the British funeral. Cremating and burying three thousand citizens a year on an ungenerous local authority budget does require a slick and efficient operation, but it also imposes severe bureaucratic rationality at the most emotional time of your life. If you really try, you can get through life without paper, but it is almost impossible to get through death without multiple form-filling. The helpful Consumers' Association booklet *What To Do When Someone Dies* accurately documents this: the booklet is all about the medical and bureaucratic procedures that the next of kin must go through, with little or nothing about emotional, spiritual or social needs. As one funeral director said to me sadly, 'All the sentiment has gone out of funerals these days.'

The crematorium building itself rarely has the 'spirit of place' of the old parish church, nor is it a significant community building like the town hall. It burns bodies, but pretends not to; hypocrisy is built into the place. You hardly feel you are approaching the resting place of the ancestors as you drive through the parkland towards a building that could be a library, could be a school, could be a factory, but is none of these.

Then there is the problem of mystery turning into mistrust. Do they reuse the coffin, and just burn the body? How do you know the ashes have not got mixed up? What on earth does the undertaker spend all your money on? Despite official inquiries which generally justify funeral directors' costs, despite crematoria frequently inviting local groups to tour backstage, the mistrust continues. Despite hygienic crematoria being originally introduced to replace literally stinking Victorian graveyards, neighbours today are more upset by the smoke from the nearby crematorium than they are by the graves of a nearby cemetery. Instead, a nearby cemetery is likely to add value to a house, guaranteeing eternal suburban greenery!

It is as though we have tried to replace religious mystery with scientific hygiene, and missed the point. To all human beings, a corpse is a perplexing, repulsive object, neither with us nor gone, neither here nor there, with human form yet no longer human. Religious mystery and ritual once provided a framework to help us face this and protect us from danger. Now instead we pay professionals to handle our corpses, yet resent paying them to do what we no longer know how to do. And when the corpse enters the crematorium, the ritual of the modern funeral director fails to protect us; the stainless steel trolley with its rubber wheels, upon which the coffin glides, does not defend us from this most terrifying of objects.

Periodically, attempts are made to reform the funeral business. The reformers usually want cheaper funerals – yet the cost of a funeral is not high, compared with former times and compared with other places. Take a trip to the Egyptian pyramids or to the Taj Mahal, or even to an ancient British long barrow, and you will be amazed at how much some ancient cultures spent on some of their dead. In many countries plagued by poverty even today, the funeral is the most elaborate part of a person's life.

If we want no fuss, if we want a funeral that is not painful and is over and done with as quickly as possible, yet afterwards feel vaguely dissatisfied that it was all rather plastic and unreal; if we pay the funeral director to do things for us that we could have done ourselves, and then feel it is cold and impersonal – do we really have anyone to blame but ourselves? The truth is, we are not prepared to think about it.

But where people have thought it through, things have changed rapidly. In Melbourne, Australia, the past ten years have seen a meteoric rise in the number of funerals conducted in a highly personal way by non-religious celebrants; and the competition is keeping religious funerals up to the mark. In some English parishes vicars have decided to reuse old churchyards – this digging up of old bones, far from creating an uproar, is quickly accepted by local people who appreciate having an alternative to the regimented municipal cemetery or to the crematorium in an alien town. The gay community in London has recently developed a new tradition in which the dead person writes his own funeral and goes out not with a whimper, but with a bang. In many towns now, someone who dies with no obvious religious faith (nor obvious lack of it) will not be dispatched by the duty cleric at the crem, but by the local vicar, who will visit the family beforehand and is able to put them in touch with befrienders afterwards if they so desire.

Everyone I have talked to who has been to half a dozen funerals or more has described at least one funeral which really worked, alongside the others that were dire. It is a myth that funerals cannot be improved, save by making them cheaper. But it is true that people, especially perhaps modern people, can choose not to see beyond their own myths.

Uncle Andrew

Within the space of a year Kathryn lost her father and brother. She can hardly bear to remember their funerals in the crematorium. Each time, as the doors closed so finally behind the coffin, she broke down uncontrollably, yet had to compose herself quickly for the immediately following session of handshaking with unknown relatives. Each time, she was hurt that people – even her own closest friends – assumed she was not suffering the loss as much as was her mother, to whom they directed their condolences.

Ten months later Uncle Andrew died. Years ago he had raised Kathryn's orphaned mother, so he was like a grandfather to Kathryn. He lived and died in a Scottish fishing village, and was given a Fife fisherman's funeral. On a sunny winter's day, with the snow thick on the ground, he was driven from his own home through the familiar streets, along the seafront, to the graveyard. Six relatives, including Kathryn and her frail mother, were given cords to lower the coffin into the ground: as the minister proclaimed in his beautiful Scots voice, 'I am the resurrection and the life . . .', they felt the weight in every muscle and sinew. Sad, tearful . . . but not unbearable.

What made Uncle Andrew's funeral so different? Four things, all of which are significant . . . each of which is a recurring theme in this book.

1. The central fact that the women had come to take their leave of a heavy, dead body was not hidden. Our technological civilisation, based on mastery of nature, is bad at facing up to nature having the last laugh on us: at the end, our bodies wear out and rot, and nothing science can do can stop that. So many funerals gloss over the physical deadness of the corpse. And women, perhaps more in tune with their physical bodies, are usually excluded by 'rational' men from active participation in the funeral: their physicality, their emotionality, could be too dangerous.

2. The desperate isolation of loss was mitigated by the knowledge that it was shared by the village community: the family were not alone in their grief. Our civilisation, glorifying the individual, has paid the price of isolating the individual. At no time is that isolation felt more than when a person confronts the chaos of death; at no time are we more in need of the knowledge that we are not alone as we face the unfaceable.

3. The family and community actively participated in the ritual. They did not pay the undertaker to do everything and then wonder why it was all so cold and impersonal.

4. Religious hope and faith were not only present in that Fife graveyard, they were affirmed by the surroundings. Our

civilisation, though, has become more and more secular: what sign of faith is there as we sign the forms at the registrar's, as we are interviewed in the new corporate-image office of the funeral director, as we battle through the traffic to get to the local authority crematorium?

Modern civilisation is usually pretty bad when it comes to these four things. It is not that modern civilisation makes death impossible to handle, whereas traditional societies have handled it well. Human societies have *never* handled death well. Death shatters our faith, whatever it be. It undermines our faith in a loving God; it shatters our dreams as we ponder the contents of the coffin – the dead child, the dead brother, the dead partner, the dead parent. It shatters our illusions of health, of safety, of self-fulfilment, of happiness. The challenge of death has to be met with faith, whether faith in God, faith in the modern family, or faith that good old English stoicism will see us through. It is never easy.

But modernity makes things more difficult with its naive faith in all-conquering macho technology, its isolating faith in the individual, its harsh faith in secularism. And these three aspects – the technical, the emotional, and the spiritual – no longer seem to tie up.

In the Fife funeral the movement from life to death, from being with Uncle Andrew to being without him, was expressed in physical movement – along the sea front, into the graveyard, lowering the cords, throwing in handfuls of earth. This kind of symbolic movement is lost in the modern traffic jam or motorway dash to the crematorium; once there, the mourners are reduced to passive spectators (though there is nothing to see).

How can the physical plant of the modern crematorium or cemetery be rescued to meet the emotional and spiritual needs of the modern mourner? How can they proclaim the significance of our mortal human life to the passer-by, as did the churchyard of old? Can a crematorium become a hallowed resting place for the community's ancestors?

As well as raising the deepest spiritual questions, the funeral has a physical task to perform: to dispose of a corpse. This is why I have devoted a whole section, Part Four, to the places in which funerals take place and to some of the issues raised by the physical task of the funeral.

Each chapter is self-contained, so this author for one will not be offended if you omit what you are not interested in, and read what you want, in whatever order you like. Some chapters will be of particular interest to the ordinary person who may one day have to arrange a funeral. Other chapters will be of more interest to the reader who actually has to conduct funerals.

This is not a comfortable book. I offer no convenient scapegoat for the pathetic non-event that is so often the modern funeral. I point to ourselves, our own attitudes, and our own modern culture from which there is no escape.

And yet it is a book of hope.

Richard died in his fifties, within a month of being diagnosed as having cancer. Living on the outskirts of London, he was not part of a community with age-old funeral traditions to draw on, yet his funeral involved much of the realism, sharing, and participation of Uncle Andrew's.

Richard had been involved in many local groups; most notably, he was a leading and colourful figure in the local morris dance group, and he had been Assistant District Commissioner for Cub Scouts. His body was piped into church by a friend playing the bagpipes; on his coffin was his morris hat, which many found the most moving aspect of the whole funeral – there was no mistaking who was in the coffin. Nor was there a dry eye as the congregation sang the hymn:

> Dance, then, wherever you may be;
> I am the Lord of the Dance, said he,
> and I'll lead you all, wherever you may be,
> and I'll lead you all in the dance, said he.

Then a group of morris men danced in the aisle – a celebration of life, yet a poignant reminder that Richard was no longer able to dance with them. A scout leader read one of the lessons – acknowledging that they too had lost a valued colleague. In his address the vicar spoke with personal knowledge of Richard's life, without once looking at his notes.

This is a book of hope because there are many, many funerals like Richard's happening today. A secular funeral held in a friend's house; a crematorium funeral for an unloved old lady; a burial for a stillbirth – this book is full of late twentieth-century ceremonies where thoroughly modern people imaginatively use elements old and new to create funerals that mark positively the passing of a human life, even in a society that no longer believes in God and which may not even believe in humanity.

Not only can funerals be different, but the time is ripe for change. Maybe the modern era is waning. Maybe we are moving out of modernity into what some observers of late twentieth-century life call post-modernity. The green movement and the women's movement are pointing us towards a more realistic view of nature; many are searching for community and wholeness; and despite the predictions of over twenty years ago, religion is far from dying out. The way these trends are already shaping new forms of funeral may be seen in the wholly new phenomenon of funerals for stillborn infants, in the gay community, and in the hospice movement: atheists and Christians, parents and clergy, are inventing new ways of marking death. Yes, funerals are too often bad – but they can be different, and they will be different.

I have written this book for the general public – for those who have been to a funeral and felt less than satisfied; for those who would like to do things better next time they are themselves responsible for arranging a funeral, but do not know how to think about the issues. I hope too that those professionally involved in the funeral business – clergy, funeral directors, local authority staff, and crematoria and cemetery managers – will not look askance at a book by a mere sociologist and attender of funerals.

Ultimately this book is for the 'consumer', for funerals will never improve until the general public think about what they want – and think about it long before they actually have to arrange a funeral. Blaming the professionals simply absolves the public of any responsibility and perpetuates the problem. In my experience, the professional providers of funerals generally do their best for a public that offers them little interest or support – just think of how few votes there are for a local authority that decides to upgrade its crematorium or cemeteries at the expense of services for the living.

Funerals will improve only when ordinary people ask for something better, and know what to ask for. That is why I have written this book.

2

DEATH AND NATIONAL CHARACTER

Masai tribesmen leave their dead out for the hyenas to eat. Parsees leave theirs in towers for the vultures to pick at. Hindus burn their dead on open pyres. The British too burn most of their dead, but indoors – maybe because of the rain? Like many other Europeans, the British used to leave their dead three feet under the flagstones where they stood to sing psalms every Sunday morning, but then the smell got too bad. North Americans like to embalm their corpses and then bury them in everlasting lawn cemeteries. Belgians bury theirs, but dig them up after a few years so they can use the grave again. Neapolitans store their corpses in lockers, and take them out every now and then to see how they are doing. The Jivaros of the Eastern Andes bury their women and children under the floorboards of the family hut, but males they place in a sitting position and then set fire to both corpse and hut. Some hunter-gatherer tribes just leave their dead behind, up camp, and move on. Elsewhere they eat parts of their corpses and are then sick; or place them in caves, as they did Lazarus and Jesus; or weight them and sink them in the river.

It's not just what people do to the dead that is so astonishingly varied, it's also what mourners do with and to themselves. The English, along with the Mescalero Apaches of North America, may refuse to talk of the dead. The Irish get drunk, talk endlessly, and become maudlin. Some Australian aboriginals used to lacerate themselves, so much so that occasionally another of the living joined the dead. Orthodox Jews do not go that far, but tear a piece of their clothing – and they talk too, for seven days, sitting on wooden stools.

In our Coca-Cola world, where national and ethnic differences are withering in the face of a neo-American consumer culture that is extending its tentacles even into remotest Africa and into the strongest bastions of communism, you might expect funerals, like everything else, to look more and more alike. But you would be wrong. You will find Coca-Cola cans in the African bush, but you will not find American-style funerals there. Nor will you in communist countries. Nor in Britain, or any other European country.

The stoical English

In England, where the ideal of cosy suburban family life reigns, people are devastated when their father, or wife, or child dies. But England is also the land of emotional privacy, of the stiff upper lip, so the funeral becomes a public stage on which to show you can stay under control, a heroic attempt to keep up your cherished English reserve at the very moment it is most threatened. 'Didn't she do well?' people say afterwards.

Elaborate mourning rituals, Baroque and Gothic memorials, may have been *de rigueur* in Victorian days, but nowadays we just try to keep going as though nothing had happened. Those expected not to be able to control their emotions, children and sometimes women, may not be allowed near the funeral at all.

You don't have to go far, though, to see emotional funerals. In Belfast, or in cities like Liverpool that are influenced by Irish immigrants, there is much talking, crying, laughing. There is not the English need to keep the proceedings as short as possible lest the family crack – processions, requiem masses, wakes, rituals abound.

Throughout Britain graveyards are run according to rules to keep them neat and tidy – especially in an era of conservation, we do so like other people's headstones to be of the right material, the lettering to be in good taste. But this can run headlong into intense family love, into my desire to commemorate my husband or my child in my way. I put flowers on mum's grave, and then get told to move them. No such problem in Italy, where every tomb, grave or niche for the ashes is turned into a family altar.

The British like to think of themselves as pragmatic and

realistic, but we are neither when it comes to funerals. We stick to a sombre dignity that denies both true joy and real sorrow, and is a leftover from the Victorian funeral. We are squeamish about reusing graves, unlike those practical Europeans who dig up the bones and start again. Though we like to think we pioneered cremation in a big way as a practical response to lack of land for burial, we actually went for cremation because we were squeamish about digging up bones.

It is widely believed that cremation 'saves land for the living', land that would otherwise be used by graves.

Multiple stacking of coffins in insanitary urban churchyards led to Victorians demanding individual, out-of-town graves
(From the collection of Prof. James Stevens Curl)

The great increase in the number of graves in England came in the mid-nineteenth century when there was both an unprecedented increase in deaths (which has hardly been surpassed even today) and an unprecedented number of people wanting perpetual and individual graves.

The first official cremation (1885) was performed as England was nearing its peak of 550,000 burials per year (1890s); 500,000 burials had materialised by the 1870s. If there was a land shortage, however, it was lived with for another seventy years, as it was not until the 1940s that cremation began significantly to reduce the number of burials (Figure 1). This suggests that any shortage of land was *cumulative*, due to the English penchant for perpetual graves rather than to the absolute number of burials.

Figure 1
Burials and Cremations in England and Wales,
1720–1989

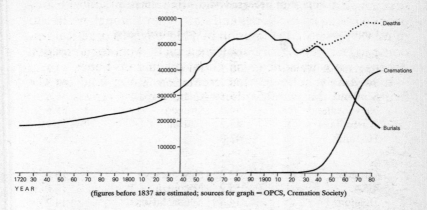

(figures before 1837 are estimated; sources for graph = OPCS, Cremation Society)

If land became scarce after only seventy years of burying 500,000 people a year in individual graves, it is clear that reusing graves on a ten to twenty year cycle (as in much of Europe) would be perfectly adequate to dispose of all the corpses produced in England in this century and the next.

Even with a population ten times bigger, no more people were buried in 1989 than were in 1700.

The real reason for cremation is not an absolute shortage of land, but has to do with values and people's perceptions. Canada – one of the sparsest populated countries – cremates more than crowded Belgium, and Australia more than Holland (Table 1).

Nor does a head-start always help: Italy pioneered cremation in the late nineteenth century, but cremation there still symbolises secularism, and this predominantly Catholic country – along with the Irish Republic – is today at the bottom of the cremation league.

In the United States the 15.2 per cent overall figure covers a wide variety. The West Coast states compare with Protestant European levels; New England and the upper Midwest steel belt are at the average for the country; while in the Deep South cremation is virtually unknown. Again, availability of land explains very little.

Table 1
Cremation: National Comparisons

Percentage of deceased who were cremated, 1986/7

Countries		The United States	
Japan	95.7	Nevada	55.8
England & Wales	70.5	Hawaii	49.2
Sweden	58.7	Washington	40.8
Scotland	55.6	California	36.6
New Zealand	54.3	Oregon	35.6
Australia	48.6	Florida	31.2
Holland	42.0		
Canada	27.3	New Jersey	18.8
USA	15.2	Michigan	15.0
Belgium	14.4	Massachusetts	14.7
Finland	13.3	Illinois	11.5
Spain	10.5		
France	3.7	Tennessee	2.5
Eire	1.5	West Virginia	2.3
Italy	0.6	Alabama	1.9

(The figures are grouped thus: the top group represents more than thirty per cent; the middle group between ten and thirty per cent; the bottom group less than ten per cent)

Almost all British funerals are religious, even though less than one person in five is an active member of any religious faith. Some of us want a religious funeral as an insurance policy, others like the Shakespearean language, others find it all a bit hypocritical but don't know what else to do. The established church seems to have a monopoly on funerals for the non-churchgoer (even though more Catholics than Anglicans go to church each week).

In Holland, though, there has long been a tradition of giving equal rights to every religion, a right which extends also to humanism. So, many funerals are performed without any religious ceremony. In Australia there is automatic respect neither for clergy (who along with police, politicians and all other authority figures have to prove themselves before being accepted), nor for the obscure language of Shakespeare; the clergy's monopoly on funerals collapsed like a pack of cards once an alternative became available.

The American way of death

Meanwhile, the United States of America is a case on its own. In this society of immigrants, no one has really arrived until they have achieved material success. The funeral, the final statement about a person's life, must demonstrate that this citizen has been successful – much as it did in Victorian Britain. This means that an American funeral should be as expensive as possible, without going over the top and claiming you were someone you clearly were not. It means that the wake – viewing the embalmed and made-up body displayed in a splendidly lined casket – is all important. Once the casket is closed and the splendour of its contents no longer on show, public interest wanes; fewer people come to the funeral service than to the wake; and only close family to the actual interment.

Jessica Mitford's exposé in 1963 of *The American Way of Death* supposes that the expense is all engineered by the funeral trade. She misses the point that Americans have showy funerals because many of them want showy funerals. Those who have taken her thesis to their hearts and abandoned the expensive American funeral are typically Americans of a third, fourth or later generation who no longer have anything to prove, or who have retired thousands of miles away to Florida or California and no longer have anyone to prove it to. Such people are more likely to go for direct disposal – cheap cremation without a ceremony.

Direct disposal is on the increase because there are more and more Americans whose families have been in the country for several generations. Cremation has risen steadily from four per cent in 1970 to fifteen per cent in the late 1980s, and in parts of the West Coast it now accounts for half of all disposals. Meanwhile, in the Midwest and Deep South millions of Americans still have never known a friend or relative cremated (Figure 2; Table 1).

Figure 2
The Increase of Cremation,
Great Britain and the United States, 1885–1989

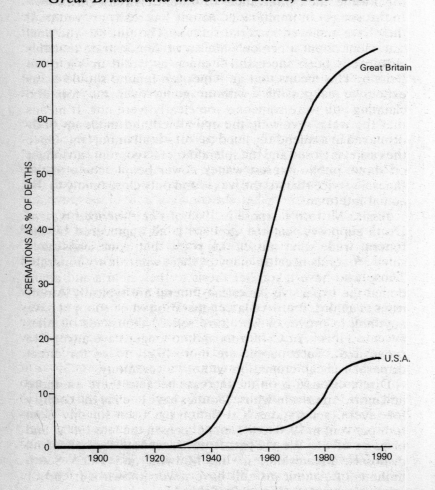

But Mitford is right in her assertion that the American funeral trade (like all American business) is driven by profit, in a manner that the British trade finds distasteful. She is right when she says that the American funeral trade has pushed for legislation to ensure their profits remain high. By the time she wrote, the trade had notched up several notable successes. In some states it had forced through legislation that families have to pay a funeral director or medic to register the death – the family cannot do it themselves, as they can in the United Kingdom. In most states, transport to a crematory must be provided by a funeral director, thus preventing do-it-yourself and cheap funerals. In California cremated remains cannot be scattered by the family, but must be kept permanently in urns at registered cemeteries or mausoleums, thus ensuring that someone makes a buck or two even after the body has been disposed of.

Americans are also infatuated with the permanence of the grave. Mitford rightly ponders a paradox. In the country where everything has built-in obsolescence, the one object that can do no other than decay – the coffin and its contents – is suffused with expensive images of permanence! The construction of the casket, the concrete walls of the grave, the embalmed corpse, are all advertised as lasting for ever. Nothing has changed in the twenty-five years since Mitford wrote, with American funeral trade catalogues still dominated by ideals of permanence quite unknown in the United Kingdom.

Why is this? Partly because hyping up the funeral is the only way to make an all-American profit when all that's actually needed is a six-foot-by-two cardboard carton, but also partly because of the Americans' need for roots. Go to any cemetery in any land of immigrants, and look at the love lavished on the graves of each family's founding fathers and mothers. Look at the graves in Melbourne of Poles who forty-five years ago escaped the concentration camps to set up a new dynasty in the lucky country. Look at the graves in Boston of Italians who arrived with one suitcase at the turn of the century; their descendants too need a permanent grave to visit. It is the third and fourth generations, who know their place in the land, who can go along with Mitford and dispense with trying to preserve what cannot be preserved.

Nationality or modernity?

So can the shape of a funeral be explained entirely in terms of national eccentricities? Though these explain much, they fail to explain three things.

One is the great variety of funeral traditions within any one modern nation. There is a big difference between the traditional funeral of the East End of London, with its horse-drawn hearse, flowers, and top-hatted undertaker, and the modern East-End funeral with a few relatives and neighbours in a not-so-local crematorium. There is a big difference between the English country churchyard funeral, with relatives carrying the coffin from the lych-gate to the church and then out again to the grave, and the domination of many rural areas today by the Co-op funeral director and a crematorium twenty-five miles away. The funerals on the Outer Hebridean island of Barra described by the anthropologist F. G. Vallee in the 1950s – with the whole island involved, with watchers through the night talking around the body about seamanship, fishing and sheep, and with the women arriving every now and then to pray around the body – are further removed from the experience of most British people than is the funeral of a Hopi Indian. Even within the family described in Chapter 1, Uncle Andrew in Fife was dispatched totally differently from Kathryn's dad and brother just down the road in Perth. And how does national character explain the dramatic change in England and Wales between 1945 and 1987, when cremation rocketed from only eight per cent of deaths to seventy per cent? Has our character changed?

National character cannot make sense of these differences and changes within one country. What does begin to make sense of them is the movement from a traditional, religious, community-based, rural society, to a modern, urban, secular society. Modernity, as well as national character, impresses itself on how we dispose of our dead, and this is what I explore in Part Two.

Religious traditions also help explain some differences within any one country. In Belfast in 1988, of the 1,705 people cremated only forty-four were Catholics. And in many countries, secular people influenced by Catholicism still stress the wake, are more likely to opt for burial, and retain rituals that enable them to interact with the dead. Secular people influenced by Protestantism tend to have thinner and fewer rituals, are more likely to opt for cremation, and are likely to have a minimalist view of what the funeral can achieve. The conflicts of the Reformation still echo in the chambers of today's municipal crematoria (see Table 1).

The second thing that national eccentricity cannot explain is certain funereal tendencies common to all modern nations, especially in cities. Here death tends to be hidden away in hospitals and funeral parlours, people are uneasy with its physical messiness, and the bereaved lack community support.

Third, the emotional privacy and self-control that at first seem so typically Anglo-Saxon are also requirements of the modern industrial age. As the jumbo jet takes off, I trust that our pilot will keep under control any memories of the previous night's row with his wife, that he will not swoon with sadness at leaving his home country, and that he will not go into ecstasies at the sunset. Keeping your emotions under control is essential for anyone handling complicated machinery. Maybe it is no coincidence that it was peoples with disciplined characters and rational forethought, the Flemings and the Dutch, the English and the Scots, who got capitalism and the industrial revolution going in the first place.

And I wonder how far back our 'English reserve' goes anyway. The historian Philippe Ariès reminds us that throughout the early middle ages brave men swooned on every conceivable occasion. By the Romantic era of the nineteenth century women (though not men) were still allowed to behave like this, and only now are we all meant to bear misfortune with our feelings carefully hidden. Emotional self-control may therefore have as much to do with modernity as with national character.

Modernity, but . . .

So, to understand today's funerals we have to understand the influence of modernity – but with the following reservations.

Reservation One: How modernity affects the funeral is worked out differently in different countries. In the United Kingdom we got rid of overcrowded slums by building modern high-rise flats in rolling parkland; in much the same way, worried by the prospect of full and ageing cemeteries – potential slums of the dead – we built modern crematoria, also in rolling parkland, and soon to be declared as soulless as the high-rise blocks. In the United States the problem of the city slum was attacked through upward mobility into sub-urban villas – an equally modern solution, and equally reflected in the suburban lawn cemetery.

Reservation Two: The principle, 'What America does today, the rest of the world does tomorrow' is not true, least of all in funeral customs. When I say that funerals today are deeply influenced by modernity, I am not saying this means we are all following a generation behind the Americans (or the Japanese, or the Germans, or anyone else). True, the flamboyant and media-conscious Howard Hodgson is intro-ducing some American commercial practices into the British funeral trade. But in the matter of cremation, the Americans are slowly catching up with the British. And remember, the two most trenchant critics of American funeral practice, Jessica Mitford and Evelyn Waugh, were both British, and have done more than any two other individuals to change American practices.

Reservation Three: To say that modernity influences funeral practices does not mean that it *determines* them. Modernity has its own conflicts and contradictions, it is itself on the move. There are enough examples around of people rejecting the typically thin modern funeral to show that modernity is something we can respond to, as well as be seduced by.

3

IN THE MIDST OF LIFE?

Jackie died at the age of twenty-three, hill-walking. She had loved life and loved her friends; her enthusiasm, her sense of fun and her joyful giving of herself to others came from an understanding that this is the only life we have. At her funeral was read this poem, found among her belongings:

Last Day

If we knew that life would end tomorrow,
would we still waste today on our quarrels?
Would we waste the precious hours away,
taking refuge behind that wall of icy silence,
creeping out only to hurl another barrage of angry words –
invisible missiles, but in every way as deadly as broken
   bricks or bottles?
If we knew that life would end tomorrow,
would we keep a tally of wrongs,
determined not to be the first one to give in?
Or would we cease to care who started it,
knowing that no one is completely in the right,
and that in this kind of war we shall both end up as losers?
If we knew that life would end tomorrow,
surely we would treasure today,
fill the hours to the brim with love and laughter instead of
anger and bitterness,
creating jewel-bright memories which would lighten our
   hearts
instead of dark regrets which could twist and destroy.

If we knew that life would end tomorrow . . .
but who can say that it will not?
The only time of which we can be certain is today.
So today I will reach out for your hand.
Today I will say I am sorry and I love you.

Perhaps the most striking thing about death in the West today is that it is uncommon. Ours is the first century in which most children (in the West at least) grow up with no personal experience of death and bereavement. All infants think they are immortal, but today many of us grow up right to adulthood without our childhood illusion of immortality being challenged by personal bereavement. What is so unusual about Jackie is that she knew she was mortal, and lived accordingly.

Most human beings probably both accept that they are mortal, and yet have to deny it for practical everyday purposes. Were we to accept it too readily, we would all commit suicide; were we to deny it utterly, we would be a danger to ourselves each time we crossed the road, thinking ourselves immortal.

'Death and the sun are not to be looked at steadily' – so wrote La Rochefoucauld. We would go mad thinking of death all day; but as with the sun, so with death: without staring at it, the wise person lives in its light. The growth in maturity that can accompany the onset of middle age or the first close bereavement comes from the realisation that we are not, in fact, immortal. We realise there is no time to achieve some of our youthful ambitions, and we become more realistic. At the same time, the shortage of time gives us a new impetus to reach out to our fellow human beings, to tell them we are sorry and that we love them.

But it is no longer true, as the 1662 Prayer Book burial service has it, that 'In the midst of life we are in death.' Apart from those in the gay community, and soldiers under fire, we do not regularly find death in our midst. The era of the plague has gone, we hope; so too has the long, long era of high infant mortality.

Much of Gustav Mahler's sublime music was inspired by his awareness of death. His older brother died when Gustav was little, and Gustav became the oldest remaining child.

He was the typical Victorian child, having close and frequent acquaintance with death. To his first piece of music, written at the age of six, he soon added a funeral march. Later, in his mid forties, came one fatal summer in which his four year old son died and he was diagnosed, out of the blue, as suffering a fatal heart condition – no wonder much of his music was obsessed with death, funerals and resurrection. How different, thankfully, is the experience of most of us today.

But have medicine and hygiene not only reduced bereavement's frequency, but also removed a straightforward awareness of our mortality? Have modern crematoria, discreetly tucked out of sight, also hidden death from view?

Let us look for a moment at the modern Western person's experience of death, from childhood to old age.

First, childhood. Last year, I visited an Islamic funeral director in London's Whitechapel Road. His office is behind a gleaming new mosque, and as we talked little Muslim boys ran past on their way to their daily religious instruction; a short while later, out they ran to go back home, dodging the parked hearse. Only some time afterwards did it dawn on me how rare this mundane awareness of mortality is for most British children. At Glasgow's main mosque the hearse is parked in the main car park outside the *front* door, so adults too pass it on the way to their prayers.

At rural Greek funerals the village women sing laments. The words differ only slightly from the laments sung at weddings, for both are occasions of loss. Parent and child 'lose' one another when the child marries. In the West today most of our parents do not die till after we have ourselves left home: parents do not usually separate themselves finally from us until we have already separated ourselves from them. I am not denying the trauma for an adult of losing a parent; what I am saying is that the loss is not usually the total rupture that it typically was for the pre-twentieth century person who lost their parents while still themselves children.

Let us now move on a few more years. The parents not only outlive the children's leaving home, they also outlive their own working lives. On retiring, they may move far away from their children – from North London to Margate, from Liverpool to Devon, from Pittsburgh to California, from

Melbourne to Queensland. They may make friends; they may have several years before they die. But when they do die, they are not surrounded by kin, by old workmates, by childhood pals. Their new friends and neighbours join the few close family who come down, or fly over, for the funeral, but it's not the same as a whole community losing a member.

I know. I live in a small Georgian square in Bath; it's very neighbourly, and I know everyone in the square. Several have retired here from other parts of the country, so when someone dies there are always a few of us neighbours at the funeral, and truly we mourn the person's passing. But what we are mourning are friendships of a few years, not bonds of a lifetime.

It is in such places of retirement, on both sides of the Atlantic, that cremation is most common. What need is there of a grave to tend when there are no kin to tend it? How can you be buried in California when all your ancestors are under the soil of Philadelphia, in Torquay when the family plot is in Bolton? Get burned instead. And have the ashes sent home, if anyone still cares.

People today do not expect to die young, but in ripe old age, without pain, after a fulfilled life. The hospice movement has helped many put their affairs in order, make peace with their families or their Maker, and die as human beings but without pain. I thank God for this, but it has made us think that death should always be like this. Unfortunately, it isn't. Many die suddenly of heart attacks, others from obscure diseases the medics do not know how to handle, others from being hit by automobiles.

We are finding these deaths increasingly difficult to cope with. Increasingly, we define them as out of order, caused by faulty technology which a public inquiry will put right. The most frequent cause of death to males between the ages of four and forty in the United Kingdom, road traffic collisions, we refer to as 'accidents', as though they are somehow uncaused, not in the ordinary scheme of things. We kid ourselves it won't happen to us.

Death is not only relatively uncommon these days, it is also hidden. Either physically hidden by removal to a hospital or hospice – though it is only since 1945 that most deaths have not occurred at home. Or mentally hidden, by the fiction of the 'accident', the 'tragedy', or by the fiction that the dying person is being removed to hospital not to die, but because the hospital will be able to care for her better. Death is no longer in the midst of life.

I therefore doubt that death is a taboo today. A taboo is something very much present that people are not allowed to talk of, or even think of, as sexuality was for many Victorians. But death is *not* very much present today: it is irrelevant rather than repressed, hidden rather than forbidden. If the bereaved person finds others embarrassed, crossing to the other side of the street, I suspect it is not so much because they dare not, cannot, confront death, but because they have had little practice at it, do not know what to do, are scared of saying the wrong thing.

It is good that people less often die before their 'time', and good that they less often die in pain. But we pay a price if we forget we are mortal, if we forget to live like Jackie.

If we no longer see death itself stalking the streets, funeral rites have more work to do than in the past in dramatising our mortality, in helping us come to terms with the fact that this person is dead, that I will die.

But in fact these public rites too, and the places in which they occur, are now hidden. John Claudius Loudon – whose book *On the Laying Out, Planting, and Managing of Cemeteries and on the Improvement of Churchyards* (1843) provided the pattern for the Victorian cemetery – wrote that the cemetery 'ought to be conspicuous at a distance, because, from its buildings and tombs, it will generally be an ornament to the surrounding country, and an impressive memento of our mortality'. Anyone who knows Glasgow will know that this statement is entirely true of that city's necropolis, set on its Calvary-like hill just above one edge of the city's business district.

By contrast, the British don't build crematoria in such conspicuous locations; instead the aim seems to be to tuck them away out of sight. By further contrast, when I was in Bangkok as a tourist, in only two days I stumbled without trying onto two funeral halls, one crematorium and one actual funeral. Few tourists would have the same experience in Britain.

Rhythms of life and death

Britain's Remembrance Day, commemorating the dead of two world wars, was originally held every 11 November. This is how the Manchester *Guardian* of 1919 described the first Remembrance Day:

> The first stroke of eleven produced a magical effect. The tram cars glided into stillness, motors ceased to cough and fume and stopped dead, and the mighty-limbed dray horses hunched back upon their loads and stopped also, seeming to do it of their own volition . . . Everyone stood very still. The hush deepened. It had spread over the whole city and become so pronounced as to impress one with a sense of audibility. It was a silence which was almost pain . . . And the spirit of memory brooded over it all.

Only after the Second World War was the remembrance service transferred to the Sunday before 11 November. Two minutes' silence during a British Sunday morning, when most folk are still abed or quietly at home reading the Sunday papers, makes little impact. The silence is no longer noticed.

But things can be different. On Saturday 15 April 1989, at 3.06 p.m., the semi-final at Sheffield's Hillsborough stadium between Liverpool and Nottingham Forest was stopped as the referee realised something was seriously wrong. Exactly one week later, at 3.06 p.m., the city centres of Liverpool, Nottingham and Sheffield, thronged with Saturday shoppers, stood still for one minute, remembering the ninety-five football fans who had died the week before. As I watched this on the TV at home, I realised how Remembrance Day must once have felt.

The day after the Hillsborough tragedy, there had been another reversal. Not of busyness into silence, but of a Sunday silence punctuated by a muffled noise. Great George, the master bell of Liverpool's Anglican Cathedral, sounded ninety-four times, once for each of those who had by then died. Normally tolled only after the death of a monarch, the bell reminded a sad city of the last time it had been rung, four years before for the thirty-nine victims of Heysel.

A bell shattering the quietness of a Sunday afternoon; a

minute's silence in a crowded Marks and Spencers; a day off work to attend a funeral. These reversals signal that there is more to reality – not just for the immediately bereaved, but for the sake of humanity.

Arnold Toynbee once said: 'Death is un-American, an affront to every citizen's inalienable right to life, liberty, and the pursuit of happiness.' Fine ideals, but questioned by death. Good funeral rites both affirm and question our ideals, they provide a bridge over the chasm, they mediate between surface reality and the depths we cannot bear. As their chaplain told the British paratroopers the day after the Argentines had surrendered to them in Port Stanley, 'Think how you felt and never forget how you felt when you thought you were going to die.'

Just as weekly worship dramatises to the believer that there is a divine as well as a human world; just as Sunday or the Sabbath dramatises that there is more to life than making money; just as going to the match on Saturday dramatises that there is play as well as work, fun as well as graft, ecstasy as well as tedium; so the funeral dramatises that there is more to human existence than life. Worship, Sunday, football, funeral rituals, none of these denies ordinary life, but they all speak of something more. They affirm ordinary life, yet challenge it too.

The funeral offers us a chance to explore some of reality's awkward corners – and then get on with living, in the light of what we have found.

At University College Hospital, London, medical students practise on human cadavers. They learn about livers and hearts and appendices. They forget this was once a person. Perhaps they *have* to forget this was once a person, if they are to attend to anatomical detail in the rush to accumulate enough knowledge and experience to pass demanding exams. But they are encouraged to go to the final service of cremation, and once a year they go to a thanksgiving service for those who have donated their bodies. There the students mingle with their cadaver's family.

Hopefully, they not only pass their exams, but as doctors go on to treat their patients as people. Such rites both challenge and affirm the students' work, and in so doing, transform it.

The TV

Most of us do not participate in such rites that in the midst of
life remind us of death. But an unexpected mediator has
arrived to bridge this gap between life and death – the
television news.

As we are eating our dinner after a day's work, on come the
pictures of the motorway pile-up, the collapsed Armenian
apartment blocks, the grieving football fans, the funeral of a
head of state. It may upset the immediately bereaved to see
such pictures arriving unbidden in their living-room, but
there are also the needs of the millions who are not personally
bereaved by this particular tragedy. We are reminded by
these pictures that, even as our own children are eating their
tea, other children are dying. We cannot cope with the
immensity of this, especially not when eating our tea, yet
nevertheless, here in the midst of the family tea-time, is
death.

While few children in the West today encounter death at
close quarters, surveys have revealed nuclear or ecological
catastrophe to be the number one anxiety of many teenagers.
But what can death in such a catastrophe actually be like? The
TV hints at answers, for most of the televised mega-deaths
are caused by technological or ecological mistakes, and the
pictures hint at the consequent human suffering.

When you attend the funeral of someone you did not know
well, it is not unusual to find yourself unduly affected. This is
because you are grieving again the loss of someone closer,
who died some time earlier: your tears are for that person, not
just for the one in the coffin. As funeral attendances and other
occasions for grief decline, images of death and funerals on
the TV can have the same effect on the casual viewer,
reminding us of the deaths of those we have loved. They can
remind us that death cannot be packaged out of the way so
easily.

The TV cameraman has replaced the priest as the one who
mediates, for the ordinary person, between life and death.
That is no mean achievement. It was, after all, what stopped
the Vietnam War.

A question

So, a key question is: How do funeral rites relate to the everyday life of society? How do they challenge, affirm, and transform human life?

Behind these questions lies a different perspective on funerals from that which is usual in the West. Usually experts think, if at all, of how the funeral meets the needs of the bereaved: How does it help the grief process? I do not believe this is always the most helpful way to approach funeral rituals, though I do not ignore it. Indeed, it cannot be ignored, especially in an era that is obsessed with psychology and personal growth. But I believe that helping the bereaved is rightly a by-product, not the aim or purpose, of the funeral. Furthermore, I hope you will see by the end of this book that always to make helping the bereaved the main purpose of funerals can be counter-productive, and may not end up helping the bereaved at all.

PART TWO

PROBLEMS

A funeral has several aspects:

A physical aspect – the disposal of a dead body.
A social aspect – the need for support at this most isolating of times.
A spiritual aspect – the relation of the mourners to the current state of the dead person.
A psychological aspect – helping mourners grieve.
An economic aspect – who does what for whom, at what price?

The modern world has particular problems with each of these, and often each aspect does not relate to the others – creating a sense of unreality, thinness, or hypocrisy. Part Two explores why this is, and offers hope that things are beginning to change.

4

NATURE'S WAY

After all, what *is* death? Just nature's way of telling us to slow down.

American insurance proverb

I chose cremation for my husband because he died of cancer, and I didn't want a burial plot for his rotting body. After all, it was his body that let him down.

Australian secretary, 1987

I don't like the idea of slowly decaying in the cold ground. I'd rather be gone quickly.

Elderly lady in Bath, England, 1987

There is more dignity in cremation than in the messy, muddy business of burial.

Official of the Federation of
British Cremation Authorities, 1988

Whatever else it is, death is the final triumph of nature, the triumph of inevitable physical decay over our will to stay young and healthy. Avoiding this all-too-physical reality is at the heart of modern funeral practices.

People often choose cremation because it is more 'hygienic'. Many people do not like to contemplate their own – or their loved one's – body decomposing in the ground. For those of us accustomed to milk coming from a sterilised bottle rather than a warm udder, to garden fertiliser coming from a polythene bag rather than the compost heap, and to the household rubbish disappearing once a week in a lorry, it is more seemly for our bodies ultimately to be consumed by a 'hygienic' technological process than by dirty, smelly old nature.

Most people die in the winter, and most winters are wet and cold. Graves can fill up with water within minutes of the pump being turned off, the surrounds can become muddy and slippery. Mourners struggling to keep umbrellas up against driving rain and blustery wind may not feel the proceedings have much dignity: it can be a very messy, untidy business, and I don't blame people for preferring to be inside in the warm and dry.

But death *is* a messy, uncomfortable business. To have this borne inexorably on your rain-sodden shoulders at the graveside, even as the minister proclaims the Christian hope, can be surprisingly appropriate. Chaos and hope are there together. Too often in the crematorium there is neither – just bland mediocrity.

One must wonder also whether funeral staff as well as customers prefer to be insulated from nature. Surely many funeral directors and local authority personnel prefer to work in the warm and dry? It is not lost on monumental masons covered in dust in their workshop, or on gravediggers ankle deep in water, that their compatriots in the funeral-directing business have risen above such artisan status and carved out for themselves a nice desk job. Were I a funeral director, I'm sure I would prefer a neat series of cremations for the day; even one muddy, wet burial, and I have to polish up the black shoes again before the next outing. The funeral trade's promotion of cremation must involve a degree of self-interest.

There is no smoke without fire. But, if all goes well, the modern crematorium produces fire without smoke, for the one natural process the crematorium does employ, fire, is hidden. Fire is humankind's most primeval technique for controlling nature, and could be a potent symbol of our ability to destroy even the decay of death, yet barely one in a thousand would want to see the flames, and crematoria are built with this knowledge in mind. (Some non-Christian religions, however, insist on seeing the coffin enter the cremator, and most crematoria have facilities for one or two mourners to witness this.)

The British crematorium, through its blandness and its plastic flowers, its hidden chimney and its hygienic efficiency, makes one statement: that technology, not nature, has the last say.

Earth to earth, American style

You might have thought that North Americans, infatuated both with technology and with eliminating all bodily odours, would have gone for cremation in a big way. But they haven't.

They have another infatuation: the American soil. ('This land is my land, this land is your land'; 'The land of the free.') So they go for burial, in the land.

But because they also love technology and cleanliness, it has to be clean land. Artificial grass is spread around the grave so the mourners don't get their shoes dirty. The plastic grass is spread over the mound, so the mourners are spared the sight of too much real earth. The minister is handed a brass shaker, from which he can shake the symbolic 'handful' of earth on to the coffin, without actually getting earth on his hands. A graveside tent is provided to keep the heat of the day off the mourners, and is heated in winter to keep them warm. A stainless-steel trolley is provided so that the 'bearers' need exert no physical effort.

What about the corpse? Symbolically, though hardly in reality, it is protected from the decomposing power of the soil, first by embalming, secondly by encasement within a stout watertight casket, and thirdly by encasement of the stout casket within a concrete vault.

Americans have twin gods: the American soil – a mythical goddess of nature; and technology – a practical, and very male, god. The American burial uses highly practical gadgets to enable the loved one to rest mythically for ever in the American soil. For believers in these twin gods, it is therefore highly satisfying.

Pampering the dead

The Reverend William Jones, Vicar of Broxbourne, wrote in 1815:

Fine gentlemen and ladies shudder at the very idea of viewing a corpse. After all the anxious care they bestow to pamper, adorn, perfume, etc. their own frail bodies, how mortifying must it be to them to think of the havoc of death, how soon they will be loathsome and a prey to worms.

Americans have not taken Reverend Jones to heart. Though more than any other nation they love to pamper, adorn and perfume their own frail bodies while alive, they insist on seeing that frail body once it is deceased. But that deceased body is pampered, adorned and perfumed perhaps more than ever it was in life. The American wake is, I suspect, a valiant attempt to avert the havoc that death plays on the body beautiful. The purpose of embalming, as by now surely every American knows, is not to preserve the body in the ground, but to preserve it long enough above ground, long enough for it to be viewed peacefully asleep. The viewed body epitomises the good death, in good time, after a long and full life. The satisfied customer comes away pleased, saying how the corpse looks almost alive. Should the family be so indiscreet as to comment how dead the corpse looks, the funeral director will make some last-minute adjustments before re-presenting the corpse for public display. The burial a day or two later is a comparatively minor matter.

Body and soul

In his book *The Denial of Death*, Ernest Becker pictures the world of the little infant. The infant believes himself all-powerful. He has magical powers. He yells, and the breast arrives; he screams, and mother comforts him; he gurgles, and dad smiles.

One of the first of life's many hurdles is the realisation that his early assumption is wrong. All-powerful he is not. It is not just the will of mum and dad that he comes up against, it is the natural world. Mum's menstrual blood smells, and he can do nothing about it. So do other people's poo. If he sees his parents making love, he is petrified by the pure carnality, by the loss of control in those he thought he knew and trusted. A battle begins in the little human being between the mental and the physical. Human life becomes a heroic attempt to stay in control, to push down the animality, what Freud called the id. By the time we are adults, we are terrified of looking inside, of discovering the dirt, the sin, within.

But every now and then nature forces herself upon us. We become ill. Like our parents, we too are overcome by the physicality of sex. The physical needs of our children impose themselves on us. Eventually we die.

How do we repair these dents to our heroic self-image? How do we keep the animal from destroying the soul?

Is this why both sex and death in almost all human societies are surrounded by taboos, why these two most physical and natural of acts are dressed up in the most elaborate human ideology? Is this why we so need the support of others when we are dying or bereaved, why we so need to know we are loved? Is this also why we need to know we are loved when we make love? Both sex and death have to be tamed.

Sex, parenthood, illness, death and bereavement – each undermines our frail façade of omnipotence. We can respond either by repairing the façade, or by using the trauma, or the joy, to demolish a chunk of façade and discover a chunk of reality.

Surely this is why Christian conversion, Buddhist meditation, and psychotherapy all involve a dying to self (the outer self) that leads to a discovery of the real self (the inner self). They each perceive the busyness we employ to run away from the truth; they each perceive the terror of handing over control; they each perceive the breakthrough that comes from stopping doing, and starting being. Our activist modern culture finds this difficult to accept, but it is what so many discover at the last hour in the modern hospice.

The last laugh

The struggle of the human soul to dominate nature is not just a struggle of the individual. It is also the struggle of human society. Human civilisation attempts to carve out a home for ourselves on this planet: we humans have to create – not just adopt – ecological niches for ourselves.

At least according to a male view of history, human culture

is in large part the story of how we have used and developed tools to control nature for our own purposes. Just as death threatens our fabricated, heroic individual selves, so it threatens human culture. If culture is the attempt to control nature, this heroic endeavour is undermined by the fact that our bodies will eventually rot. Nature has the last laugh. Always. With or without ecological catastrophe.

This conclusion is galling for all human beings, but never more so than for modern technological men, who like to think they really have got nature beat. For city dwellers who never need touch the muck of the earth, it is galling to think that their bodies will eventually become part of that muck. For those who can at the flick of a switch turn night into day, winter into summer, it is puzzling to understand how the light can eventually go out for good. For people who think every problem has a technological solution it is disturbing to discover that for some illnesses there is no cure. For people who are used to taking the car into the garage for a service, knowing they can buy a new model if the news is bad, it is disturbing to find themselves frightened as they enter hospital for a check-up.

Is this not why so many British prefer cremation, and why Americans embalm and beautify their corpses?

Christians today are not necessarily any better at this than other modern people. The instructions in the old 1662 burial service referred earthily to 'the Corpse':

> The Priest and Clerks meeting the Corpse at the entrance to the Church-yard, and going before it, either into the Church, or towards the Grave, shall say, or sing . . .

> When they come to the Grave, while the Corpse is made ready to be laid into the earth, the Priest shall say . . .

> Then, while the earth shall be cast upon the Body by some standing by, the Priest shall say . . .

But the 1980 Alternative Service Book of the Church of England spares both priest and people from such infelicities. No mention of corpses or earth; instead, we have 'the committal' and 'at the graveside'.

Interestingly, the American Episcopal Prayer Book of 1979 is less squeamish, referring to 'the body' and 'the coffin'. This is quite radical when you consider that the American funeral trade insists on referring not to the 'coffin' (a container for a dead body), but to the 'casket' (a jewel box).

Gaining control, losing control

If human culture is the attempt to control nature, it unfortunately controls its citizens too. This is perhaps more true of modern technological civilisation than of most. Though complex technological systems give us great power over nature, as individuals we notice them only when they break down. We turn on the light without thinking, but are frustrated by the power cut. We drive to work half asleep, but fume when the traffic jam stops us. Many of the new powers given to ordinary people by education, by medicine, by efficient organisation, only lead to many of us feeling we are in the power of teacher, doctor or bureaucrat; even as we gain more control over nature, we feel we are losing control of our very lives. Never is this more true than at death. The be-tubed hospital patient may live longer than her Tudor counterpart at home in her hovel, but the modern patient has less control over the circumstances of her dying. The hospice movement is, thankfully, changing that.

The funeral directing profession – like the medical profession – disables ordinary people in their handling of death. It has been doing this ever since the late seventeenth century, and had made a pretty good job of it in urban areas by the late eighteenth century. But it is only in this century that most rural people have not organised funerals for themselves, with a local carpenter making the coffin, local women laying out the body, friends and neighbours digging the grave and carrying the coffin. The automobile has enabled the hospital, the funeral director and the crematorium to sell their wares to rural folk as well as urban. In Britain only the remoter parts of the highlands and islands of Scotland are beyond driving distance of a crematorium, funeral parlour or hospital. Death is now controlled by the hospital, the crematorium, the funeral director.

The individual, desperate for control over his own life, has forfeited control over his own death.

Subtle denials

If we deny death more than did previous generations, it has to do, in part, with its threat to our control over nature. But let those of you who agree with me not be smug.

Christians are sometimes smug, using their hope in the resurrection to deny death. Some Christian funerals are nothing but joy, denying the very real sadness of loss and parting; other Christians believe in a continuing inner essence, or soul, that never dies. Such funerals, such beliefs, are not truly Christian, for Christianity believes that people really die, that death is tragic and obscene, and that Christ can and does raise those who have died. There is real death and real resurrection, real sadness and real joy. To forget the death, to ignore the sadness, is to deny the reality of death; far from transforming the normal human tendency to deny death, it simply repeats it.

The smug can also misuse psychology; and this is especially the case in the United States. The psychiatrist Elisabeth Kübler-Ross has close and personal knowledge of dying people, and has detected various stages they go through as they die – shock, denial, anger, bargaining, depression, acceptance. Several experts believe the bereaved go through similar stages. It can be very helpful to someone experiencing these disturbing emotions to know they are normal and temporary. But the idea of stages can also be used, and has often been used, to kid ourselves that we now understand death. Dying and bereavement are no longer mysteries, paradoxes, but predictable processes – we cannot control the inexorable physical processes that lead to death, but we can now control, manipulate and predict the psychological processes that precede and follow death. We have regained control over nature.

This is a particular danger for Americans, who believe every problem can be fixed. I must admit to admiring, in general, this practical American optimism; we British could do with a lot more of it. But when it comes to the unfixable, this kind of practical optimism can get you into trouble. And there does come a point at which death cannot be fixed. The British psychiatrist Colin Murray Parkes, in his book *Bereavement*, wisely refrains from giving a set order of discrete stages, in either dying or bereavement; he simply lists the emotions that may, or may not, be felt. This approach comforts sufferers that they are not round the bend, without tempting well-meaning helpers into becoming Mr Fix-Its.

Paradox

Modern technology can, however, help us with death: its practical attitude to life's problems may help some people accept death as something which is there and must be faced, reasonably and responsibly, rather than evading its reality through spiritual or sentimental sophistry.

But in general, modern *technology* as a way of *doing*, with its apparent mastery over nature, seems to deny death. However, modern *science* as a way of *knowing* most definitely has helped people accept death, for science reminds us that we are a part of nature, subject to natural laws of change and decay. Freud once observed that the three big scientific revolutions – the Copernican revolution (demoting the earth from the centre of the universe), the Darwinian revolution (linking *homo sapiens* with the other creatures of this planet), and his own Freudian revolution (revealing the power of animal instinct over rational will) – are history's three biggest blows against human narcissism. Science doesn't half take us down a peg.

The mysteries of the earthquake, the stars, the human being, all are now understood as natural processes. For many in our age of science, death too is no longer an act of God, but a natural event; it can no longer be spiritualised away. The technological hubris that makes death an unpardonable offence is balanced by the scientific humility that accepts the human being as governed by the laws of nature. Many people today seem to be returning to the age-old awareness that bodies wear out and that death is not to be feared. They are helped in this by secularism and by the hospice movement.

Indeed, some people opt for cremation not as a denial of natural processes, but in order to become part of the natural elements again as their ashes are sprinkled on field or ocean. This is how folksinger Ewan McColl expressed it:

Take me to some high place
of heather, rock and ling.
Scatter my dust and ashes,
feed me to the wind,
so that I will be part of all you see,
the air you are breathing.
I'll be part of the curlew's cry
and the soaring hawk,
the blue milkwort and the sun-dew hung with
    diamonds.
I'll be riding the gentle wind
that blows through your hair,
reminding you how we shared
in the joy of living.

While many opt for cremation in order eventually to be reunited with the elements, others reject cremation because the hygiene feels to them cold and clinical, the practicality feels banal. The crematorium gives them the creeps, just as others get the creeps from worms and damp earth.

I suspect there are a fair number of scientists in the pro-burial camp. One university biology lecturer I know went on a backstage tour of the local crematorium and did not like what she saw. She particularly disliked the electrical machine that grinds up what bones remain after cremation. As a biologist, she'd rather be returned to the earth.

Hope: The greening of death

Probably all societies simultaneously accept and deny death; our modern technological, scientific society is no exception. So far this century, the denial seems to have outweighed the acceptance, but things may be beginning to change. The green movement surely must lead to a more realistic acceptance of the fact that human beings are natural creatures who must die. This movement has prompted all of us to question our technological hubris; we all know now that we are part of a delicate natural system; we are less able to split a heroic, rational soul from an inconvenient body.

This new attitude surely underlies the natural-childbirth movement. Giving birth may be painful, but it is part of the natural human experience, and many women would not wish it anaesthetised away. Nor do they want to be socially isolated; they want to share this miracle of nature with their partners and their other children.

It seems to me that precisely the same attitude undergirds the hospice movement. Death is also a natural part of being human, and therefore I do not wish to be drugged into oblivion: I want the pain to be controlled, but I would like to be conscious and in control as far as is possible. And I would like to share this unrepeatable and important event with my partner and my children.

It is surely only a matter of time before this greater acceptance of death as a natural process to be shared with our family and friends begins to influence the funeral. To date, though, too many funerals are still where hospitalised technological death and hospitalised technological childbirth were a generation ago: isolating and unnatural.

5

THE FEMALE WAY

Last year, when I was visiting Antwerp, I attended the Catholic church funeral of a middle-aged man who was both a husband and a father. The female family members sat in pews on the left-hand side, the males on the right, so the dead man's two little boys had to sit next to an uncle, separated from their mother across the aisle. Dividing the sexes is normal in Antwerp's Catholic funerals; in this instance it struck both myself and my academic hosts as cruel.

Village funerals in Majorca are similar, except that the women sit on the right-hand side of the church, the men on the left.

In the Yorkshire fishing village of Staithes, as observed by the social scientist David Clark in the mid 1970s, funeral processions took the following form: first the priest, then the coffin, the close family, the female villagers, and finally the male villagers.

A female Dutch funeral director told me that when there is a death in the family of a Moroccan guest worker, only the father is involved in the Muslim funeral ritual. Even if it is a baby that has died, the mother never sees it again, staying at home while the father washes the baby at the mosque, and it is he who then goes back to Morocco for the funeral. My informant found this behaviour very strange.

In many places in Britain, from the Hebrides to parts of Southern England, women do not go with the coffin to the burial ground. They stay at home preparing the funeral meal. In rural Greece, though, women take the leading parts in funerals of high drama, and five years later it is women who dig up the bones, ensure they are clean, and place them in the communal ossuary.

In Britain women are generally given more freedom than men to cry during a funeral. But on some Hebridean islands it is the women who display a stoicism born of a lifetime of seeing their children depart the island for secondary school, never to live on the island again, while it is the men who get maudlin over the whisky once they've put the coffin in the ground.

Virtually every society has rules instructing women to behave differently from men at funerals. The rules can be reversed from one country to another, but rules there almost always are. These rules puzzle intellectuals and death professionals such as my Belgian hosts and my Dutch informant. They puzzle me too. You often find that in the literature on funerals these sex differences are noted, but rarely does anyone try to discover what they are all about. They seem incomprehensible to those of us who want to be next to our closest kin, of whatever sex, in our time of need. Why have such rules?

Earth mothers

A physically healthy man can get well past retirement without ever being physically limited by his body, but when the old man's body begins to wear out he can get very frustrated: his fantasies of omnipotence and independence may never before have faced such a challenge. Barbara Myerhoff, who studied a Jewish old folk's club in Los Angeles, observed that the men found it much more difficult than the women to accept their physical dependence on others.

Women, by contrast, have got used to a life of being limited by biology. With the onset of menstruation the young woman has to take account of her body; later on, pregnancy, nursing, and the menopause all give rise to a life that has to be lived within the limits of the body. Physically healthy men simply do not have this particular set of physical considerations.

It is men who can live with illusions of omnipotence over nature. It is men, more than women, who find death the ultimate insult. It is men whom my previous chapter was largely about.

Men fear women's familiarity with the body and its

processes. They like to develop an image of the rational male, to distinguish themselves from the female and her dangerous intimacy with nature. Along with this, particularly in the West, goes the idea that women are emotional. The detached mind is opposed to both body and emotion.

Women will often be more in touch than men with the natural, emotional processes of dying, death, and bereavement. It is women who nurse the dying, and women who lay them out; often it is women who make the arrangements for the funeral. It is women who are used to losing children, either through death or marriage. It would seem that women can be more in touch with death, literally more in touch with the corpse as they lay it out, and more in touch with the emotions aroused. Men, traditionally distant from all this, take care to distance themselves from women in the funeral rituals. Women are too dangerous; their in-touch-ness, their emotion is too scary. Bereavement plus female emotion could destroy the whole macho edifice.

Evidence for this assertion comes from the centrality of female emotion in the sex rules for funerals. Rules for handling emotion at funerals take two, opposite, forms.

The most obvious rule is to keep women away from the funeral. Whenever I ask why this is, some people just say that they don't know, or that it's traditional. But time and again, in different societies, I have heard both women and men say, 'Oh, women are too emotional, they'd break down.' But these emotional women are the very ones who have been nursing the dying person – emotionally demanding work, surely? What is so disastrous about the pain and emotion emerging from the sick-room to the graveside? I suspect the men are afraid that the women's grief will overwhelm the occasion – and overwhelm the men. Is this not what the mourning veil is for, to hide the woman's tears when she is in public?

But in many societies the rule is reversed: women take the leading part in the funeral and in public mourning. This is most dramatic where the women lament and wail. Wailing is a ritualised crying; no doubt it is genuinely felt, but it is socially expected rather than a spontaneous eruption of emotion. It is as though the women do the grief work for their menfolk: the emotion, the contact with physical reality, may be too much for the men, so they get the women to do the emotional work for them.

Take Victorian Britain. Its elaborate mourning rituals applied almost entirely to the women. Victorian gentlemen's clothes were black anyway, so for them mourning dress was little different, but for women it was (then as now) an irksome restriction on their choice of an ever-changing fashion. Moreover, the woman's mourning dress was physically uncomfortable, rough, heavy, and eventually abandoned as unhygienic. The woman's social life was severely restricted while she mourned for a relative of her husband, while the man's public life was little affected while he mourned even his own parents, wife or child.

All this began to be questioned as women's equality gathered pace. *Woman's World* spoke out in 1889: 'the custom of mourning presses far more heavily on women than on men. In fact, so trifling are the alterations made in a man's dress . . . that practically the whole burden of mourning wrappings would seem to have fallen on women . . . they [men] positively manage to mourn by proxy!' Victorian mourning went out of fashion in large part because of female emancipation.

Either way, whether women are banned from the funeral, or mourn in public on behalf of men, female emotion and familiarity with death has to be controlled. It cannot be let loose.

Feminine funerals?

But in our age of equality has not all this changed? Well, some of the rules for male and female behaviour at funerals are indeed being relaxed as modern urban culture kills local traditions, but the funeral itself is still overwhelmingly in the hands of men.

Women care for the dying. Mother Teresa has received the Nobel Prize, the psychiatrist Elisabeth Kübler-Ross the Teilhard de Chardin Prize, the hospice-founder Cicely Saunders the Templeton Award. No man has received equivalent acclaim for care of the dying. Women are also leading the way in the care of the bereaved, in listening patiently hour after hour to the pain of the bereaved. Women seem to know how to handle both the dying and the bereaved.

Nothing, therefore, has surprised me more when researching this book than to discover that every official meeting or conference to do with funerals that I have attended has been dominated by men. I am a social scientist, and an active member of both my local community association and my local church, so I am used to being at meetings where females are present in good numbers and often predominate. So why, when it comes to the funeral business, do I find row after row of men?

A conference of 250 crematoria managers and owners: eighty-five per cent of them men over forty. A national inter-church committee on funerals: all men. Though I have met female funeral directors most funeral directors are men, and almost all funeral-directing firms are controlled by men. Every funeral I have attended, religious or secular, has been conducted by a man. When on TV you watch a major funeral or memorial service – for example, following the Lockerbie plane crash or the Hillsborough soccer disaster – you see at the front of the church serried rank after serried rank of male clergy. No woman spoke at the Lockerbie service. The behaviour of the Moroccan migrant who keeps his woman in purdah during the funeral begins to look uncannily familiar.

It is as though women's work with the dying and bereaved must be kept quiet, private, out of the way, sitting by the hospice bed or in one-to-one counselling. Death has become privatised, and the men who control the public face of death – the funeral – continue their impersonal, bureaucratic, ecclesiastical ways, as though developments within the private face of death – hospice work and counselling – had never happened.

But when women *are* involved, if they do their work well, demand for their services quickly materialises. An Australian funeral celebrant suggested that his wife, having herself given birth, would be better at conducting the funerals of young children, and she now regularly does these. A female Anglican cleric in London's East End, who conducted several funerals in a neighbouring parish when they lacked a vicar, now finds people specifically asking for a woman to conduct the service. These women often handle the emotions of a funeral congregation in a more direct way than do many of their male colleagues. Maybe this is more painful, but it is more personal.

I suspect some male clergy reflecting on this will be petrified. The clergyman, unsure of his role in a literate and non-churchgoing society in which his small congregation may well be better educated and qualified than he, may cling to the funeral as one of the few things that only he can do, or that people still want him to do. Male clergy often encourage female staff, and female laypeople, to be involved in post-funeral counselling and befriending of the bereaved, but I have yet to meet a clergyman who offers the funeral itself to female lay members of his church.

There is nothing in law to stop this. And for the clergyman with 150-plus funerals to do each year, surely it would be in his interest to delegate some? But no. 'It's delicate work, and they're not trained,' male clergy object. I have yet to meet a clergyman who was trained to conduct funerals – often they comprise half his workload, yet he may have got only one afternoon on the subject in his three-year theological training. 'People want a proper vicar to dispatch them,' male clergy object – that can change remarkably quickly once a feminine alternative is available.

We desperately need the female touch at funerals. Perhaps the single most practical conclusion clerical readers of this book could draw is that they seek out female members of their congregation who might be good at conducting funerals. The consequence could be a quiet revolution.

Hope for the future

The problem is as old as patriarchy. Yet in another sense it dates only from the 1830s. At this time, through sermons and Factory Acts, women and children were being firmly told that their place was in the home. Is it any coincidence that this was also the period when the modern rational approach to death was developed? Death became something to be counted, ordered, recorded; the registrar of births, deaths and marriages took over from the priest, who gave way at the bedside, too, to the doctor. Cemeteries were reorganised on a rational basis, with concern not so much for spiritual well-being as for public health.

A male rationality that insists on tidy, legal distinctions is still very much with us. In Britain (at the time of writing) a baby born dead before twenty-eight weeks[1] is legally a miscarriage, after then a stillbirth. The state will pay for a basic funeral for a stillborn infant, but not for a miscarriage. But what if the mother wants a funeral for a miscarriage or termination? Does she have to pay for it? What is the difference between going through labour at twenty-seven weeks and producing a dead baby, and doing the same at twenty-nine weeks? Surely such legal niceties are meaningless for a grieving parent?

Thankfully, some hospitals ignore the rules. I have some friends whose twenty-six week miscarriage was given a free funeral, and I have talked with a hospital chaplain who has performed funerals for infants born dead as early as sixteen weeks.

The grip of the old male 'rationality' must surely weaken. Just as the green movement cannot but undermine the technological grip in which funerals are currently held, so the women's movement cannot but undermine the male grip in which they are held. The re-entry of women into public positions must at some stage begin to influence the funeral industry. Women priests and women funeral celebrants signal that, slowly, women are refusing to be confined to the one-to-one care of the dying and bereaved.

The women's movement can have either of two effects. One is the masculisation of women, where they must become more like men if they are to succeed in public life. If a tough, 'Big girls don't cry', mentality is needed for a woman to succeed in business and public life, we may find more female, as well as male, mourners approaching the funeral as a heroic exercise in stoicism. I know of one highly competent woman, active in local politics, who refused to let anyone, even her children, attend her husband's funeral. She went alone. She had never broken down in public, and was determined she never would.

[1] This may change as a result of new abortion legislation currently going through Parliament.

The other possible consequence of the women's movement is not the masculisation of women, but the feminisation of culture. A culture dominated by aggression and competition, by high military spending and high-tech medicine, may begin more seriously to seek peace and co-operation. It is no coincidence that women have been in the vanguard of removing dying people from high-tech hospitals to hospices in which the personal and spiritual, as well as the medical, affairs of the dying are attended to.

If some mourners are becoming more 'masculine', I suspect the funeral business is becoming more influenced by the feminine. Many men became undertakers because their fathers ran carpentry or haulage businesses; undertaking for them is basically about the physical handling of a corpse. Men who run crematoria may have risen up through the registrar's department or the city's parks and recreation department (which in Britain often runs both cemeteries and crematoria), and often they see their job in terms of running a technical production line. On the other hand, women often go into the funeral business because of an interest in bereavement and even with a degree in psychology. This must introduce a different attitude. Whatever one thinks of those avant-garde funeral directors who are getting into bereavement counselling and 'death education' – especially in North America and Australia – they surely reflect the effect on male funeral directors of female staff who are more concerned with the emotions of the bereaved than with hearses and coffins.

Perhaps the high period of modernism, dominated by technically minded males, is waning. Or maybe at least it is changing. The effects on the funeral cannot but be felt.

6

THE TRAGEDY OF THE CREMATORIUM ROSE

He first deceas'd; she for a little tried
To live without him: lik'd it not, and died.
> Sir Henry Wotton (1568–1639), 'Upon
> the Death of Sir Albert Morton's Wife'

In the grounds of many British crematoria is a memorial garden containing rows and rows of identical rose bushes. Each commemorates an individual.

People today spend their lives trying to create some sense of uniqueness, of personal meaning, in the face of an increasingly mass-produced society. We each try to become an individual. In our families we create the privacy to insulate ourself from the forces of the mass society; we try to create islands of individuality, even as our cars increasingly look the same, even as we all shop in the same hyper-market, even as we become more and more dispensable as machines and systems come to rule the work-place. And what happens at the end of this brave struggle to be, to become, an individual? Consummation by the conveyor-belt crematorium; and memorialisation in a rose bush, planted by the local municipality, identical to thousands of other rose bushes.

In a Jewish cemetery eight thousand miles from Israel I did not get this sense of the tragic. Every gravestone was the same, every rose bush the same, but this symbolised to me that those buried there were common members of the Jewish community – a comforting and appropriate last statement for people who in life had fought to keep their ethnic identity alive.

Nor is this loss of individuality tragic in a military cemetery. Here, identical graves speak of death in a common cause.

But identical rose bushes for the rest of us who have struggled to wrest individuality from an impersonal society, these make a truly appalling last statement. These rose bushes say one thing: 'You failed.'

It's not just the crematorium and the cemetery that operate like a production (destruction?) line. Funeral directors do their best to provide something meaningful, but too often their ideas do not fit the unique personality of the one who has just died. Maura Page, who conducted a detailed study of the funeral trade in a northern city in the 1980s, writes:

> One bereaved lady was most distressed after the funeral because her father had been attired in a pink gown. 'Grandad was a real man' she said. 'A man's man. He wouldn't have liked to think that we put him in that pink gown.' Similarly, a young man who had been bereaved complained that he found his father in 'a kind of salmon coloured dressing-gown with a kind of cravat thing at his throat.' If there was one thing his father loathed, it was dressing-gowns; nor would he have appreciated looking like Noel Coward's understudy.

Maura Page also interviewed local clergy and found a great deal of conflict between their attempt to impose a theologically 'correct' funeral and the increasing desire of many families to personalise services by playing their own music – anything from light opera to pop songs. Many clergy do not seem to realise that 'if the bereaved are not churchgoers and not familiar with the service, there is nothing memorable in it, unless it is personalised in some way'. Bereaved people who are not churchgoers 'remember little of the content of the funeral service, but they can remember if the vicar mentioned the name of the deceased and whether he said anything about him or her'.

Too often in England those who have no great religious conviction have no real choice as to who conducts the funeral. Depending on the local arrangement, they will get either the minister of religion who is on duty at the crematorium that week, or the local vicar – which is fine if the minister takes care to personalise the service, but too often the production-line mentality takes over. Some funeral directors would like to have more choice as to which clergy they can call on: they are frustrated by a system that forces them to use some clergy they know will give a poor service. One funeral director said to me that more and more people are coming and asking him, 'Get us a *decent* clergyman – someone who's gentle and kind and will say something nice about our Albert.' In desperation, this funeral director – himself a practising member of the Church of England – will take the funeral himself when his customer is a non-believer and he cannot find a sympathetic minister or other celebrant.

If the bereaved can be upset by the fearful sameness and impersonality of the funeral, they can be upset still more by social isolation in the months to come. The two problems are related. They are the product of a society that on the one hand lauds the worth of the individual to the skies, while on the other hand isolating the bereaved individual and, through bureaucracy and mass production, destroying individuality. In a word, what makes funerals and bereavement so trauma-tic is individualism.

Taming death

Many traditional societies, in the historian Philippe Ariès' word, succeed in 'taming' death. They tame the intense personal pain by stressing the permanence of society.

Among the Shona people of northern Zimbabwe the months of personal mourning are ended by the ceremony of 'hitting the grave': the grave is beaten with sticks to wake up the dead person's spirit, in preparation for one final cere-mony. In this final ceremony of 'settling the spirit' the people invite the spirit back home, invite it to return to the community as one of the ancestors.

There is good psychological and sociological sense behind this ceremony. Once born, a human being loves and hates, works and plays, becomes a part of the community; the community never dies, and in this sense the person never dies. 'Settling the spirit' affirms what is in reality already true, for the dead person does indeed live on in the community.

This is why the Shona, like many other Africans, talk not of the dead, but of the living dead.

Contrast this with our modern view of bereavement. When after some weeks a widow senses her husband is physically with her in the room, next to her in the street, in the garden – and over half of British widows at some time experience this physical presence of their dead husband – she is told this is a phase of grieving, which will pass. In Britain, usually it does. According to Western experts, the eventual purpose of grief is not to reconstitute the dead man as one of the ancestors but to reconstitute the widow as a free, and freed, individual. Freed from ties with the dead person, she is now free to move on to form new relationships, and to this end the living dead must sooner or later become the dead dead.

We therefore have a major problem. By stressing the individual and not the group, we remove one of the strongest bulwarks against mortality. Groups are immortal, or appear so to their members. Individuals, unfortunately, are not.

Philippe Ariès traces the origins of individualism in Europe. In the twelfth century a people who had for centuries been confident of Christ's taking them to heaven became anxious about whether or not they would pass the test at the day of judgement. The stress shifted from the communion of the saints in heaven and their communion with us on earth, still expressed today in the Orthodox church, to the question of the eternal destiny of the individual. So acute became this anxiety that the church succumbed to the temptation to exploit it, selling people ever more and more prayers for their souls, more and more indulgences, to guarantee the individual entry into heaven. This exploiting of religious fear finally precipitated the massive clean-up known as the Reformation.

But individualism merely gathered pace. Though offering a different path of salvation, Protestant churches exceeded the Catholics in inducing fear in individuals as to their eternal destiny.

Meanwhile, the Renaissance stressed the earthly achievements of the individual. The hero became not the loyal member of the group, but the uniquely creative artist, the successful trader, or the inventive scientist. Life came to be seen as a book, in which the earthly works and religious faith of the individual would be scrutinised – by posterity or by my Maker. The group gradually came to be seen as the enemy, not the source, of personal identity.

Nowadays we take this to extremes, believing the ultimate aim of life to be the happiness of the individual. 'We don't mind what you do, dear, so long as you are happy.' A Victorian father would never have said this; more important to him would be that his offspring led Christian lives and fulfilled the expectations of society.

Most modern of all, perhaps, is the idea of individual self-fulfilment as the purpose of life. This idea has gained currency only in our society where infant mortality has been all but eliminated and most can expect to live to their 'three score years and ten'. It would have been cruel to believe in self-fulfilment when most people died at five, or fifteen, or twenty-five. In those days people believed instead that the good life meant obeying God's and society's values; one who did that, and died young, could be a hero, an example to all. Nowadays we say of his unfulfilled life, 'What a waste.' The only good death today can be the death of the old person, fulfilled, fading away gently and peacefully.

How far our attitudes have changed came home to me at one Greek Orthodox funeral, for the Orthodox espouse – remarkably successfully – a pre-modern view of the purpose of life. Theodora died at nineteen after a lifetime's illness and mental handicap. Knowing she might not survive the last of her many operations, she had called the whole family to her hospital bed the night before to say goodbye, to comfort and encourage them, to tell them she wanted to go to heaven. At the funeral, we wept not for a life unfulfilled, but for a saint who had left us behind and entered heaven.

Thy death

Any churchyard containing stones from the period 1650 to 1850 – in Britain, Europe or North America – displays a major change in tombstone wording and decoration. On the late seventeenth-century tombstone the deceased's name is tersely given, with little more detail. The carving displays the same earthy approach to death to be found in the 1662 Prayer

Book, with skeletons, death's-heads, and skulls and cross-bones in abundance. But on the late eighteenth-century tombstones these have given way to cherubs, harps and willows, the wording becoming effusively sentimental. Why the change?

The Renaissance, which stressed personal achievement, had by then evolved into the Romantic movement, which stressed love of one's sexual partner and children. The individual was still pre-eminent, except now the individual was not so much me, as my beloved; as Ariès puts it, preoccupation with my death gave way to preoccupation with thy death. Death, far from being the familiar natural continuity experienced by the pre-twelfth-century European (or indeed by the twentieth-century Shona), became the most devastating personal break. The more people invested emotionally in their spouse, lover or children, the less able they were to cope with their loss. Or perhaps it was more the case that the Romantic movement allowed us to express a grief that had always accompanied the loss of one we love. Either way, there was an explosion of sentiment expressing the pain of bereavement. Till her own death forty years later, Queen Victoria never got over the death of her consort Albert, and she let everyone know. Catholics were no longer endowing chantries to pray for their own soul, but paying to have masses said for their loved ones.

We may not be so effusively sentimental today, but the Victorian equation of death with personal bereavement is now totally taken for granted. We suffer from what the psychiatrist Colin Murray Parkes calls 'the cost of commitment'. A classic study in 1967 by W. D. Rees, a Welsh general practitioner, showed that in the year following a death close relatives were seven times more likely to die than those who had not been bereaved, and widowers ten times more likely.

But there is a final twist to this story. Out of love, people began to keep from their dying parent, spouse or child the knowledge that he was dying – and when the dying person discovered the game, he colluded with them in it. As Ariès puts it, 'the dying man's relations with those around him were now determined by a respect for this loving lie'. At this most traumatic time in maybe more than half a lifetime of love, deceit enters, and the dying man no longer conducts his own demise; Victorian sentimentality thereby joins modern technology in denying death.

Today we experience a terrible combination of *thy death* and this *hidden death*. Death is on the one hand uniquely painful and isolating, and on the other studiously ignored and hidden away. This is why bereavement counselling has had to come on to the scene to fill the gap left as old communities and old community attitudes have withered. It is also why widows and widowers say they want no fuss at the funeral, but come away sick at the very anonymity of the plastic occasion they have ordered.

Funerals in the seventeenth century were decidedly anonymous. The 1662 Prayer Book made no provision for mentioning the name of the deceased, but I have yet to come across evidence that people were offended. The problem we face today is not just that funerals are so often impersonal, but that they are impersonal to mourners who are desperate for personality.

Privatised death

Bereavement today is not so much a taboo subject as a private experience that cannot be shared. It could be once, at least in some communities, for if the whole of life was lived within one community, when a member of that community died everyone felt the loss. The whole community had to readjust. When a character in the fictional BBC radio village of Ambridge dies, every other character mourns the loss, but in urban or suburban reality what the geographically mobile widow feels after forty or fifty years of marriage cannot be shared by others. They may have experienced similar losses, but they have not lost this particular person.

This is why death is dealt with privately, why so often the bereaved want to keep their emotions private. It is why funerals are often small, family, private affairs. Bereavement counselling respects this desire for privacy, while at the same time attempting to get the bereaved person to express her feelings – to one person even if she cannot share them with a wider community.

Geoffrey Gorer, in his *Death, Grief and Mourning in Contemporary Britain,* detailed mourning practices in Britain in the early 1960s. There used to be several ways of indicating publicly that a death had occurred: in the North of England drawing the blinds, in parts of Scotland sending mourning cards, in a few areas of the North East hanging on the front door a wreath ornamented with white ribbons. In traditional cities like Belfast and Liverpool you announce your sympathy for the bereaved publicly in the local paper, which each day may devote several pages to such notices. Gorer found that people in clerical and professional jobs, and those living in the South East, were much less likely to keep up these traditions. Since these are precisely the groups that are increasing in the long term, it is not surprising that public and local acknowledgement of a death is decreasing overall in Britain. The widow weeps at home, by herself, unacknowledged.

Incidentally, Gorer's is the only such study of mourning to have been carried out in the second half of the twentieth century in Britain. Sociologists have done dozens of studies on football crowd behaviour, industrial relations, bias in the media and scores of other publicly observable phenomena, but just this one and now rather dated study of mourning customs. Psychologists and psychiatrists have studied the individual's experience of grief, but not the public face of mourning. It is not just local communities that are privatising death, but social scientists too.

Philippe Ariès astutely observes that the grief described by modern psychology is the grief following 'thy' death. The best-known textbook on bereavement in the United Kingdom, the psychiatrist Colin Murray Parkes' *Bereavement,* draws heavily on his 1971 study of twenty-two widows whose husbands had died before they reached the age of sixty-five, and on a study of sixty-eight Boston widows and widowers under the age of forty-five. They had all endured the classic romantic loss: the untimely death of a spouse. Selecting this particular kind of bereavement for his book, Murray Parkes reflects our preoccupation with 'thy' death, the death that really scares us, and to use this particular data to develop a more general theory of bereavement suggests that we believe romantic death to be what death is all about.

Geoffrey Gorer, observing a much wider cross-section of

widows and widowers, found that the picture of pain painted by psychiatrists examining particularly traumatic bereavements cannot be generalised to all bereaved people. In particular, he did not find the anger and guilt the prematurely bereaved typically feel. Moreover, Gorer criticised the picture painted in many psychiatric studies of grief, a picture of the solitary patient with nothing to do but get over her grief; in practice, in many parts of the country there are still support networks. Gorer's point is not that the psychiatric studies are wrong, but that what they portray is only a part of the picture – that part called romantic death, privatised death.

And yet Gorer's study is itself trapped within a psychological framework. For him, funeral and mourning rituals have one main purpose: to assist the mental health of the closely bereaved. This is a typically narrow and modern view of the funeral. Though accepted by the intelligentsia and the caring professions, this view of the purpose of the funeral is not shared by more ordinary folk. For them, the funeral is an occasion to show respect for the deceased, perhaps to pray for that person's soul, perhaps to put on a good show, but certainly to affirm what is of value at this time when everything has fallen apart, and to show support for the close family. Funerals are about the deceased, about God, about values, not just about psychological recovery for the next of kin. You cannot privatise death that easily.

Hope

I do not believe we will ever succeed in privatising death entirely. Time and again, the widow, numb with grief and believing no one else shares her pain, is surprised at the number and variety of people who attend the funeral, who come to show their respect, even their love, for the person who has just died. Unlike her, they have not shared his bed for forty years, but they too feel a gap; that they too know and respect what that person lived for can be a great comfort to the close family.

A friend of mine recalls when he was a teenager and his father died. For the first time since they were little children, his sisters and he brought mattresses and slept in their mother's bedroom with her. This was not a conscious decision, it just happened, out of a natural desire to be with one another at the very time that threatens to destroy all relationships.

It is not just at death that we find this desire for connectedness. A major thread in both the women's movement and the green movement is to re-establish connectedness in a fragmented world. Isolated suburbanites move out from the city – in Britain to little villages, in the United States to small towns – not only for fresh air but also in search of community. Many, many people reject the isolation of the modern individual and are re-creating structures of connectedness. Mobile people, especially in the United States, are great joiners – joining churches, sports clubs, baby-sitting circles – in order to connect themselves with others. People are not taking modern isolation lying down.

It is this desire for connectedness that, in part, motivates the hospice movement. Why should the struggle to relate be abandoned at the precise time when relationship is more important than ever? 'The loving lie' is being challenged.

At the same time that new forms of connectedness are being formed, many of the old forms are still alive and kicking. Where there is community, funerals too become communal. Go to a Jewish funeral, a Muslim funeral, a not-yet-commuterised English village funeral, a funeral in Northern Ireland or Liverpool.

When ninety-five Liverpool football fans died at the Hillsborough stadium in April 1989, an entire city, and an entire footballing community, went into mourning. The pain of individuals was unimaginable, but hardly anyone in Liverpool was unaffected. Of my three Liverpudlian friends, one was there, but escaped; another's son lost his best friend; and the other had bereaved colleagues at work. In addition, Liverpool has a uniquely strong sense of communal identity, an identity symbolised by football, so a footballing tragedy attacks the city's very heart.

In the week following the disaster the whole city went into mourning and Liverpool Football Club's Anfield stadium became a shrine, filled to the half-way line with flowers. One million people, twice the population of the city, visited

Anfield that week. Old rivalries between the city's two football clubs were abandoned, with their different coloured scarves hung together in tribute all over the Kop end of the ground (Plates 5–7).

The communal grief at Anfield seemed different from the fragmented grief following the major train, plane and boat accidents that had happened in Britain in the preceding twelve months. With each of these, most of those who had died were strangers to one another. The grief was the same, but how could it be shared? What Anfield showed was that, where there is connectedness in life, there is connectedness in death – even in the late twentieth century.

If the increasing desire for connectedness is a sign of hope, so too is the increasing confidence of consumers – including the consumers of funerals. I have the impression that a small but steadily increasing number of people are rejecting the assembly-line funeral, and either doing it themselves or insisting on it being done the way they want.

The city of Bath was shocked when a local man in his early twenties, Chris Beechinor, was accidentally stabbed in a

Corfu nightclub while on holiday there. He had once told his sister that if he died he would want his friends to come to his funeral as though they were going out to the pub. At an emotional funeral, his mates came in the tennis shoes, T-shirts and shorts they had bought while with him in Corfu. They said goodbye in the way he would have wanted.

The Salford Funeral Planning Society, set up by Age Concern, enables local people to file details of the kind of funeral they would like for themselves. This ensures not only that the funeral director cannot foist things on to the bereaved family; it also helps prevent a family (through guilt) spending more than the person would have wished, or (through wanting to get its hands on as much of the estate as possible) spending less than the person would have wished.

Organisations such as Age Concern encourage elderly people to make informed choices while they are able. There may come a time when an old person is no longer able to control events, and it is important that she decides in advance what she would like to happen in various circumstances: if she can no longer live at home, for example, and ultimately of course, what should happen to her after death. Filing your wishes for your funeral is all part of the process of making informed choices in advance of the event.

More personal funerals are also becoming more common in England because in many towns the Church of England is relying less on a duty cleric who has to do dozens of funerals for the week he is on duty, and more on using the dead person's local priest who has time to visit the family beforehand. In the past, when many more people were churchgoers, the rota system was a useful way of providing a minister of religion for the few who had no contact with their local church; but with declining church attendances, the rota came to provide for the majority of bereaved families. The Church of England was woken up to the fact that a system which worked well as a back-up became terribly impersonal once it became the norm. (The new system, of course, works only if the local vicar takes his new responsibility seriously; funeral directors claim that not all do.)

If many contemporary funerals are cold, clinical and impersonal, I have great hope that they need not continue to be. Some people are rediscovering how to reconnect with one another, even in their grief; others are discovering the courage to ask for what they want; still others are thinking about their funerals as part of the process of making informed choices about their old age; and the church is facing up more to its pastoral responsibility, even in a largely non-churchgoing country.

Progress and the ancestors

I walked into a plush funeral parlour in Australia to the accompaniment of the piped strains of Bob Dylan's 'The Times They Are A' Changing'. I was with the director of the funeral parlour chain, who observed it would not have been his choice of music, but he gives the manager of each parlour the freedom to run their own show.

Bereavement is obviously a time of great change, but is it helpful for the bereaved to be reminded of this?

Earlier in this chapter I described how many traditional tribal societies tame death by affirming the continuity of society. Such societies usually see time as cyclical. The seasons follow one another predictably, the rains come once a year, the game migrate at the same time each year, dawn reappears every morning. Nothing changes permanently; society doesn't change. The rules of your parents, the elders, the ancestors, the laws from time immemorial, these are what govern life yesterday, today, tomorrow.

The rupture caused by death is profoundly disturbing to the social order of such societies, for the social order cannot cope with change. So funeral rituals reaffirm the values of society; they affirm the transition of the deceased from elder to ancestor; they proclaim that, just as birth inevitably leads to death, so death inevitably leads to some form of rebirth (in Britain, for example, prehistoric burial mounds are full of symbols of fertility).

But we moderns have a very different view of time. For us time is linear: it moves on, and things are never the same again. We believe in history, in progress, in novelty, in youth. We ditch the elderly, proclaiming that the future belongs not to the ancestors but to the young; for many elderly people, physical death merely completes the social death that they have already suffered. The ending of an elderly human life is not a problem for modern culture, but it is a massive problem for the modern individual.

Today the individual opposes him or herself to society. Death, not a problem to an ever-changing society, is *the* problem for the individual. How society reacts to death is different from how the individual reacts. This surely helps explain why death is simultaneously both a taboo and not a taboo: it is too awful for the individual and their family to discuss, yet part and parcel of modern progress. The bereaved feel bereft and isolated, and neither they nor their comforters seem to know what to say, and yet society itself happily produces image after image of death and disposability.

How then are we to comfort the modern individual? Do we remind them that change is inevitable, that the old must give way to the young? Do we play 'The Times They Are A' Changing' in the funeral parlour? Do we proclaim, as does the 1662 Prayer Book funeral service, the words of St Paul: 'We shall not all sleep, but we shall all be changed, in a moment, in the twinkling of an eye, at the last trump, (for the trumpet shall sound,) and the dead shall be raised incorruptible, and we shall be changed'?

Or do we confess that the modern faith in change is not strong enough to tame death? Do we turn the Christian hope in resurrection into a hope that we will be reunited with our loved ones, in a heavenly replay of family bliss on earth? Do we stress God's unchanging love, that 'underneath are the everlasting arms'?

We have to do both. Even as the priest proclaims 'we shall all be changed', the Tudor language he uses and the vestments he wears proclaim that nothing changes. Even as we process through the village churchyard, our movement speaking of an irreversible change, yet we are aware of the stones of ages all around us, speaking of unchanging community. Soviet funerals point to both continuity and change in formulae such as: 'Life continues, and everything that the deceased has managed to achieve will continue. His causes are alive in ours, his beginnings we shall complete, everything is left to men.' Secular funerals in the United Kingdom often quote Bertrand Russell's image of life as a river that can never flow back uphill, yet we know that water eventually goes back to the ground via the clouds:

> An individual human existence should be like a river – small at first, narrowly confined within its banks, and rushing passionately past boulders and over water-falls. Gradually the river grows wider, the banks recede, the waters flow more quietly, and in the end, without any visible break, they become merged in the sea, and painlessly lose their individual being. The man or woman who can see his or her life in this way, will not suffer from the fear of death, since the things they care for will continue.

However much we believe in the private individual, we shall never prevent people facing the insult of death together. However much we believe in change and progress, we will never cease to gain comfort from the knowledge that our ancestors also faced the death that we face. However secular we become, we will never cease to believe that, in some way, the person does not die. We cannot but try to tame death.

7

THE COST OF FUNERALS

At length the day of the funeral, pious and truthful ceremony that it was, arrived. Mr Mould, with a glass of generous port between his eye and the light, leaned against the desk in the little glass office with his gold watch in his unoccupied hand, and conversed with Mrs Gamp; two mutes were at the house-door, looking as mournful as could be reasonably expected of men with such a thriving job in hand; the whole of Mr Mould's establishment were on duty within the house or without; feathers were waved, horses snorted, silk and velvets fluttered; in a word, as Mr Mould emphatically said, 'Everything that money could do was done.'

'And what can do more, Mrs Gamp?' exclaimed the undertaker, as he emptied his glass and smacked his lips.

Charles Dickens (1812–70), *Martin Chuzzlewit*

It is within the last half century that prodigious funerals, awful hearses drawn by preternatural quadrupeds, clouds of black plumes, solid and magnificent oak coffins . . . have spread downwards far beyond the select circle once privileged to illustrate the vanity of human greatness.

The Times, 2 February 1875

The most common response from those who have heard that I was writing a book on funerals has been to tut-tut about the price of funerals, and what a hardship and anxiety it can be for the elderly nowadays, and to ask whether I was going to expose the dreadful way in which we are ripped off by undertakers.

In Britain the first man known to set himself up as an

undertaker was a painter and decorator by the name of William Russell, in London in the 1680s. Ever since then, from Richard Steele's 1701 comedy *The Funeral – or Grief à-la-Mode*, through Dickens' astute send-ups of the greed and trappings of the Victorian undertaker and Evelyn Waugh's delightful satire on the modern American funeral *The Loved One*, to campaigns to reduce the cost of funerals portrayed in books such as Jessica Mitford's *The American Way of Death*, those who make a profit out of other people's grief have been exposed and lampooned. From the Victorian fear of a pauper's funeral to the shame of the widow of the late 1980s who finds herself in debt to the Social Fund, funeral charges have been a worry. Indeed, the British system of National Insurance goes back, in large part, to Victorian savings schemes designed to ensure that, if nothing else, the funeral could be paid for. There was no shame in poverty, but great shame in a pauper's funeral.

"The insurance money didn't amount to much then?"

Though worry about the cost of funerals may be a modern (that is, post-seventeenth century) Western phenomenon, it does not derive entirely from the greed of undertakers. In Staithes at the turn of the century – before undertakers had penetrated to this remote Yorkshire fishing village – poorer villagers had to save very carefully or else a funeral could break them. They must provide for not only the cost of the traditionally elaborate coffin, but also a funeral tea of smoked ham, fruit cake and Madeira cake for the whole village.

From 1666, before undertakers had appeared on the scene, Acts of Parliament made burial in any other than a pure woollen shroud illegal – in this case, it was the wool trade that was protecting a nice little number. The Acts were not repealed until 1814.

Today, at the same time that we bemoan the cost of funerals, blaming it on the greed of modern funeral directors, as tourists we enjoy the infinitely more elaborate mummies and pyramid tombs of the ancient Egyptians along the banks of the Nile, we wonder at the gold finery buried along with the Saxon king at Sutton Hoo, and we marvel at the tumuli funeral mounds dug with meagre tools and prodigious effort by the infinitely poor inhabitants of prehistoric Britain. They must have spent half their time digging houses for the dead.

On the Indonesian island of Sulawesi, the main attraction for Western tourists are the funerals of the Toraja people. They are described in the Lonely Planet guidebook *Indonesia* (1986 edition, p. 646–7):

The great funeral ceremonies of today seem to have lost none of their ostentation. In the village of Langda I watched a funeral for a woman which was spread over several days and involved hundreds of guests. The wooden effigy of the woman alone cost about 200,000 rupia – a year's wage for many Indonesians. The funeral was held in a quadrangle bounded by bamboo pavilions constructed especially for the occasion, with the death tower at one end. After the guests displayed their presents of pigs and buffaloes, the traditional *Mabadong* song and dance was performed . . . cigarettes were circulated, pork and rice dishes, washed down with alcoholic *tuak*, were served to the guests by immaculately clad women, their hair tied back in large buns, playing the part of waitresses and squishing barefoot through the thick mud of the compound.

Funeral ceremonies last from one to seven days, depending on the wealth and social status of the deceased. For the longest and most ostentatious ceremonies months, even years, may be required to accumulate sufficient money and plan the ceremony. Hundreds of buffaloes and pigs might be slaughtered . . .

How can modern tourists, enjoying such costly and elaborate funerals, believe that the sole cause of the high cost of funerals is the greed of modern funeral directors? Elaborate funerals, making our twentieth-century examples quite feeble, have been common throughout human history. What is modern and Western is not elaborate funerals, but our resentment of the cost.

How to get cheaper funerals

By almost any standard the cost of funerals in the West is not excessive – though this is not to say it can't cause hardship and worry. The average funeral in Britain costs much less than a wedding, and about the same as a colour TV plus video – about three times the average weekly wage. Forty years ago it was nine times.

In Britain the very old are still haunted by the fear of a pauper's burial. The historian Ruth Richardson, in her *Death, Dissection and the Destitute*, has recently revealed the shocking source of this fear. After years during which dismemberment and dissection were used by the state as the ultimate deterrent against certain forms of crime, the 1832 Anatomy Act exchanged the qualification for dissection from crime to poverty: the unclaimed corpses of those who died 'on the parish' were now available for medical dissection. The most feared of punishments was now reserved for the 'offence' of poverty. Ever since then British people have been terrified of what might happen were they not able to afford their own funeral.

This fear is presumably evaporating as each generation is that bit further removed from the mid-nineteenth century, but there is another factor which makes a funeral a greater burden for the low income family in Britain today: the loss in value of the death grant. When introduced in the late 1940s it covered the cost of a basic funeral. When it was abolished in the late 1980s it had become almost valueless, and people now have to find the cost of the funeral out of their own pockets, unless they are virtually destitute.

Government reports on funeral directing in the 1980s, in both Britain and the United States, though critical of certain aspects of the business, have confirmed funeral directors' claims that their costs are reasonable. A basic funeral takes about forty hours of work. The work of making coffins, carrying heavy bodies, maintaining vehicles, and paperwork, is comparable to work in the construction and transport trades. £10 per hour, including materials and equipment, is quite normal in both trades.

The only way to get repairs to your house done substantially cheaper is to do it yourself, and/or get a friend to help you. This is the nub of the problem with the cost of funerals. We have abdicated – or had stolen from us – the old tradition of ourselves performing the tasks of caring for and transporting the corpse, and now we no longer want to do it ourselves.

This is clear when you listen to satisfied customers. 'The funeral director was marvellous – he took all the pressure off . . . all we had to do was pay the bill' (*Funerals*, Office of Fair Trading, January 1989). Exactly. In the early nineteenth century the idea got around that at a time of grief you and your whole household should go into mourning, paying someone else – the undertaker – to arrange the entire funeral for you. Today we have dispensed with most of the Victorian funeral trappings, but we have kept the basic attitude underlying them: that at a time of grief we cannot handle things ourselves and have to hire a professional to take over on our behalf. We pay for what we are no longer prepared to do ourselves. In the United States people even pay the cemetery to look after the grave for them. They call it 'perpetual care'.

Most funerals done for less money than the funeral director's minimum are achieved through relatives, friends and neighbours performing some or all of the tasks of transporting body and soul, as an act of unpaid duty or love. The Secretary of the Bristol Jewish Burial Society told me that the Society's voluntary workers who lay out the body, carry the coffin, and do the paperwork, perform these tasks as an honour. Caring for the dead is the only thing you can ever do without any thought of being repaid or thanked; it is an act of pure love.

In London's East End an Islamic funeral director, who delegates as much of his work as possible back to the families, told me that the imam (unlike Anglican clerics) does not charge for his services; and that at the burial anyone can read a verse or even lead the ceremony. Mr Ali added with passion: 'Prayers cannot be bought or sold. They are not a commodity.'

The problem with funerals is not that they cost too much, but that they cost at all. The funeral that communities used to provide for themselves has been stolen, and then sold back to them, at a price. We are now so used to this that all we can complain about is the cost at which it is sold back!

This is, of course, how capitalism operates. Many of the things that people used to do for themselves they now hire others to do – and then complain of the impersonality, loneliness and isolation of the modern world! As Marx so perceptively observed, we have 'resolved personal worth into exchange value'. Unpaid acts of love, duty, and respect, have been replaced by the cash nexus; even dignity for the dead is now bought and sold.

This is the nub of the problem with funerals. If we do not understand this, things will never change – reformers will continue to call for more official inquiries, which will continue to find the funeral directors' charges reasonable. The problem is not that we pay too much for funerals, but that we are not willing to take responsibility for our own funerals.

Both the would-be reformers' revelations of the cost of funerals and the justifications of funeral directors and government commissions are beside the point. The underlying reason for the cost of funerals is revealed by asking a more pertinent question: 'Who is performing funerals? Them or us?'

A friend of mine attended a military funeral. He commented on how odd the funeral director looked in his black top hat and tails, walking near the front of this procession which was really the army's show. What was this man in black tails doing among the combat fatigues, the Hussars' splendid tunics, and the clerical robes? A military unit capable of transporting personnel and equipment half way around the world at a moment's notice, capable of thrilling the world with the pomp and circumstance of a Royal Tournament or an Edinburgh Tattoo, and which incorporates a medical and nursing unit able to care for the wounded – a unit such as this is surely capable of transporting its own departed from deathbed to grave, with dignity and decency? Yet even here we find the funeral director – redundant, but still getting his cut.

Of course, only a few families want to arrange a funeral totally on their own. It is no use telling an anxious elderly person that if she is to reduce the anticipated cost of her dying husband's funeral she will have to do it herself. The way forward, if you truly wish to reduce the cost of funerals for most people, is to form co-operative burial societies in which members do the work for one another, though in Britain only certain traditional religious groups seem willing to do this.

Goods and services, such as coffins and international transport of corpses, which the burial society may not be able to provide for itself, can be procured by negotiating a contract with a local funeral director. This kind of contract always incorporates a cut price; this can be negotiated because the people with whom the funeral director is negotiating are not in grief and are quite prepared to go elsewhere if the price is not right. If the funeral director's service turns out to be poor, the burial society will go elsewhere in future, and the funeral director knows this. Some large funeral directing chains refuse to deal with burial societies, but for independent local firms the burial society's custom is better than none.

In peasant communities which have elaborate funerals, people do not complain so long as they and their friends do most of the work.

I have an English friend who is a single mother on social security. She spends each summer with her friends making from papier mâché and old polystyrene packing the most elaborate float, which they take to each of the local carnivals that September; they love it, enjoy each other's company, and take great pride in what they create, win or lose. The product is similar to the funeralia of many traditional societies. My friend does not complain about the cost, because it doesn't cost a penny; it is a shared act of love, even of joy.

Weddings in Britain are increasingly elaborate. Many cost

a lot. Many cost not so much, because friends and relatives make dresses for the bridesmaids, arrange flowers, make the wedding cake, or do the photography. It is a family, a community, affair. Dad may mutter about the cost of it all, but the cost of weddings is not a public issue like the cost of funerals. Even so, weddings cost more than funerals.

If we complain about the cost of funerals, it is because we look at the work involved – transporting coffins and bodies – and conclude that it is not very onerous. We are correct – it is the kind of thing we could easily do ourselves. But we are rarely prepared to do it ourselves, and there's the rub.

Either we should get our act together, as families or in co-operatives, and organise funerals ourselves, or we should stop complaining. It is a lot less skilful than plumbing, and a lot less complicated than a wedding; physically, there is no more to laying out a body than there is to changing a nappy. But it does involve contact with death, and that is what we pay funeral directors for.

Burial societies are almost all run by religious groups. An alternative, popular in Canada and the United States of America, is the memorial society, which is a consumer group. The memorial society, unlike the burial society, does not actually use its own co-operative labour to do the funeral; instead, it negotiates a good price for its members from a local funeral director. The society can certainly reduce the cost of a funeral by a certain amount, but the benefits are limited since members are still paying someone else to do the work. (Also, inefficient small funeral directors may be put out of business, extending the power of the major chains.)

In North America funerals are much more of a rip-off than in Europe, and memorial societies draw on the established North American tradition of consumers organising to oppose commercial malpractice. In Britain we have neither such expensive funerals nor such a strong consumer tradition, so memorial societies have never really taken off. British people who fear the cost of funerals don't really want – or don't know how – to do anything about the problem; we just like to moan, and expect someone else to do something.

A few borough councils in areas where there is much financial hardship, like Salford and Lewisham, offer a guaranteed-price funeral for local residents; like the memorial societies, the council negotiates a contract with one funeral director who has to offer a good price if he is not to lose the considerable trade the council can offer. Such initiatives, however, are being superseded by the growth in Britain of funeral directors offering pre-need contracts; these increase competition between funeral directors and enable not-so-well-off people to avoid anxiety about whether they'll be able to afford the funeral (see Chapter 24).

Guilt, status, and cost

It is well known among psychologists and funeral directors that those who mourn hardest are those who had a close but difficult relationship with the deceased. (Queen Victoria was the classic case.) When the person is dead, and you can no longer say sorry, how do you make up for the bad times? The American *National Funeral Service Journal* for August 1961, quoted by Jessica Mitford, provides the American funeral profession's solution:

> A funeral is not an occasion for a display of cheapness . . .
> the most satisfying funeral service for the average family
> is one in which the cost has necessitated some degree of
> sacrifice. This permits the survivors to atone for any real or
> fancied neglect of the deceased prior to his death.

In twentieth-century America the funeral director grows fat through ordinary people paying him to deal with guilt and sin. In late medieval Europe the priest did the same.

If you truly are guilty, in addition to the guilt that bereavement ordinarily induces (we always could have done more, loved more), then I suggest – in true Protestant style – that you confess it to your Maker. And perhaps do it communally with others, as described in Chapter 22. Don't try to atone by paying the undertaker for all the trappings: it's expensive, and it doesn't work.

When we come to *status* – the other major reason people lash out on expensive funerals – I can give no such clear-cut advice. This needs exploring in some more detail.

To go back to a bit in the *National Funeral Service Journal* quotation that I missed out: 'A funeral is not an occasion for a display of cheapness. It is, in fact, an opportunity for the display of a status symbol which, by bolstering family pride, does much to assuage grief . . .' Some of the most elaborate funerals are indeed among those groups which have had to struggle through poverty.

Michael Harrington, in his influential book *The Other America* (1962), wrote:

> Death plays a peculiar role in the life of Harlem. One first realises this by walking the streets and gradually noticing the enormous number of funeral parlours . . . For the Negro poor, death is often the only time when there is real luxury . . . Dying is a moment of style and status, at least in the impoverished world of the racial ghetto.

Like the Pentecostal church, 'the funeral can provide a moment of release, even of ecstasy, in the midst of so many troubles'. British people often do not realise that many American funeral directors are themselves black and know well the desire of poor people for the spontaneous binge that celebrates life even in the face of death.

But there is more to it than the poor person's desire to inject an occasional binge into the routine of drudgery and poverty. The funeral is the final statement about a person. To be a pauper may be just bad luck, but to have a pauper's funeral, stating that you are nothing but a pauper, is intolerable.

In north-east Brazil the first peasant league was formed in 1955 not to improve living conditions, but to ensure for its members a coffin and a single grave. The Brazilian recorder of this movement comments,

> Why this desperate desire to have a coffin of one's own in which to be buried, when during their lifetimes these outcasts of destiny had never been the owners of anything? It is death that counts, not life, since for all practical purposes life does not belong to them.

Philippe Ariès, who quotes this, adds, 'Death gives them back their dignity.'

So it is that the poorest people often have the grandest funerals. As one Victorian music-hall song ran, 'Ain't it grand to be bloomin' well dead.' There was never any grandeur in life.

Rich and influential people also have grand funerals, but for a different reason. When the head of state or the head teacher of a school dies in harness, a time of great anxiety follows. Many relationships have to be renegotiated; the direction of the state or the school may change, as other factions move into the vacuum. The funeral therefore has much work to do – to reaffirm the value of the threatened institution, to enable people to meet and renegotiate relationships.

The smallest funerals are often for those who, in old age, have already wound down many relationships; and for folk of middling status who have neither substantial property nor power to hand over, yet do not need the funeral to mask any lack of status. In the United States, for example, those who are dispensing with the all-American funeral and opting for the simplicity of direct disposal are, it seems, Americans whose ancestors arrived across the Atlantic or Pacific generations ago, Americans who no longer have anything to prove.

Would-be reformers of the funeral (whether American, European or Australasian) often come from this middling group of folk who have made it, yet not attained the very heights of power. I would guess most readers of this book are also in this group. Such folk may opt for a simpler funeral for themselves, but they should beware of imposing this on those of lesser status.

Whether or not a grand funeral can give a psychological boost to a poor family, it can cripple them financially. The spectacular funeral, far from displaying an economic status that in reality does not exist for the poor family, may actually destroy what little economic stability the family had. And if most people in Victorian cities lived in insanitary conditions, one reason was surely that one whole room of their tiny dwellings – the front parlour – was reserved for the formal lying in state of their dead.

People will comment on the funeral trimmings or lack of trimmings. But their comments imply something not about the deceased, but about the surviving family members and their care for the deceased. The real mark of respect for the dead is the number of people who turn up.

This too used to be bought. Mutes were paid to attend Victorian funerals; in the middle ages, beggars were paid to turn up at a rich man's funeral to create a good show, just in case the contempt in which he was held by tenants and serfs in life should be revealed by their staying away at his death.

50,000 years of funerals

The anthropologist V. Gordon Childe published in 1945 a key article on 'Directional Changes in Funerary Practices During 50,000 Years'. From his survey of archaeology, anthropology, and history, he concluded that funerals are most elaborate at times of social instability.

This sheds extra light on the status business. It is at times of great social change that individual status is most in doubt – not only doubt about how far up the ladder you are, but even which ladder you are supposed to be on.

In Hong Kong and Singapore, where peasants are turned overnight into industrial workers, funerals are indeed elaborate. One Singaporean student complained to me about this. His father's funeral had cost £6,000 and was of the kind Dickens lampooned. The student also mocked the purchase of elaborate paper houses and a paper Mercedes to equip the body for the next life. (The student himself doubtless had a more secure social status than his parents, and was therefore able to criticise the elaborate funerals of the socially more unstable previous generation.)

Though it has been criticised, Childe's thesis makes a lot of sense. In Britain the disruption of the industrial revolution saw the source of status change from blue blood and land-holdings to money. Millions fled the poverty of the countryside for the slight hope of betterment in the industrial towns. It was in this period, when so many did not know where they stood, that the funeral emerged as the final and definitive statement about a person's social standing. It was not until the 1880s, when Britain's industrial and imperial power was at its seemingly invincible height and bourgeois people felt more secure, that the movement for funeral reform began.

In the nineteenth century the funeral was simpler in the United States than in the United Kingdom. It was in the early twentieth century, as wave after wave of Sicilian and Polish peasants arrived off the boat, that the elaborate American funeral really took off. And it was only in the 1950s and 1960s, with America at her peak of world domination, that the funeral reform movement, symbolised by Mitford's book, got under way.

So we find a long-term cycle of priests or funeral directors hyping up the funeral, followed some time later by puritans and secularists downplaying and reforming funerals, followed some time later again by emotionally starved people ready to pay for something richer and more elaborate. This cycle of elaboration and abuse, abuse and reform, reform and elaboration, according to Childe, runs in synchrony with cycles of much wider social change and social stability. It is this wider social stability that triggers reform, and then a wider social turmoil that motivates elaboration, of the funeral. Childe's thesis helps explain why reform comes when it does, why people are concerned with the cost of funerals at some times and not others. Their concern certainly does not correlate at all well with the actual cost of funerals.

Conclusion

One of the main criticisms of funerals today is that they are impersonal; another is that they cost too much.

The two are linked. One reason that funerals are impersonal is that they are bought with money, not organised by family and community. Impersonality, in the funeral as in so many other areas of life, is due in large part to the inexorable spread of the cash nexus. The strange men in black who wheel granny in and out of the crem are weird and impersonal *because* they are strangers; if you want something more personal, you'd better find bearers who knew granny – they'll probably do it not only for love, but also for free.

There is no reason why we should not perform some, or even all, of the funeral director's tasks for ourselves. Then we would regain not only our bank balance, but the funeral itself.

This need not mean simpler funerals. Whether a funeral is elaborate is a separate issue from whether we pay for it or choose to organise it ourselves. Before cash came to rule over all, the world saw great variety in funerals – some were simple, some were elaborate. Some were dominated by priests as much as funerals today are dominated by funeral directors. However, the bereaved family and community themselves organised and participated in the funeral, and no one complained that funerals were impersonal.

"Hardly worth building if he's not going to stay."

8

RELIGIOUS FUNERALS, SECULAR PEOPLE

From sense of grief and pain we shall be free;
We shall not feel, because we shall not Be.

Lucretius (94–55BC)

Men fear Death as children fear to go in the dark; and as
that natural fear in children is increased with tales, so is the
other.

Francis Bacon (1561–1626)

In a secular age it seems strange that so many people who
have hardly ever been to church should end up with a
traditional religious funeral. Does this reveal some hidden
religiosity that surfaces only under the duress of death? Or
has official religion got an unfair monopoly on funerals? Or
are many of us hypocrites, cashing in the eternal life insurance
policy even though during our lifetime we have failed to pay
regular premiums?

Such questions all assume that the traditional religious
funeral is in fact traditional and religious. But in fact, in the
past five hundred years the Christian funeral has gone
through some extraordinary about-turns. If you dig behind
the religious façade of the contemporary funeral, you discover that some of the basics, such as a belief in heaven and
hell, seem to have evaporated; and if you dig further, you
discover that Protestants have never really made up their
minds what the purpose of a funeral is anyway. Research
into the religious history of the funeral reveals a surprising
amount about the problems that funerals, both 'secular' and
'religious', face today.

The funeral triangle

In rural Greece, for five years after the funeral the body lies in a splendid marble grave. Each evening, the widow or closest female relative comes to tend the grave, to pray for the dead person, to remember; at their nightly vigil the women talk with each other and swap stories. At the end of five years they dig up the grave and inspect the bones, a traumatic business for the widow as she sees before her eyes what her husband or son has been reduced to. If the bones are white and clean, the women take this to mean that the soul is now cleansed of its sins and is in paradise. They collect the bones and place them in the communal village ossuary, and the mason can reuse the marble stone for the next burial. If the bones are not clean, they are replaced in the grave, prayer is multiplied, and another year or two elapses before the women try again.

All this seems very strange to Anglo-Saxon sensibilities that do not like to contemplate the decaying matter under the churchyard grass, and digging it up still less. However, it is all very logical. There are three actors in funeral and mourning rites:

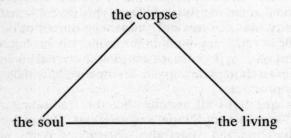

In Greece, what happens over time to each of these actors is mirrored in each of the others.

The corpse is decaying. Its putrid flesh is consumed by the earth, till after a few years only clean bones are left. At this point the bones lose their individual identity as they are tossed into the ossuary and become unidentifiable bones of the ancestors.

The soul is being purified, aided by the prayers of the living, on its way to paradise.

The widow is mourning the loss of a husband or child. This pain is unique to her, but once the mourning is over the deceased moves from being uniquely grieved by one person to being one of the village ancestors.

All three actors proceed in parallel, each reflecting the state of the others. What happens to the corpse reflects what is happening to the soul and to the widow. The widow's tending of the corpse's home through her gardening, the church's tending of the person's soul through its prayers, and the women's tending of each others' bruised selves through their talking and sharing, all proceed in parallel.

You might say this kind of logic may apply to rural Greece, but it doesn't make any sense in modern Britain or Australia. In fact it does. The Reformation banned praying for the soul of the deceased, since it believed the soul's fate to be determined already; after death, nothing more could be done. If the mourners cannot interact with the soul of the departed, that simply leaves the body to dispose of. If the body is deemed important, its disposal can be a reverent and religious act; but if the body is ignored, all you are left with is the living, narcissistically contemplating their own grief. As I suggested in Chapter 6, this is precisely the view of the funeral held by some modern psychologists. Corpse and soul are ignored, leaving what the Australians call the 'life-centred funeral'.

But corpses and souls don't go away quite so easily. Hidden from the bereaved in the days following death, they suddenly reappear in the funeral service itself: centre-stage are the coffin and a cleric. Both are all too often an embarrassment to be endured by the grieving family, and this is one reason why what happens in the funeral does not relate at all well to the life of the family in the days before and after.

Though in rural Greece the fates of body, soul and mourners all mirror one another, in most modern societies the three fates do not relate to each other. The physical, the psychological, and the theological constantly jar, mainly because we pretend to ignore the physical and the theological. This, surely, is one reason why people find funerals unreal and lacking in integrity. To regain integrity there are only three options:

1. Explicitly exclude the body from the funeral, as is often done nowadays in California.

2. Explicitly exclude the soul from the funeral, as in secular funerals.
3. Explicitly reintroduce both body and soul back into the funeral.

The Puritan ethic and the spirit of cremation

Catholic theologians in the late middle ages went over the top in stressing the importance of praying for the deceased. The quiet confidence of the Orthodox believer that the departed were growing into God was replaced by the Western tradition of purgatory, with its inherent anxiety as to whether the soul would enter heaven at all. This anxiety enabled the church to dominate the people, since only the prayers of the church could help the soul's passage.

The linchpin of the Reformation was that neither the good works of the living nor the prayers of the church could affect the eternal destiny of the soul. Only the grace of God could save the human being.

Condemning popish funeral customs became a prime concern of the reformers. Read the words of Thomas Becon, Cranmer's chaplain:

> After the departure from this life all go straightways either unto eternal glory or else unto everlasting pain . . . Here are reckoned but two kinds of persons, faithful and unfaithful . . . and the preacher saith, 'when the tree falleth, whether it be toward the south or north, in what place soever it fall, there it lieth. As we depart so shall we have our place . . .' Therefore your prayers for the dead are in every condition frustrated and unprofitable. Heaven needeth no prayer, hell refuseth all prayer . . . If these things be true . . . what need you then to stand nodding in your Memento, praying for the dead. Ye might as well pray for dead swine.

In the more extreme reformed funeral, not only the requiem mass for the dead, but any funeral service in church was banned. The service was meant to take place entirely at the grave, and it was simply a matter of dumping the body in the ground, saying a quick prayer, and going home. What more was there to do? More to the point, what more dare you do if you were not to be accused of popery? The Anglican funeral service was based on the old medieval rite's final committal to the earth, leaving out the mass in church entirely; this turning of the postscript into an entire service is why to this day there is no satisfactory rite for an Anglican funeral in church.

When I ask Catholics why they officially disapproved of cremation until the 1960s, and Orthodox Christians why they still do, they usually reply, 'Because of the resurrection.' World religions (Christianity, Judaism, Islam) that believe in resurrection of the body bury their members, while those that believe in reincarnation of the soul (Hinduism, Buddhism) cremate theirs. The earthiness of burial seems to 'fit' the physicality of the belief in bodily resurrection, while the dissipation of smoke into the air and of ashes into the river frees the soul to find another incarnation.

But this does not account for why many Protestant Christians have readily accepted cremation. They would claim that if God has the power to raise a pile of dry bones, especially if all mixed up with other bones in the ossuary, he certainly has the power to raise to life six pounds of ashes. Admittedly, it is easier to imagine the dead rising on the day of resurrection out of their coffins, as depicted by the medieval sculptures on the west front of Wells Cathedral, than it is to imagine dispersed ashes rematerialising. But this is a matter of ease of human imagination, not of God's power.

I am convinced that Catholic and Orthodox Christians prefer burial because, unlike Protestants, they believe in a process that occurs after death, during which the soul is purged of its sin (traditional Catholicism), or at least under-goes a growth towards God (Orthodoxy, and some modern Catholicism). The intermediate period when the corpse is rotting – still with the semblance of human form but not yet in its final state, smelling of corruption before it becomes clean and pure – matches the post-death cleansing of the soul. Protestants, who tend to believe the person goes to heaven or hell instantly on death, are much happier with cremation, in which the body is reduced instantly to ashes.

Certainly this reasoning is why the Puritans had just one quick service, for a lengthy series of rituals would have implied the soul going on a spiritual journey. Bishop Hooper, in Edward VI's reign, was most concerned to root out 'month-ends or anniversaries . . . which is the maintenance of the purgatory, and false belief and state and condition of the dead'.

As one New England Puritan divine put it in 1679, 'We must leave the dead with the dead, and live with the living.' This is remarkably similar to the motto of the Cremation Society of Great Britain, 'Leave the land for the living.' There is a clear affinity in attitude between the minimal funerals of the Puritans and modern cremation: both say that the person is dead and there is nothing you can do about it, save get rid of the corpse and get on with life.

Sir John Millicent, in his will of 1577, was concerned that elaborate funeral ritual was not only superstitious but also, like its modern American counterpart, chargeable, a rip off. He instructed that 'the burial be done without any manner of pomp, and without the wearing of black gowns or coats, or the jangling or ringing of any bells, or any other ceremonies to be had thereat, for they are but vain, chargeable and superstitious'.

These Puritan criticisms of popish funeral rituals are similar to modern criticisms of the elaborate American way of death. In the one case the Catholic church exploited ignorant people's anxiety about their status in the eyes of God; in the other case the American funeral industry exploits rootless people's anxiety about their status in the eyes of men. Direct disposal, Californian style, is a secularised replay of the Puritan funeral. It is no coincidence that among once-Christian but now secular countries it is those with a Protestant heritage that have spawned the most vigorous movements to stop elaborate funerals.

Then as now, not everyone was happy with this: ordinary folk wanted something to mark the passing of a friend or neighbour. Luther was sympathetic to this and, unlike Calvin, tolerated the ringing of the church bell to signify the death, though not of course to call people to pray for the dead.

Luther also stressed the funeral sermon. The point of the funeral shifted from assisting the deceased in their passage to heaven, and became instead an object-lesson for the living. Some of us today have been to Puritan-influenced funerals in which the living have been harangued from the pulpit. One Dutchman told me of a work colleague who had defected from the Puritan 'black-stocking' church in which he had been raised; when the colleague's father died, the three-hour funeral was directed mainly at reminding the son of the joys of dying with and the terrors of dying without Christ, calling him to repent and return to the fold.

If ordinary people shut their ears to funeral sermons, in other ways they took to heart the new stress on the living. The historian Clare Gittings reckons that people found a way around the Puritan ethic by replacing the now non-existent religious ritual with secular feasting. After the burial in 1649 of James Lawes, a Lincoln plumber, there were consumed sixteen gallons of ale, five and a half gallons of muscadine, ten pounds of biscuits, eighteen dozen cakes and forty-eight and a half dozen loaves of bread and buns, not to mention two pounds of sugar and an ounce of nutmeg and ginger! If religious ritual smelled of Rome, elaborate secular rituals were safe – so much for the 'abstemious' Puritans!

The funeral became a display of social status, with the funeral sermon giving way to the funeral eulogy (a rarity even today in Catholic countries). As the spiritual meaning of the funeral all but vanished, so the social meaning expanded. Earthly status came to replace spiritual status.

In death as in life, Protestantism paved the way for secularism. Protestantism helped dig its own grave, in more senses than one.

The abolition of hell

In ancient Egypt the dead embarked on a journey. To help them through the perils of the Underworld, they were provided with a papyrus containing excerpts from the magical *Book of the Dead*. Any visit today to Egypt or to the Egyptian room in the British Museum is replete with images of bodies mummified so they can enjoy the next life, of the mummy being rowed in a funeral boat, of pyramids stocked with provisions for the next life.

Ever since, we have thought of death as the start of a journey. Successful completion of this journey depends, in part, on the ritual actions of the living. The funeral is a rite of passage where the task of the living is to assist the spiritual passage of the dead. That is the rationale for most pre-modern funeral practices.

No longer. The Reformation told people that, although the soul did indeed go on a journey, the journey was over in a flash and there was nothing we could do to assist it once the person had died. So, in the Victorian era, the spiritual stress was not on the funeral but on the deathbed, with clergy and family praying for the last-minute conversion of the unregenerate sinner, or listening for the last whispered prayer of the faithful.

But the nineteenth century saw a further change. Somehow, hell began to disappear. It became difficult to believe that the spouse or lover you had put on a pedestal in life might be rejected by God in death. There was nothing more likely to erode a clear fundamentalist belief in heaven and hell than being in love with someone whose eternal destiny was unclear. (It still is. Shirley du Boulay's recent biography of Cicely Saunders, the founder of St Christopher's Hospice, touchingly reveals how falling in love with first an atheist and then two Catholics softened her once clear-cut evangelicalism.)

So, romantic love undermined the belief in hell. The problem was not lost on the Victorians, whose theologians spilled much ink debating the nature of heaven and hell.

Other currents fuelled the debate. In feudal times you might be hung for stealing a sheep from the king but not for stealing a sheep from a serf, for the status of the person offended against was more important than the offence itself. In such a world, sins against an infinite God certainly deserved infinite punishment. But by the nineteenth century the scale of punishment was related to the scale of offence, so why then should mortals be given infinite punishment for finite offences? Hell was no longer plausible. Moreover, social science was beginning to suggest that sins are caused not by the evil heart of the sinner but by the environment, making any kind of divine punishment unreasonable.

But it was the First World War, hell on earth, that really finished off hell below. How could anyone believe that half of all those brave young lads, dying for their country, were destined for hell? By 1920 hell had disappeared.

Where did this leave the funeral? Protestants could use the

occasion neither to pray for the deceased nor to warn the living of the perils of hell. If the Reformation had killed off the medieval requiem mass, the century leading up to 1918 killed off the Puritan funeral sermon. All that was left to do was to commit the deceased into the love of God, and thank God for her life.

So in the 1920s the Protestant funeral turned into an occasion to comfort the living with the hope of heaven. In North America ministers in liberal churches criticised the 'hell-fire and damnation' funeral sermon as psychologically damaging. Enter instead around this time the twenty-third Psalm and flowers; exit all talk of hell and worms. The congregation are not to be frightened, they are to be comforted, and in the process reduced to total passivity. There is nothing for them to do but be thankful for the life of the deceased, and be grateful she is now in heaven.

But as hell disappeared, so heaven lost shape, for it could no longer be hell's opposite. If you are a romantic, you cannot believe in hell because you cannot conceive of your lover being in hell, so heaven became the place where you will eventually be reunited with your beloved. Philippe Ariès tells a delightful story of one pious Victorian eulogising about the bliss of seeing his wife in heaven, and then suddenly, as an afterthought, guiltily remembering the joy of seeing his Saviour too! Spiritualism also became attractive, offering a more immediate contact with the departed, blossoming in the Victorian period and then again after the First World War.

Rite for the dead, or right of the living?

In this chapter I have traced how the Christian funeral has changed over the centuries. Originally performed to assist the passage of the deceased, after the Reformation it turned into a display of social status for the living, and in the present century into a therapeutic act to comfort the intimately bereaved. First the deceased, then the social group, and finally the bereaved individual have succeeded one another as the focus of the Western funeral.

This shift has most affected secularists and Protestants. As part of my work, I teach final-year Anglican theological students in a largely evangelical college. When I ask them what in their three years of training they have been taught about death and funerals, they usually list the items in Pastoral Theology to do with care of the bereaved. I have yet to hear a student refer to the sections in Christian Doctrine that deal with the resurrection! The only issue for them, apparently, is the psychological state of the bereaved.

Roman Catholics are holding out against all this. One study in 1959, by the American sociologist Robert Fulton, found that Catholic priests saw the funeral as an occasion for prayer for the salvation of the deceased's soul, while Protestant ministers saw it as an opportunity to offer peace to the survivors and hope of a future life. Since Vatican II, however, Catholic funerals are paying more attention to the congregation of the living and downplaying the sins of the deceased. This worries some Catholics, who fear a replay of the Protestant débâcle.

You might think that the Orthodox church, with the resurrection central in its ancient liturgy, would hold out the longest. However, several studies in the Soviet Union have found that although Russian Orthodox believers are holding out against secularism in many other ways, half of them no longer believe in a life beyond the grave; these now attend funerals not to pray for the soul of the departed, but to express and share their grief.

So it is that, starting with Protestant countries, gathering pace in a secular twentieth century, and now affecting Catholic and Orthodox traditions too, the funeral has changed from a rite which the mourners perform for the dead, into the right of the living to be comforted by the minister. From this derive most of the problems of the modern cremation service, in which joy and sorrow, participation and any sense of reality, have collapsed into a pseudo-dignity designed not to upset.

The dilemma of the modern funeral is how to devise a rite for the living. How can the congregation be involved in their own therapy, now there is precious little for them to do for the deceased? Should we perhaps abandon the funeral, and just cry alone at home or talk to our bereavement counsellors? What is the funeral for?

9

BEYOND TABOO

The English have by far the most unhealthy attitude to death, especially the middle class; they're so repressed. And as the Eighties have seen the growth of middle-class aspiration, there has been a growth in emotional repression. The working class used to spend a lot of money and let it all out. Now it's more stiff upper lip, forty-five minutes down at the crem and pretend it never happened.

Howard Hodgson, funeral director, 1989

I see little reason to believe that our society is more death-denying than previous ones – it is, simply, dead ignorant about death.

Dr Colin Murray Parkes, psychiatrist, 1984

A friend of mine from Manchester recalls that when her uncle died in the 1950s, he was laid in the front parlour and everyone came to pay their respects. When in the 1960s her mum died, there was a post-mortem and she was a bit of a mess, so she was not on view; but people still came to the house expecting her to be on show. When a year or two ago her dad died, he was neither taken home for viewing, nor did anyone call.

Funerals, and attitudes to funerals, are constantly on the move. What one social class or ethnic group accepts without question, another finds offensive. What one class accepted in a previous generation, another class will today. The picture at any one time in any one country is complex, and just as soon as you think you have captured it, it has already changed.

In Britain in the 1960s and 1970s, even as the rituals of

taking off your hat as a hearse passed and having to wear black at the funeral were disappearing, so Geoffrey Gorer was putting death back into focus and Elisabeth Kübler-Ross became required reading in the medical schools. So, was death at that time becoming less visible, or more? Is the ever-increasing pile of newspapers and magazines publicly proclaiming death as the greatest taboo of the twentieth century evidence for, or evidence against, the supposed taboo?

One reason for the constantly shifting funereal sands is the presence of opposing forces within modern society.

Some aspects of modernity make death rather easy to deal with. Most of us now die in old age, by which time a pension for a surviving spouse and their own careers and families for our grown-up children mean that we rarely leave survivors financially destitute – as we typically would have done in previous centuries when many died during their working lives and with dependent children. Should one be so inconsiderate today as to die while still in harness, it may upset our family but not our employer: bureaucracies require trained competence rather than personal flair, so can replace the dead employee without upset. Secularism and science enable many to face death as the natural end rather than as a religious ordeal. We expect change as the natural course of things.

At the same time, as previous chapters have suggested, other aspects of modernity make death peculiarly problematic. Nature's final victory over the human being comes as a shock to macho, technological man; the old person who dies at eighty, written off by society, is also the husband of fifty or more years, leaving a gap in the life of his widow unknown by her forebears who expected death to end marriage within a decade; capitalism has long since stolen communal ritual; and secularism leaves us unable to communicate with either the dead or with a God who cares for the dead.

When people are moulded by such varied and conflicting forces, there is no predicting how attitudes will change in future, though they may help us understand why attitudes have changed in the past.

White-sliced or wholemeal?

Recent generations have seen major shifts in lifestyle: from country to city; from local to cosmopolitan; from having out of poverty to do things yourself to paying professionals to do things for you; from traditional working class to affluent working class, lower middle class or underclass. Each shift usually involves a loss of what we like to think of as tradition, including the traditional funeral.

Some may accept the loss of the old-style funeral, arguing that with funeral directors, automobiles, hospitals and crem"toria there is no need for old-fashioned behaviour such as relatives carrying the coffin. Others may find positive status in *not* having to carry the coffin. The services of the funeral director reflect both your ability to pay him, and – like Coca Cola and white-sliced bread – your entry into the modern, sophisticated world.

Those whose forebears moved out of the rural or working class several generations ago may be one stage further on. They may have gone so far down the rational, secular, cosmopolitan road that they eschew the funeral altogether, preferring to fly their busy friends in from around the world a few months later for a secular memorial service. Jessica Mitford is their guide to funeralia, and they complain, even when wealthy, at the cost of funerals. Why should they pay for services they do not want?

Then there are those of a more green persuasion, who reject white-sliced for wholemeal bread; it may not taste so nice, and the kids may object, but it is better for you. A green holistic view of the human being also implies a more whole view of death, a hospice death in which body, mind and spirit cannot be divorced. It may also lead to a more wholemeal kind of funeral, bringing the kids with them, letting the emotions go. Like wholemeal bread, it may be harder to digest, but it is better for you, and for the kids.

The Victorian bench-mark

Many people, when they think about how funerals have changed, take the Victorian funeral as the starting-point. This

is understandable, for many old people grew up at the end of
the Victorian era, and the changes since then have been
remarkable. Some of us look back with horror at all the black
crêpe, and thank God that things are more dignified now.
Others, especially some social scientists, look back sentimen-
tally to the public mourning rituals of the Victorian period,
arguing that they were therapeutic for the grieving individual
and that we have abandoned them to our own loss.

What the Victorian period did was impose on death both a
rational, male approach, and a romanticism that opened the
floodgates of sentimentality. The conflict between these two
irreconcilables, rationalism and romanticism, is still very
much with us. We want to be practical, orderly, scientific,
medical about death, at the very moment that we are paying
the cost of commitment to a lifelong partner. In an age when
the death of a partner may hit us harder than in most previous
ages, we abandon elaborate ritual and sentimental gravestones in favour of the plastic anonymity of the modern
crematorium. Funerals today look utterly different from a
hundred years ago, but we are still playing out the tension
between rationalism and romanticism that the Victorians
created.

Historical studies all point to other forces, going back much
further than a hundred years. Modernity has been a'coming
for several hundred years. When you take the middle ages as
your starting-point, as I have generally done, you come up
with a different picture. The rise of the individual dates from
at least as far back as the twelfth century; our power over
nature has been steadily developing since the seventeenth
century, although it is only in the past few decades that
ordinary people have felt much benefit; secularisation, again
only consciously experienced recently, has roots going back
to the Reformation; the entry of capitalism into the funeral,
and the claims of undertakers to know better than ordinary
folk, began in the late seventeenth century. All these currents
have profoundly affected both how we handle death, and the
format and function of the funeral.

But individualism, male pride in technology, the conning of
consumers by self-proclaimed professionals, and secularism
are all under attack in the late twentieth century. In the 1960s
pundits saw them as the inevitable fruits of modernity; but

now things look very different, and the pundits talk of post-modernity. The search for community and connectedness, the women's movement, the green movement, the renewed interest in religion, and the education of consumers all cause us to wonder whether modernity has had its day. And if so, whether the modern funeral has had its day too. It is this possibility that encouraged me to write this book.

The cross and the chimney

Following the Hillsborough disaster of 1989, local Liverpudlian musicians cut a single of the local song 'Ferry 'Cross the Mersey', which immediately went to the top of the charts. A fitting memorial perhaps, but people across the country must have found it strange for this to be plopped into radio and TV pop music programmes. Nothing was done to phase people from entertainment into contemplation of human tragedy, nothing to phase them back again into light-hearted entertainment, just entertainment and tragedy plopped next to each other.

Such an experience is typical of death today. For the bereaved, the days following the death involve getting death certificates signed, seeing lawyers and funeral directors, reading the will, releasing bank accounts, finding life insurance policies, deciding on the hymns. Into this acute bout of rationality is suddenly injected the archaic mystique of the 1662 Prayer Book's funeral rite, which relates neither to the form-filling nor to the grief of modern individuals.

Nothing hangs together. There is no link between efficient combustion of the body and a preoccupation with the emotional state of the bereaved; no link between the funeral director's view of the corpse as an object to be transported and prevented from going off, and the bereaved's perception of it as a person; no link between the psychiatrist's view of death as another emotional process to be identified, controlled and managed, and the priest's view of it as a mystery to be left in the hands of the Almighty.

These contradictions must not be brought into the open. When considering the cover design for this book, it struck me that a forceful image would be a crematorium chimney with a cross on it. I have never seen such a thing: it would be as shocking as a cross over the door of a brothel. What has the crematorium chimney, symbolising death as a technically manageable process, in common with the cross, the symbol of Christ's victory over the ultimate human mystery? So instead, we find the priest and the cross inside, and the chimney hidden around the back.

This contradiction between sacred and profane has perhaps always been a feature of funerals throughout human history. We humans have always struggled to find the meaning in death. But the feeling that nothing 'hangs together' is a key feature of post-modernity, for nowadays we have only partial perspectives, partial truths, about life as well as death. With computers, we have so much information, but so little knowledge, and even less wisdom. We are rediscovering religion, but don't know how to apply it to economics, or to politics. As the modern certainties of science, of reason, of secularism wane, we are left with patchwork knowledge, patchwork architecture, patchwork art, patchwork funerals.

Post-modernity opens up our approach to death in a way not known, perhaps, since the Reformation. But it also fragments things, so that our handling of the funeral could collapse altogether. That is the challenge taken up in the rest of this book.

PART THREE

PRINCIPLES

This part attempts to answer the following questions:
What exactly is a good funeral? What is its purpose?
Who is it for? What are the ingredients of a good
funeral?

10

WHAT IS A FUNERAL?

Backwards or forwards?

In the past, in some Australian aboriginal tribes, people unrelated to the person who had died might lacerate themselves, sometimes with dire consequences, presumably symbolising that every member of the community shared the pain of loss. In Europe in the late middle ages, the poor were often just stitched up in a shroud and dumped in a communal grave of five hundred or so souls, without any religious service.

Do not imagine that I am a romantic, wishing to turn the clock back to the good old days, to a golden age before individualism, technology and secularism had made life – and death – so complex. There was no golden age.

Do not imagine, either, that returning to Victorian funeral rituals will solve anything. Like the United States today, that period suffered from a surfeit of undertakers, who could make a profit only by elaborating the funeral, adding value to their services. From 1840–3, London averaged 114 deaths a day, including unprofitable workhouse deaths, and these had to go to around 1,025 undertakers, all of them trying to make a shilling or two out of on average less than one funeral a week.

The Victorian funeral became in large part a display of status, again as in the United States today. And the severe restrictions imposed on women in mourning were a kind of social death endured not only on behalf of a deceased husband, but also on behalf of distant relatives, which must often have created rather than softened their emotional distress. Worse, the physical discomfort of the mourning dress smacks of a self-mutilation not so different in spirit from the lacerating aboriginals, except with the Victorians it was only women who were expected to suffer.

Nor is there much hope to be found in the headily atheist and egalitarian days following the French Revolution, in which public officials attempted to take over from clergy and undertakers. Here is what one critical observer said:

> I must describe a scene that will inspire you with a righteous horror. These men who transport the dead of the town to the common cemetery often become intoxicated along the way and quarrel, or what is even more revolting, sing gaily, and the public official who goes with them is unable to impose silence.

Religious fear, financial exploitation, bureaucratic incompetence, and even plain chaos are there in abundance in the historical record, as much as today. Such problems were worst in the cities, where hundreds could die each week, for how do you retain the uniqueness of each death, its spiritual significance, the involvement of family and community, when the authorities have to run a mass-production – or rather, mass-destruction – line?

No, there is no golden age to which we can return. Human society has perhaps never handled death that well, and probably never will.

In particular, death raises questions:
1. What is our relation to natural forces?
2. How are we to be supported at this most isolating and devastating of times?
3. What is the meaning of life, and of suffering?
4. Is there a God?

Modernity, despite its many benefits, is particularly bad at helping us with these four questions. Our macho technology and urban living isolate us from nature; our individualism isolates us from our fellow human beings; our secularism rules out of court some of the questions asked by the bereaved.

The way forward is to be found neither in tradition nor in modernity. But we can learn from tradition, extracting those features of traditional funerals that make good sense even today. And we can face up to the peculiar problems of modernity as we seek to move on beyond the modern understanding of death. We can seek out community where it exists, to counter the isolation of the individual. We can look to the female and the green, as we suspect male technocrats of not having a monopoly on truth. We can face up to both the problems and the possibilities offered by secularism. We can challenge the insidious idea that everything, even respect for the dead, must be bought and sold through an impersonal market. This is what the next few chapters attempt.

What is a funeral?

Before proceeding, we must have some idea of what a funeral is. What is its purpose?

For many bereaved people, the funeral is an ordeal to be endured. For others, not immediately bereaved, it is a rip-off. For clergy, it is a time for committing the deceased to God's care. Psychologists say it is a minor part of the grief process. Funeral directors, especially those in Australia and the United States, say it is a major part of the grief process; though for them it is also a way of making a living. For anthropologists, it affirms or creates social structure. In the eyes of some sociologists, it is a display of status and an atonement for guilt.

Apart from the ongoing war between some angry customers who attack the funeral as a rip-off, and the funeral directors who respond by claiming the funeral provides invaluable psychological help for the bereaved and is therefore good value for money, these different views exist in splendid isolation. Only historians seem able to integrate these various views and put them in some kind of perspective.

In the United Kingdom publicly owned cemeteries and crematoria in some towns come under Environmental Health, in others under Parks and Recreation (itself a part of Leisure). I would have thought more directly appropriate would be Housing, or Transport; after all, graves provide homes for the dead, and, whatever else a rite of passage is, it provides transport for both body and soul. Funerals seem to fit everywhere, and nowhere.

What then is a funeral?

I would resist any attempt to reduce the funeral to any one of its many aspects, though unfortunately this happens all the time. Some churches so stress the bliss of the deceased in heaven that the emotional grief and social loss of the mourners is not acknowledged; years later, some of these mourners end up on the psychiatrist's couch, with unresolved grief. In the United States, the funeral has come to be dominated by the profit motive; even the industry's critics – such as Mitford – have adopted a purely materialistic concept of the funeral, in which the sole purpose is the physical removal of the body. They have thrown the spiritual, social, and personal baby out with the economic bathwater. In the United Kingdom, by contrast, municipal bureaucracy is the driving force behind most of what happens before, during and after a funeral.

Psychology too has been staging a take-over bid for the funeral. We are asked to believe that the funeral is all about therapy, oiling the bruised emotions of the grieving. Habenstein and Lamers, two sociologists who in the early 1960s were commissioned by the American funeral industry to write the massive tome *Funeral Customs the World Over*, note in their conclusion that there are three aspects to a funeral: disposing of the body, relating to the departed spirit, and therapy for the bereaved. Whereas the first two aspects get only two-thirds of a page each, therapy gets over eight pages. The book's penultimate sentence states categorically that the function of the funeral, 'basically, is therapeutic'.

The anthropologists Huntingdon and Metcalf, in their *Celebrations of Death*, rightly question this. There is no reason to suppose that funeral customs are driven by a desire to heal the emotions. Indeed, in many societies, traditional and modern, the grieving person has to survive *despite* local funeral customs. And as I suggest in this book, preoccupation with therapy for the bereaved can be counter-productive, not to mention distorting the spiritual and social purposes of the funeral.

An answer

The only occasion on which funeral rites are deliberately withheld is when the public consider the dead person to have been inhuman. This is why war criminals have no memorial. Goering's ashes were taken into the countryside and dumped in a ditch. Nor is there any stone to mark the life and death of Michael Ryan, the gunman who killed thirteen of his fellow villagers in Hungerford and then turned his gun on himself. To quote one newspaper: 'His ashes were to be scattered across the countryside, leaving no grave or mark to show he ever existed.'

Oliver Cromwell was buried in grand style. But a few years later, at the restoration of the monarchy, he was redefined as a war criminal, so Charles II had the bodies of Cromwell and two others who had assisted in the regicide of Charles I exhumed, dragged through the streets to Tyburn, hanged, and beheaded. The heads were stuck on poles at Westminster Hall, while the bodies were flung into a common pit for criminals. In the seventeenth and eighteenth centuries, to be denied a funeral and cut up instead by the anatomist was the ultimate deterrent in English criminal law, more feared than capital punishment.

All this suggests that the funeral has something very basic to do with human dignity. Only when the person is deemed inhuman can the funeral be dispensed with, or even reversed as in the case of Cromwell. Only when we would rather this person had never lived do we feel it inappropriate to pay him the respect implied by a funeral.

So I agree with Roger Grainger's definition: '*The main purpose of a funeral is to signify the event of a death*.' It marks that something valuable, a human life, has passed. Whatever else a funeral does or does not do, it must do this.

When a pauper dies, with no one to grieve her, and no one to make a profit out of her, do we just tip her into the cremator or into the ground? If it were just a matter of economics, of public health, or of psychology, or even all three, we would; yet no civilised society does, nor ever has done. We provide her with a coffin, and a religious or civic service of committal. Poor people the world over fight for the right to a decent funeral above almost anything else, for they know there is something appalling about a human life ending, and no one noticing, no one marking it.[1]

Grainger works as a hospital chaplain, so he knows what he is talking about:

> When the number of patients in the female psycho-geriatric ward at the mental hospital is reduced by the death of one isolated old woman, and the sister in charge brings along half-a-dozen patients, all equally old, equally isolated, to pay their last respects 'because she hasn't anybody, you know'; these are the times when the funeral really counts . . . [These funerals] are not prompted by the desire to make a show and impress the neighbours or reinforce the social hierarchy. They are not ways of assuaging guilt . . . indeed, these archetypal, critical, front-line funerals are noted for their absence of display. They are not particularly valuable as outlets for powerful feelings of grief on the part of the bereaved, because there is often no one present who comes into the category of a bereaved person. On these occasions it is neither an individual nor a community that is bereaved, but humanity.

This is why throughout the world paupers always want a proper funeral, even if they have no family left. It is why, even in modern wars, soldiers risk life and limb to collect their killed compatriots, to give them 'a decent burial'. It is why, as Grainger puts it,

> the bereaved person attends the funeral of someone whom he has greatly loved, making himself go, often against the advice of family and friends who are as frightened as he is

---

[1] With the 1832 Anatomy Act, dissection in Britain ceased to be a punishment for crime and became a punishment for poverty; many workhouse occupants were therefore denied a funeral, and dying 'on the parish' became a thing greatly to be feared. Ruth Richardson, in her book *Death, Dissection and the Destitute*, argues that this is why ensuring they receive a decent funeral has been so important for poor people in Britain. But the fact that poor people in many other parts of the world also go to extraordinary lengths to ensure a decent funeral suggests that there is also something much more universally human going on.

that he will not be able to bear it. Such people are aware of a greater priority than that of keeping calm and avoiding pain: the instinctive compulsion to assert the dignity and importance of persons.

A funeral may or may not help the bereaved, may or may not signal social status, may or may not make someone a profit – but these are no way to judge the value of a funeral. Like weddings, coronations and other ceremonies where people come together, a funeral may 'provide an opportunity for alliances to be established, to entertain, to remind people of obligations, to enable people to test whom they can trust and whom they cannot, to transmit news', to quote another survey of world funeral customs. But these functions, often valuable in themselves, are even further from what the funeral is essentially about.

Basically, a funeral says that something significant has happened, that a human life, *this* human life, has ended; and it goes on to interpret this event in some way. When funerals today fail, it is because you would never guess that something significant is being marked. When crematoria today fail, it is because their sheer mediocrity denies the significance of the life that has passed.

One friend of mine recalls when he was a teenager being driven in the funeral director's limousine to his father's funeral. He remembers clearly how extraordinary and how comforting was the way people on the pavement, total strangers, stood still and took off their hats. Somehow the world was recognising that a human being, they knew not whom, had left them.

In the old days, a passing bell was rung as a man lay dying, so he and his neighbours should know the end was near. Was John Donne thinking of it being rung for one of those unknown, unloved geriatric patients when he wrote:

Who bends not his ear to any bell which upon any occasion rings? but who can remove it from that bell which is passing a piece of himself out of this world? No man is an island, entire of itself; every man is a piece of the continent, a part of the main. If a clod be washed away by the sea, Europe is the less, as well as if a promontory were, as well as if a manor of thy friend's or of thine own were: any man's death diminishes me, because I am involved in mankind, and therefore never send to know for whom the bell tolls; it tolls for thee.

Clods as well as promontories deserve recognition. They too deserve a funeral.

11

WHOSE FUNERAL IS IT ANYWAY?

Until this century, most people would have said that the funeral is performed on behalf of the deceased, either as a way of helping them on to the next world or of paying them respect. Admittedly, St Augustine long ago said that all the elaborations that go with burial 'are rather comforts to the living than helps to the dead', but it is only in the twentieth century that the view has really gained ground, mainly among clergy, undertakers and other professionals in the grief business, that the funeral is performed essentially for the sake of the next of kin.

In law, the funeral does indeed belong to the next of kin. You can state in your will with the force of law what should happen to your property, but you can state only a preference as to what should happen to your body. It could hardly be otherwise. If you want to be buried, and your husband ends up cremating you, there is nothing you, being dead, can do about it; nor can any judge order your widower to reverse his decision, since you are already reduced to ashes. Your stated preference can be no more than a stated preference, for the funeral belongs not to the dead, but to the living.

Prince Albert, for one, must be turning in his grave. Despite the fashion for elaborate mourning, he wanted a simple funeral, but his distraught widow, Queen Victoria, did not accede to his request, in particular to his request that no busts of him be made. She put up statues of him all around the land, culminating in London's Albert Memorial. Her grief overcame the wishes of the one now six feet under.

This is no academic issue. Take a young homosexual man who dies as a result of AIDS, and whose parents have rejected him for his homosexuality or may not even know of his sexuality. Losing an adult offspring can be one of the most difficult of losses, for you have sacrificed much to bring up the child, are just about to enjoy his or her adult company, and then . . . nothing. The parents of the person with AIDS would seem to have a good case for arranging the kind of funeral that helps them. But if relations have really broken down between the man and his parents, is it right for the funeral to say or imply things about him that deny everything he lived for? After all, he was a grown man.

And what about the man's lover? Is he not equally traumatised? Not only does the lover have to cope with the loss of the one he loves, but also he is all too aware that what killed his partner may in the coming months kill him too. So whose funeral is it – the deceased's, the lover's, or the parents'? There is a big risk of the parents arranging something inappropriate – with the lover, whom they may have never met, suffering silently at the back of the crematorium. So it is not surprising that in the gay community in London, people with AIDS often plan their funerals together with their partners.

The problem is not just whether for a funeral to have integrity it should reflect the values of the deceased or of the next of kin. There is also the problem of who is the next of kin: the parents or the lover?

Legal resolutions are not very helpful. One funeral celebrant told me of a man who, unknown to his parents, had entered the country via a marriage of convenience, and had then died unexpectedly. He had met his wife just once, at the wedding ceremony. Technically, the wife was the next of kin, but fortunately the celebrant was able to contact her and she was very happy to forgo her legal rights and allow the man's parents to arrange the funeral. I think she came to the funeral.

More commonly, an old person may in effect have swapped her own family for the 'family' of friends and staff in the old person's home that has been her home for maybe a decade or more. Their loss may be greater than that of a biological family she has barely seen these past ten years.

Or take an increasingly common situation. The father of a friend of mine divorced some years ago. His recent funeral was attended not only by his children, but also by his divorced wife and his three subsequent girlfriends. The children, who decided to conduct the funeral themselves, were wise to think not of what they or any of their father's sexual partners would like, but of what he himself would have liked. They picked poems, songs and readings that summed up the man, and that incidentally all his womenfolk recognised. Some of the children are evangelical Christians, but their father was not at all religious, so to honour the man they knew and loved they conducted a secular funeral.

"It was a condition of his will – he didn't want anyone to be miserable at his funeral."

To forgo one's own beliefs and values, and arrange the kind of funeral that honours the actual life of the deceased seems to me to acknowledge something very profound about bereavement. Losing someone involves handing them over, whereas to grasp the funeral as your own possession is to cling to your unfulfilled hopes for the dead person. To hand over your legal rights over the funeral is to acknowledge that in reality you no longer possess this person.

This is not hard for many people. One British survey asked what was the most important thing about a funeral. Though clergy overwhelmingly saw its purpose as displaying the love of God in order to comfort the bereaved, the bereaved themselves saw its purpose as honouring the life of the person who had died. Only professionals – clergy, funeral directors, crematoria staff – who generally do not know the deceased focus on the bereaved. Friends and family focus on the deceased.

(One Australian funeral celebrant told me that by listening at length to the family's stories about the dead person he himself begins to appreciate the person and himself begins to grieve. Only then can he focus himself, and therefore the funeral, on the deceased. His funerals are very sympathetic, and I suspect this is because the celebrant is thinking not of the bereaved, but of the deceased.)

One further reason why some people with AIDS organise their own funerals is that they have been hurt by the condemnation of religious people. If people with AIDS do not plan an alternative funeral service, they will usually end up with a clergy-run service. The church abandoned them in life, why should it claim them in death? Whose funeral is it? They see no reason why it should be the church's. (This is something I explore more in Chapter 20.)

It is often appropriate, though, for the dying not to be concerned about their own funeral. Letting go is what dying, as well as bereavement, is about. So, for a dying person to allow the living to control the funeral is for him, too, a letting go that reflects the reality of dying. Persons with AIDS are perhaps unusual in having been so misunderstood in life that retaining control over the funeral is a final statement of their own personal dignity.

To sum up. Legally, the funeral belongs to the next of kin, but this is one occasion when people would be wise not to stand too firmly by their rights.

Enter the group

A soldier dies in Northern Ireland, and his body is flown home to his regimental barracks in England. The funeral service is held in the barracks, not a local church or cemetery chapel. For the journey to the cemetery, the coffin is transported not by funeral director's hearse but on a gun carriage; on the coffin rest the soldier's cap and gloves, and the flag of the nation he served. At the burial, guns are raised and a salvo fired in salute.

This funeral is not directed towards the grief of the young man's parents. It does not reflect his own unique personality. It eschews some of the usual services and facilities offered by church, local authority or undertaker. It is a military funeral.

Army recruiting offices in local high streets up and down the country stress the opportunity to see the world, learn a trade, have adventure. No mention of being prepared to kill and be killed. So when a soldier dies, especially in what is euphemistically termed peacetime, the official ethos of the army is undermined. It must be shored up, for if the death is ignored or just treated as a family matter, morale in that soldier's unit could quickly deteriorate. So what we find is a ceremony that powerfully reaffirms military values, with cap and gloves, salvo and flag. It has been said, for example, that the attention paid by military chaplains to conducting funerals helped Britain win the Falklands War.

Funerals belong not only to the deceased and to the next of kin, they also belong to groups. The tighter knit the group, or the more threatened it is by death, the more likely it will take over the funeral. It has to restate its values at the funeral if it is to survive.

When a fire-fighter, police officer, ambulance person, or other rescue staff-member dies, a funeral of the military kind ensues, unless the family specifically requests otherwise (Plate 2). When a miner dies underground, his mates have to turn out in force at the funeral, not only to pay their respects to a mate, but also to reaffirm their trust and respect of one another, without which accidents would occur every day.

Monarchies are rarely entirely safe from attack by pretenders to the throne or republicans. And there is no better time for such attacks than the death of a monarch, for in her dying days the old monarch is weak, in the first few days the new monarch is inexperienced, and key people are grieving. Is this not why royal funerals are as much about affirming the institution of monarchy as about personal grief for a dead individual? 'The King is dead! Long live the King!'

When an easily replaceable clerk in a large bureaucracy

dies, some colleagues may attend the funeral; but maybe none do. Her death does not threaten the organisation in any way. But when a school pupil dies, the school may well turn out in force, for education is about training young people for adulthood, and a child that does not reach adulthood threatens the very *raison d'être* of the school.

When a football game, played for pleasure, turns into a massacre, the values of the game have to be reasserted. In the week after the terrible tragedy at Hillsborough, Anfield stadium was decorated by fans' scarves and favours, not only the red and white of Liverpool, but also the blue and white of rival Everton and the colours of clubs from all over the world. In the face of appalling personal loss, people responded by making offerings of the symbol of the club and the game in whose support their friends had died. They created a shrine of red, blue and white that symbolised both their grief, and the city and the sport to which they are devoted (Plates 5–7).

Jackie, whose tragic death I mentioned at the beginning of Chapter 3, was a leading light of the local youth fellowship. At her requiem mass, the coffin was draped with her red youth-fellowship T-shirt. Many of the five hundred mourners came dressed in their red T-shirts, lining the path to the church. They sang through their tears 'Let there be love shared among us', and 'Make me a channel of your peace'. They were affirming not only what Jackie but also what their fellowship stood for.

When someone dies suddenly, anger is a common response, and this anger can be very disruptive. What if the parents should sue the army? What if the miners cannot face going down the pit again, or the players turning out again for Liverpool? What if the youth fellowship should collapse as the kids wander off in anger and disillusion at a God who is no longer loving? The values of the group must be asserted to be more powerful than the pain of the individual. Solidarity between the survivors must be shown. As individuals they may not come to the same answers, but there is comfort in facing the questions together, in knowing that the group goes on even as individuals go to pieces.

This power of the group to heal its bereaved members exists whenever the deceased was a member of an ongoing community. It is why, apart from any religious faith, there is usually something extra at the funeral of a regular member of a church, synagogue, mosque or temple. The mourners share their loss, and reaffirm what they as a group believe in, even at a time when as individuals they may never have had more serious doubts.

Often, the main group the deceased belonged to was his or her family. What are expressed then are the values of the family. Loyalty, kindness, hospitality, faithfulness, these are what feature in the eulogies at small private funerals. Some of the less pleasant aspects of family life may also emerge – as one undertaker in South Wales told me: 'You know we Welsh have Celtic blood in us, and we fight like dogs in our families. Weddings and funerals are the only times some families get together, and Celtic blood is often all over the floor.'

When the values of the group, the deceased and the family coincide, the funeral can be a moving and strangely satisfying occasion. When the parents of the soldier can say, 'He chose the army, knowing its dangers. It was his life,' they can attend the military funeral, pride mingling with grief.

But what of the soldier who was becoming a pacifist, and is shot the week before his discharge papers are due? What of the maverick politician who dies in harness, whose memorial service is organised by the party in which he was a constant irritant? What of the one unbuttoned daughter in a family devoted to the stiff upper lip? Or the one atheist in a fundamentalist family? Such funerals, dominated by militarism, party conformity, the stiff upper lip, or fundamentalism, can be hell for some of those attending. The needs of the individual and of the group clash.

> 'The King is dead! Long live the King!'
> 'Corporal Smith is dead. Long live the 2nd Battalion!'
> 'Ninety-five die at Hillsborough. Liverpool for the cup!'
> 'Aunt Freda has died. Long live the family!'

The group cannot but reassert itself.

The others

John travelled some hundreds of miles back to his parents' town for his father's funeral. After the service, everyone lined up to shake his hand, though he knew hardly any of them. He said to me afterwards that it felt as though they were not shaking his, but his father's hand. They had come not to help John, but to say goodbye to John's father.

The funeral belongs to the family, to the deceased, to the group. In a mobile society, there are also those who knew the deceased, but are members neither of the family, nor of any close-knit group to which he or she belonged. Often, the numbers of such people turning up for the funeral are not anticipated by the family.

When Pat Phoenix – soap opera *Coronation Street*'s Elsie Tanner – died, the church was full of her colleagues and friends. Behind a Dixieland band playing 'When all the Saints', the procession left the church to find the street outside thronged with those who knew not Pat, but Elsie. For these fans, the jazz band transmuted the mourned Pat into larger-than-life Elsie. Afterwards, just twelve close family went on to the crematorium for the committal. This funeral recognised colleagues, fans and family, in three connected but separate rituals.

Pat Phoenix's was typical of the funeral of a public figure. The most formally orchestrated are those of royalty. These too have a three-part structure: a funeral service for those whose work or ancestry connect them to the royal family; a procession through the streets for the crowd; and a private committal in the family mausoleum at Frogmore. Such funerals take care to belong to everyone.

These days, royal funerals are planned well ahead, but in more ordinary funerals certain people can get left out. Patients may never get over the death of their analyst, or post-graduate students over the death of their supervisor, yet no one stops to think that they too may need to say their farewells. A friend of mine in her sixties is angry that each Christmas two or three cards arrive, usually having crossed with hers, letting her know that a friend or colleague died some months ago. Nobody thought to invite her to the funeral. Nobody realised that person mattered to her.

It may not be practical to expect many of these people to get to the funeral. It is not just that they are often busy people and cannot fly to the other side of a continent at a day's notice. A person's circle of friends and acquaintances can be wide and varied, so that it is some weeks before everyone gets to hear of the death. Were I to die today, I am not sure how my family would know who might be interested in my demise. Certainly they are not all in my address book – some are on the membership lists of professional associations, others who know me in connection with my books have their addresses tucked away in diverse parts of my filing cabinets. It is not like Ambridge, where word that someone has died gets around the village within the hour.

Surely this is why, among mobile professional people, memorial services after a few months are becoming more popular. While not ignoring family ties, these typically address the person's contribution to public life. Moreover, there are likely to be former colleagues who are competent to speak movingly to a large and diverse congregation about the character they knew, loved or tolerated.

More often, though, letters have to suffice. When an old person dies, many friends and ex-colleagues are themselves old. They cannot travel to the other end of the country for funeral or memorial services, and in any case they may not wish to do so several times a year as friend after friend dies. Receiving memorial cards and writing letters of sympathy become the ritual through which the person is honoured and remembered. Certainly I found it very helpful in the weeks after my father died to read the letters that arrived by each post; some of them put into words what I, too close to my father, could not quite capture.

The Maoris see it as a good omen if it rains during a funeral, for it means that the gods are crying too. The Maoris wisely recognise that tears are shed not just by those most obviously and immediately affected by a death.

The gods cry for the reason given in the previous chapter, to signify the event of the death of a human being. Ultimately, the funeral is performed not just for the deceased, who is no longer there to care; nor just for the family, who may all be dead too; nor just for the community, for community there may be none; nor just for friends, who may not exist. But the death of a human being must be marked. The funeral belongs to humanity.

12

FLOW

This very day, a little while ago, you lived,
But now you are neither man nor woman.
Breathless you are, for the Navahos killed you!
Then remember us not, for here and now
We bring you your food. Then take and keep
Your earth-walled place: once! twice!
Three times! four times! Then leave us now!

Pueblo Indian song

A funeral is an occasion where change takes place; it must be located in a safe place where people can let go, and come out reconstructed.

David Durston, 1989

The death of a human being is a significant event. The funeral marks this; but how – in a few minutes – can a funeral do justice to something of such significance? One key is to understand the flow, the tone, the drama of the funeral. (This chapter will be of particular use to those who conduct funerals.)

Theatre

The lowering of the coffin into the grave, or its final disappearance at the crematorium, is the moment many of us find most painful.

I witnessed a Buddhist funeral in Hong Kong in which everyone displayed a calm detachment until the moment the coffin slid into the flames. At this moment, the widow broke down uncontrollably. In the West, very few of us are prepared to watch the coffin slide into the cremator – the disappearance of the coffin behind the curtain is painful enough.

The final disappearance of the coffin tells us brutally that this person has died. Many of us would like to avoid this knowledge, and indeed denying that the death has occurred is a common initial reaction to hearing the news. And yet until we accept that the death has happened, we cannot begin to grieve – and grief is essential if we are to move on in life. Psychologically speaking, the main function of the funeral is to ram it home to us that the person is dead: painful though it is, this frees us to enter a period of mourning, of adapting to a new life. In Christian terms, it is only when we accept the reality of death that we can believe in resurrection; Good Friday has to be endured if we are to see the joy of Easter.

Roger Grainger observes that a symbolic death can be more painful for the bereaved than the actual death. A widow may seem to be coping well, until she sells the family home, which precipitates a clinical depression. Or the widower copes, until a minor accident brings home to him that he has no one to care for him, and his confidence evaporates. It is as though only then does the widow or widower truly realise she or he is alone; until then, this has not truly sunk in, it has been subtly denied.

The funeral's final act of committal is just such a symbolic death. Placing the coffin into the ground or into the flames is not just a practical disposal of now-useless remains. It re-enacts death itself, which is why it is so painful. As Grainger puts it: 'When instinct and training urge us to leap over the tomb itself into a fantasy future, the rite brings us face to face with death and allows us to die, so that we may eventually live.'

This theatrical re-enactment can be greatly helped by a creative use of props. When a standard, closed coffin is the only prop, some mourners may not face up to the fact that the coffin contains someone they love. So, many people leave the modern crematorium funeral service feeling it was unreal. But with a hat placed on the coffin, as in military funerals or as in the morris dancer's funeral described earlier (p. 16), there is no mistaking who the unique person is within the coffin. And if the hat is also to be buried or cremated, this too is a symbolic death of something that represents the person:

somehow we can't quite imagine the body inside the coffin, but we can imagine, and may actually witness, the clods of earth squashing the hat.

Anyone who has been to a baby's funeral cannot but have been moved by the coffin's tiny size – a poignant reminder of precisely who we are saying goodbye to. The last sight of these reminders of the person – the tiny coffin, the treasured hat – is upsetting, yet the inevitable tears somehow feel positive. Later it is something visual to remember, more personal than the mass-produced coffin and the mass-packaged flowers.

There are three ways the death can fail to be re-enacted. One is that some or all of the mourners may not be there. In the United States few other than close family attend the final committal; in certain traditions, women are spared the ordeal. In these instances the body is there, but it is not disposed of in front of some or all of the mourners: it is not publicly put to death. The desire to spare our feelings at this point is understandable, but usually misguided.

If one reason for the re-enactment failing to happen is that the mourners are not present, a second is that the body is not present. This can occur after certain types of accident, or when a soldier's body is not recovered, and in other unusual circumstances. This can be very difficult for the family to bear. More frequently, the body is not present because it has already been disposed of previously, without any ceremony, and a memorial service follows as the only public farewell. Or the coffin may be present physically, but not symbolically – in some crematoria, for example, the coffin is there, but is so tucked out of the way that in effect it is not there at all. Without the body, we can share memories, affirm our ideals or religious faith, but we cannot re-enact the death.

Even when both the coffin and the mourners are present, a symbolic death is not assured if, at the end of the service, the coffin is not seen to depart . . . and things just peter out. This happens too often when the final ceremony is in a crematorium or funeral parlour. The mourners walk out, leaving the coffin there, without touching it or acknowledging it in any physical way. Or, if the coffin is hidden from view at the end of the service, the sense of finality can be disturbed by the noise of grinding machinery and uncertainty as to what happens to the coffin next. Either the coffin must move in some meaningful direction, or we must move in relation to the coffin: one way or the other, we have to say farewell to it.

If the committal is conducted without mourners present, the preceding public ceremony can still end with a symbolic death. Last year, I attended the funeral of an old family friend in central London. Since her flat was just around the corner from her church, and since most of us would have got lost finding our way through central London traffic to the crematorium and back, the funeral service in its entirety was held in the church. After the service, the vicar accompanied the coffin to the crematorium, while we all popped around the corner to her flat for sherry and cakes. The end of the funeral had been a moving symbolic death: the vicar led the procession through the congregation, proclaiming in ringing tones, as we watched the coffin being carried slowly down the aisle and finally out of sight:

> Go forth upon thy journey from this world, O Christian soul
> In the peace of him in whom thou hast believed,
> In the name of God the Father, who created thee,
> In the name of Jesus Christ, who suffered for thee,
> In the name of the Holy Ghost, who strengthened thee,
> May angels and archangels, and all the armies of the heavenly host, come to meet thee.
> May all the saints of God welcome thee,
> May thy portion this day be in gladness and peace, and thy dwelling in Paradise
> Go forth upon thy journey, O Christian soul.

Thus we bade farewell to Trix.

Like any religious act of worship, the funeral is a theatrical performance. This means not that it goes against people's real feelings, but that it dramatises them. It brings to the surface the reality that is too painful to surface safely elsewhere.

Several things follow from this.

One is that celebrants have licence to say the unsayable. They can speak without flinching of the physical reality of death. They can express anger and dismay at an untimely death, at our being hurt by the person now in the coffin: 'Man born of a woman has but a short time to live. Like a flower he blossoms and then withers; like a shadow he flees and never stays.' Religious celebrants can confidently proclaim 'I am the resurrection and the life', irrespective of the celebrant's own faith or doubts. They can instruct angels and archangels and all the armies of the heavenly host to welcome a little old lady. Not many would dare say any of this so directly in a one-to-one pastoral situation.

Most important, in the religious funeral the celebrant can articulate the faith that the mourners doubt they have, but would like to have. Even believers need to have that done for them at this time of all times when faith is assailed. Many clergy have told me what an unexpected privilege it was when they conducted their first funeral. They always use that word 'privilege'. I am sure what they are referring to is the privilege of affirming for others in their time of need what they so desperately want to affirm, but in either their grief or their unbelief, cannot.

One young Christian minister told me that, were her husband to die, nothing would comfort her; yet here she is offering hope to others in a hundred or more funerals a year. Each one challenges her to the depths of her being, and facing up to this is, I am sure, what gives her funerals their integrity.

All this means that the congregation is in a state of acute dependence on the celebrant. Upright citizens and civic leaders become upset little children, the celebrant their comforting parent. While sympathising with or even sharing their grief, the celebrant has to offer security, helped by time-honoured clerical robes and well-known hymns. The celebrant has to offer hope, where none seems to exist. It is important that celebrants understand what is happening, that they are not surprised at the over-the-top anger or thanks that may later be directed at them. Celebrants must know that, while remaining genuine, they are playing a part, and that without that part humanity collapses in the face of death. They must acknowledge despair, but not give in to their own despair.

In any performance of a play, the director is aware of the likely audience, but should not pander to them. To direct a play well, you focus not on the audience but on the play itself.

You get inside it, respond to it yourself, and then direct it in such a way as reflects with integrity both the play and your own response to it. But if you look overmuch to the audience for cheap laughs or cheap tears, the performance will lack credibility.

So too with a funeral. The celebrant focuses on the unique life and death of the deceased, death itself, God and his love. The likely feelings of the 'audience' – anger, dismay, relief – are of course crucial to how the celebrant goes about things, but they rarely take centre stage. What is on stage is not the audience, but a corpse.

Formality and dignity

To say that a funeral is a drama doesn't mean it has to be formal. A requiem mass for a civic dignitary in Halifax may be very formal; but 'down under', in Australia, they don't take kindly to formality. A priest in effeminate garb, pompously processing into the funeral parlour and incanting 'I am the resurrection and the life' and 'Go forth upon thy journey from this world, O Christian soul' will not go down as well in Brisbane as it will in an English village. More formality is appropriate for a matriarch dying in grand old age than for a cot death, for a high Anglican than for a house-church charismatic. What matters is that, in whatever way, a symbolic death is enacted and the passing of a life marked with integrity.

The word 'dignity' comes up a lot in the funeral business. A funeral is essentially about human dignity, but this can be expressed in quite informal ways. In 1989 viewers around the world could not but notice the rough-and-ready way the coffin of Iran's leader Ayatollah Khomeini was handled by its bearers and by the pressing crowd. Admittedly this particular funeral got out of hand, but such behaviour, perceived by Western Europeans as undignified, is typical of the rough-and-ready way in which coffins are handled in funeral services in many countries. Even in Venice, shirt-sleeved men almost toss the coffin into the funeral boat in a way that seems casual to onlooking tourists from North-Western Europe.

I suspect that sometimes we distance ourselves from the

pain of the occasion and the problematic status of the coffin's contents by a put-on formality and dignity. We rely on the black-coated undertaker's men to handle the corpse for us, to keep us pure. In some countries those who handle the coffin may distance themselves from the task by a put-on casualness.

So yes, the funeral is about recognising human dignity. But whether or not we translate that into a 'dignified' way of doing things depends on local tradition. Tradition must not bind us, but we should respect it or we will cause offence . . .

Limbo

When someone dies, we have to renegotiate our relationships. When my father died, it was not just him I had lost. My relation to my mother changed, my relation to my brother and his family changed, their relationships with me and with my mother changed, and other more distant relationships changed too.

None of this can happen overnight. In mourning, we have manifestly lost the old relationship with the one who died, but how other relationships will change has yet to crystallise. We are in limbo.

Funeral rituals the world over move mourners firmly into limbo, and then in due course out of it. Indeed, all rites of passage do this. In many tribal societies initiation ceremonies change a boy into a man, via a limbo period of some days or weeks in which the youngsters have to go through a series of ordeals or prove their hunting capabilities. In the modern world adolescent gangs and American college fraternities and sororities also have initiation ceremonies. So do the armed forces – as a cadet, you are neither civilian nor soldier, but in limbo, in transition. The traditional period of betrothal, during which you commit yourself to your prospective partner, but not yet irrevocably, in which you are neither single nor married, is another example. So too in pregnancy, especially in its later stages: you are burdened, slowed down, absolved from certain normal responsibilities, but not yet a mother. In each instance you are between one status and another, needing this time to renegotiate relationships with a whole range of people. As the anthropologist Victor Turner puts it, you are 'betwixt and between'.

The traditional wedding reveals the threefold nature of the transition. First comes the rite of engagement, the sharing of rings, maybe a party, the parting from the status of the free-and-easy single. The following period of engagement is stage two, betwixt and between, not single and available, but not yet married. The present makes no sense in itself, for you are in limbo, making preparations for the wedding, looking back to your days of freedom. Finally, there is the wedding ceremony and the wedding night, confirming the end of limbo and entry into the new status of married person.

The same kind of process occurs with death. The moment of someone's death – or with a terminal illness, the fore-knowledge of their death – numbs us, hurling us into emotional limbo. We may move quickly out of this emotional limbo, but we are still very much in social limbo, dominated by a series of rituals – visiting the comatose patient, arranging and attending the funeral, replying to letters of condolence. These rituals both give us something to do while in limbo, and define us as being in limbo. And then at the end of this time of readjustment we are often helped by a final ceremony such as a memorial or anniversary service.

Within this limbo of several months there are shorter, more acute limbos. The period from death to the funeral is one. It is during this period that, in Britain, relatives are most likely to come and stay and relieve you of normal chores; and it is at this time that you have to perform some very abnormal chores like visiting the funeral director and procuring a death certificate. A sense of unreality pervades this period; or occasionally a sense of utter reality pervades it, with ordinary life seeming utterly unreal.

Helping serve the funeral tea may start you back on the road to being a competent human being again. After that, the mourners leave, and you must struggle on with life, of a kind.

The acute limbo of a few days is most clearly expressed in the Jewish custom of sitting *shiveh*. The funeral usually takes place within twenty-four hours, but is followed by the week of *shiveh* (Hebrew for 'seven'). The family sit at home on wooden stools, while all the world comes to talk about the dead person, bringing with them food to feed the family. At the end of the week, the *shiveh* or limbo ends, and the family must get on with life. Many Jews who are not orthodox, and have abandoned other religious rituals, still see the social and psychological value of *shiveh*.

Roger Grainger stresses that to be in limbo is to be in chaos, a chaos other people have to handle for you. Within ritual limits there is value in expressing this chaos, which is surely why Jews rend a piece of clothing. In many societies, roles are reversed. The Shona peoples, normally very sure about etiquette and formality, get into their old gardening clothes for the burial. Informal people, like the Swedes, have absurdly formal funerals. Normal order is turned upside down.

Most dramatically, the wilder kind of pre-funeral Irish wake expresses pure chaos – drinking to excess, ribald jokes, sitting the coffin at the head of the table, playing games with the corpse – all of which is otherwise quite inexplicable. Ritual behaviour like this enables life to become chaotic without fear of the chaos overwhelming you.

But there is a more acute limbo still, the funeral itself. This may be the only limbo for secondary mourners, being the only day or morning they take off work. They drive themselves to the funeral, and only as they enter the building do they consciously feel the hush, the being in the presence of something they cannot handle. They rely implicitly on whoever is taking the funeral to handle this time when they are not themselves, and they certainly rely on the celebrant to provide a definite end to the ceremony, a point at which the deadness of the body is confirmed and they can move on. Without that symbolic death, they too can remain stuck in limbo.

Whatever else a funeral does for those attending, it must move them first into and then out of limbo. If it does not move them into limbo, they will still be thinking of whether they turned on the washing machine, and the funeral will mean nothing; if it does not move them out of limbo, they will not be able to move on.

Bruce Reed, in his book *The Dynamics of Religion*, shows how social limbo is often accompanied by a psychological state of regression. In any act of worship, people are likely to regress to a more childlike, more emotional state, in which they relate to God in a more direct way; the task of the priest or leader is to provide an environment in which the congregation feels safe to regress, and then towards the end feels bold enough to move back into the world. Nowhere is this understanding of worship more true than in the funeral service. According to David Durston, one of Reed's colleagues, the funeral is an occasion where change takes place in each member of the congregation; the funeral must therefore be located in a safe place where people can let go, and then emerge reconstructed. (Unfortunately, many people do not feel safe in their local crematorium.)

One practical problem facing many ministers of religion in Britain is the beginning of the service. There is a lot to be said for the traditional, and dramatic, procession into the building, with the priest leading the coffin and proclaiming 'I am the resurrection and the life'. Whatever else, the congregation knows that something significant has happened, and is going to happen.

The problem, though, is that people come to the funeral with their grief, and this has to be acknowledged if there is to be any chance of that grief being transformed by hope or thanksgiving. That is why many ministers wait at the chancel steps for the coffin to arrive, ask the congregation to sit down, and begin with a welcome and a comment such as: 'All of us here were shocked to hear of Elsie's sudden death last week . . .' or 'David's death was no surprise to some of us, but that does not lessen our grief and sadness. We have come here to . . .' This format is particularly appropriate when the death is not that of a fulfilled person in ripe old age, and the mourners arrive in suppressed anger or frank dismay, for until these emotions are acknowledged, the funeral will not connect. Drama is perhaps best left to later, to the final committal to earth or flames.

Sorrow and joy

I have been to funerals in which acute sorrow and joy mingled together. The death of Tony, a layman who had contributed immeasurably to our struggling church, crossing age barriers at will and respected by all, was a deep loss to the whole congregation. We were shocked at his sudden death, bereft of one we needed, and yet for the packed congregation at his funeral, among the many tears there was a tangible joy – joy in the hope that Tony was with the Saviour he so loved, joy in the way we had been enriched by him.

After Jackie's tragic death (p. 120), the funeral was full of sorrow, joy, and defiance. The priest explained it to me afterwards: 'Absolute sorrow met its match in absolute faith, the faith of her family and friends.' I know what he means.

Sadly, many people do not know what that priest means; in many funerals there is neither sorrow nor joy. Tears are suppressed in an effort to be heroic, or to appear religious. Sikhs are forbidden to cry – that someone has died must be the will of God, and to cry is to dispute with God. Some Christian fundamentalists also suppose tears reveal lack of faith. But surely to show sorrow at your personal loss says nothing about your faith in a loving God? It is for this reason that some funeral celebrants begin with an invitation such as: 'We have come here to weep for, as well as to celebrate the life of . . .' Some people need to be given this permission to weep.

If some funerals display no sorrow, others display no hope. There are many things, both religious and secular, which can give mourners courage (Chapter 21). But some congregations and some celebrants can be in such blackness that there is no lifting them as sorrow spirals downward to despair. These are possibly the worst funerals of all. I have been told by more than one priest that a minute or more's silence can be the way to break such blackness; it is certainly the way to allow hysteria to subside. Then the funeral can move forward.

Universal and unique

Are we all equal in death? On entering a graveyard, with rows and rows of headstones proclaiming we all have the same end, our first thought may be that we all end up six foot under, regardless of earthly status. One Victorian graveyard in Aberdeen is entered through wrought-iron gates proclaiming in Latin, the text circling a skull and crossbones: 'Not alone, but together.'

But on closer inspection the gravestones tell a different story. This man was well known, and will be remembered long after his death. Another was a pauper and had no friends. This woman died in ripe old age, loved by her eight children. Another died in childbirth. In old Dutch churches you still see the trademarks on the tradesmen's graves – ships and shoes, anvils and anchors; in modern Dutch cemeteries, you see the symbols of love – pink hearts, a child's cot. The effect of a person's death on others is unique, how she lives on in others is unique.

Every funeral must affirm both the universality and the uniqueness of death. We all die, but I die only once.

The affirmation need not be in words. As the funeral cortège processes through the churchyard, surrounded by the graves of the ancestors, you hardly need state the universality of death. There is comfort in knowing that the deceased is not alone, that we are not alone in our grief, that our experience is universal.

Some groups go out of their way to symbolise this. In Jewish communities there is generally only one type of coffin, only one type of grave. When any male Jew dies, they call him 'rabbi': he is as honoured as one. In one town, when a prostitute was murdered and it was discovered she was Jewish, the local Jewish Burial Society arranged and paid for her funeral as it would for any member of the synagogue. Some Muslim groups do not allow the name of the deceased to be mentioned in the funeral; what matters is his or her status *vis-à-vis* Allah.

Unfortunately, in funerals in a mass society powerful symbols of the universality of death, or of membership of a cherished community, can all too easily degenerate into sameness and bureaucratic monotony. It is therefore important in such funerals that – whatever else – the uniqueness of *this* human life is stated. Good funeral directors know they must treat each funeral as if it were the only one, even if they are doing ten a week.

Clergy and others conducting such funerals should speak personally of the deceased, but not presume intimate knowledge where there is none. Find out a little about her, even if it is only the name by which she was commonly known. Talk to more than one family member, in order to get a more all-round portrait of her. Acknowledge failures, respect the integrity of the person. Mention mourners by name, not just close family. If the picture painted is one the mourners recognise, and are included in, then they will be able to say farewell.

Some Christian ministers guard against a eulogy that replaces love of God with praise of man. There is indeed much to be said for having a requiem mass, expressing both the love of God and concern for the departed, but this need not mean that no word at all is said about the uniqueness of this individual and of what she meant to us.

Take care!

Funerals have a tone, a drama, a flow that is all their own. Respect this, and the funeral should succeed in truly marking the passing of a human life.

Do take care. Botch a wedding or a baptism, and folk will relish the joke for a lifetime. Miss a date, and you can laugh about it in your old age. But be careless about a funeral, and you have failed people at their most vulnerable, at the point when they are relying on you both to put them in touch with and to protect them from the most unbearable reality. You will have left them in limbo.

Limbo originally meant the borderland of hell, the place where they went who had not received the offices of the church. Today, still, those who have not received an effective funeral, whether religious or secular, are left in limbo.

There is no magic formula, for death is not neat. It is full of contradictions: this and every death is both universal and unique, utterly natural and totally obscene, a continuity with the past and a rupture of the present. The unique pain as we walk through the universal graveyard; the feeling that life will never begin again, even as we see the first crocuses coming up; the continuity as we go up to take mass, yet on the way pause to touch the awful finality of the coffin; the sublime perfection of Bach as we experience searing pain – such juxtapositions, such symbols, speak more than a thousand sermons or the finest eulogy.

13

PARTICIPATION

Susan had lived for twenty years in rural Spain. As in much of Europe, the commercial funeral director has not yet moved into the rural areas, so villagers organise funerals themselves. A local woman, often the midwife, comes to lay the body out; a male relative goes post haste to the nearest town to buy a coffin. All the village comes to the house to pay their last respects to the open coffin; then comes the priest, and the coffin is sealed in the presence of the family.

By tradition, the body must be buried by sundown: male kin carry the coffin to the church, where the mass is held, and then the men take the coffin to the cemetery. Over the next three or four days the women spring-clean the house, whitewashing all the walls, and only then do they go back to their work. Everything is done by local people, for local people.

Soon after Susan returned home to the West of England, her aunt died. She found what happened next 'all rather strange'. For some reason, her mother refused to talk about her sister's death or the funeral arrangements. Susan wanted to pick flowers from her own garden for her aunt's funeral, but was informed by the funeral director that this was not done. So she went to the florist, but was told the flowers she wanted were not available.

What is so wrong about offering a much-loved aunt flowers you have grown and picked yourself? After all, you would be able to do this were it a much-loved niece who was getting married; indeed the family would be delighted you had the skill and the personal touch to arrange the flowers for the wedding and they did not have to hire a florist.

British people are used to arranging weddings themselves.

They hire outside professionals – florists, hairdressers, outfit-
ters, photographers, travel agents, caterers, speech-makers –
only if they do not have friends or family willing and able to
perform these functions as an act of love. So why is 'keeping it
in the family' disapproved of when it comes to funerals?

I can understand that in their shock and grief many families
want to hand over the entire funeral to experienced professionals – this is undoubtedly one reason why we hire funeral
directors and not wedding directors. But after a long terminal
illness in which family members have nursed the dying person
themselves and look forward to continuing that personal care
after death, why are they told it is 'not done'?

Suggesting why it *should* be done, and how it *can* be done,
is the purpose of this chapter. (Taking participation to its
ultimate conclusion, doing without a funeral director or a
professional celebrant to conduct the funeral service, and
doing it yourself, is explored in Chapter 23.)

A family affair

Fortunately, Susan's experience is not universal. Monica's
father had been dying of cancer at his home in North London
for some weeks, looked after by his wife and the two
remaining unmarried children. When he died, and the funeral
director suggested he be removed to the funeral parlour, it
just didn't seem right. As Monica said to me, 'Why should his
body be handled by those who neither knew nor loved him?'
So he stayed at home until the funeral.

Steve, a Melbourne student, had a vacation job in the local
funeral parlour when his mother died. So he laid her out
himself, an experience he later described to me as most
helpful.

Ted recalls with affection the funeral of his favourite uncle
in a remote Herefordshire village, in which he joined other
relatives to carry the coffin from the lych-gate up the path into
the church. He found this very natural and satisfying, 'like
making him a last cup of tea'; his uncle had been kind to Ted,
and this mundane task was one last thing Ted could do in
return.

At West Indian funerals in Britain there is lots of this kind of participation. It is rare for the body to be moved from the house; a stream of visitors come to comfort the family, both before and for weeks or even months after the burial; and at the burial itself, shovels are provided and male family and friends fill in the grave, while the women stand around singing farewell songs and funeral hymns such as 'God Be With You Till We Meet Again', or 'Shall We Meet At The River'.

A Catholic priest describes funerals in his working-class Liverpudlian parish. Male relatives carry the body into the church. He starts with a confession, so that those who have not been in church for a while may feel able to participate in the mass; both the collection and the bread and wine are brought up to the altar by grandchildren or other relatives; if the family includes someone able to speak clearly in public, they will read the lesson.

At my father's memorial service, his grandchild and adopted grandchildren – aged eight, seven, and six – acted as ushers. At other funerals, grandchildren have played musical solos.

Roy and Jane Nichols, Ohio funeral directors, have written movingly of how their involvement following the death of Roy's father revolutionised their approach to their work. (Their story may be found in *Death – The Final Stage of Growth*, edited by Elisabeth Kübler-Ross.) Like Steve, Roy found himself performing many of the last rites himself; like Monica, he would not hand his own father over to strangers. He cared for his father's corpse himself.

Reflecting on this, he realised that as a funeral director he removed from his clients the very involvement that he himself found so helpful with his own father. So he decided to change from the all-knowing, all-providing professional into an enabler, his task henceforth being to enable families to do whatever seems best to them.

Other American funeral directors have written of how they have assisted customers who indicate they want to perform some or all of the rites themselves. A widow, who had nursed her forty-four year old husband through terminal leukaemia, wanted the funeral not in the funeral parlour but in her home. It was a hot August, and the body had to be embalmed; so the funeral director did this in the home, with the widow assisting. Funeral director and family together arranged the casket and lifted the body into it. Friends came to visit and view, and the whole process ended with a short service in the crematorium. The widow, who also wrote about the experience, describes how this working together changed the funeral director from a distant professional into a friend.

The current fashion for take-overs in the United Kingdom funeral business makes this kind of enabling more difficult. Amalgamated firms usually centralise certain facilities, such as vehicle maintenance and embalming. For example, one national chain no longer does embalming at the local funeral director's; instead, the body is transported to the area embalmer and back again. The likelihood of funeral directors who belong to this particular chain being able to provide home-embalming therefore seems remote indeed.

But in a quiet way, many funeral directors do enable families to participate. At a West Indian burial, who provides the shovels for the mourners? A good funeral director will have told the cemetery beforehand and arranged for half a dozen or so shovels to be waiting at the graveside.

A schema

It may be helpful to sketch the various possible models of funeral participation.

The community model

This exists in most traditional, rural societies (Plate 3). As in Majorca, there are no professional organisers of funerals, though usually there are religious specialists. Family and neighbours organise the funeral, buying a coffin from the local carpenter, or hiring a cart from a haulier.

The undertaker model

With time, if local community traditions begin to break down under the pressures of the modern world, the carpenter or haulier may begin to call himself an 'undertaker' – one who undertakes to provide the requisites for a funeral.

The professional funeral director

The undertaker may go further, and set up as a funeral *director*, one who directs the whole show because the family and community no longer know how to. He changes (in his eyes at any rate) from a tradesman selling services as and when demanded, to a professional adviser of ignorant and needy clients. He is given, and/or takes, control.

The enabling professional

Nowadays, the Roy Nicholses of the funeral trade are redefining their role as enablers. They are still the experts, still in control, but they aim to help clients do as much as possible themselves.

The consumer model

This can look like the enabling professional model, but is radically different. The bereaved family takes the decisions, decides what it does and does not want the undertaker or priest for, and instructs accordingly. The customer calls the tune, and reduces the funeral director back into the role of undertaker; in North America, some customers may band together into memorial societies in order to give themselves greater bargaining power. Some do-it-yourself funerals also have elements of this consumer model if, for example, the family go to their local funeral director to purchase a coffin or use his fridge in hot weather.

This is like the undertaker model, except that the consumer is motivated more by personal preference than by community tradition.

The do-it-yourself model

Here the services of funeral directors and professional celebrants are dispensed with altogether. However, unless the DIYers bury the departed on their own property, they will still need to pay for the services of a cemetery or crematorium.

The community-consumer model

A mix of the community model and the consumer model, this model is operated very satisfactorily in Britain by tight-knit ethnic/religious groups such as Orthodox Jews and Muslims. Local Jewish burial societies do most of the work themselves, as in the traditional community. For things they cannot or will not do themselves, they give a contract to a local funeral director – most commonly providing coffins and occasionally transport overseas.

Although this chapter addresses the question how families and communities can participate more in funerals organised on the professional model (which accounts for most funerals in the West today), the principles are, however, the same for all funerals.

Good and bad psychology

Psychiatrists have studied how people react to loss. Whatever the loss, whether a little child is hospitalised and separated from his parents, or an elderly person is told she has cancer and will lose her own life, or you are bereaved, similar emotions can appear. In the case of bereavement, these could be:

Shock and numbness (lasting a few minutes or hours);
Denial (that the person has died);
Anger (that the person has left you);
Guilt (that you could have prevented him dying, or about things left unsaid and undone);
Bargaining (with God);
Depression;
Acceptance.

The funeral usually takes place between one and seven days after the death. For those still in shock, the funeral can move them on to the stage where they can begin to take things in. Others will be denying the death. Their mind knows the person has died, but their heart continues to kid them otherwise. Although the order or content of the above 'stages' is by no means fixed, it is true that feelings of anger and guilt, and the eventual working through of grief, cannot begin so long as the heart continues to deny that the person is dead. The funeral's symbolic re-enactment of death painfully drives home the fact of death for those who are denying it or are still in shock. It releases them to begin grieving (see Chapter 12).

The psychological value of participation in the funeral by family and friends is that it helps make the funeral, and hence the death, real. Cutting flowers, procuring a death certificate, kissing the corpse, carrying the coffin, even just touching the coffin, are all actions which make sense only if someone has died, only if the box contains a corpse. Sooner or later, my beliefs have to catch up with my actions, and if I perform actions that imply someone has died, my heart will pretty soon come to accept this fact.

But if mourners are reduced to passive spectators, it is quite possible for some of them to return from the funeral with hearts that still do not believe the death has really happened. Psychiatrists pick them up years later, discovering they have rooms in the house kept unchanged since the day of death, veritable modern-day mummies; the psychiatrist's job is to get the person at long last to face up to the question, 'When are you going to let your son/mother/wife die?'

It is this very natural denial that, in the early days, leads mourners to want to hand everything over to the funeral director and priest. These professionals are wise if they allow – but do not pressurise – family and friends to carry out minor acts of participation. To allow, even to encourage, participation in the events of the funeral is good psychology.

But another kind of participation can be unhelpful. Death leaves us powerless; it makes us dependent on others; it reduces us to tears. Saying goodbye to the departed means handing them over – to the love of God, to fate, to memory. There is a danger that too active a participation in the million and one things to be done after a death can reflect and perpetuate a refusal to hand over, a determination to remain in control.

People used to organising and being in charge of things are particularly susceptible to this; not just because they are good at being in charge, but also because they are more threatened than most by the handing over that death entails. This is why, even in 'do-it-yourself' funerals, it is wise if the person who acts as master or mistress of ceremonies during the funeral is not someone very close to the departed. The MC must remain in control of proceedings; the closely bereaved, though perhaps reading a poem or saying a prayer, need space to grieve, to let go, to hand over.

More commonly, the temptation to busyness is not during the funeral, but before and after. There is much to do, especially if large numbers of relatives are coming from afar, and over-busyness at this time can be a way of perpetuating denial. You never have time to stop and think and feel. In moderation, of course, routine tasks are valuable as a way of keeping going, but when routine tasks become addictive busyness, that is a danger signal. So too is an unwillingness on the part of the bereaved person to delegate chores. (The genius of the Jewish *shiveh* is that delegation of chores such as cooking is mandatory.)

I have been talking in this section about the psychological effects of participation. Remember, though, that most ritual participation is motivated not by psychology, but by tradition or religious dogma. Paradoxically – and unfortunately – the greater the place we give to psychology, the more we tend to forget tradition and religion. This is the dilemma for those with a secular and psychological approach to funerals: in theory their approach highlights the need for participation in the rite, yet in practice undermines it.

Flowers

In Britain, flowers for the dead can be used in two ways. One is usual at the funeral: friends and family order from a commercial florist a 'floral tribute' which is sent by the florist to the funeral director, who places it in the hearse (one London funeral director I talked with takes great pride in decorating the outside of his hearse with the flowers). The flowers arrive at the graveyard with the coffin, and are strewn on top of the grave by the gravediggers after they have filled it in. Or they go with the coffin to the crematorium and after the service are available for viewing by the mourners as they leave the building.

At no point in this process does the giver of the flowers

touch them, nor physically offer them to either the deceased or the family. A personal note will be attached, and people tend to pay more for flowers than they will give to charity on those occasions when the family requests 'no flowers', so giving flowers obviously means a lot, yet the giving is conducted in this extraordinarily abstract, impersonal, commercial way.

How different is that other use of flowers, the laying of the wreath. Though the memorial wreath may also be commercially purchased, the central act is the mourner's laying of the wreath. On the anniversary of his death, the widow may lay it on her husband's grave; on the anniversary of a war, comrades lay it at the foot of the war memorial. The wreath is never laid by a professional funeral director or florist – mourners do it themselves!

A more homespun variant is the placing of cut or potted flowers on the grave, or planting flowers on the grave. This, together with the subsequent gardening and tending of the plants, is perhaps the most common participatory funeral or memorial act in the United Kingdom. (Tragically, it is discouraged by some local authorities who find the mourners' gardening untidy, as though the cemetery were there not for the benefit of the mourners, but to please the aesthetic taste of the park superintendent.)

In Britain, this humble placing of a flower is banned by tradition from the funeral itself. I can see no good reason for this tradition other than the profit of the flower trade. There is also, of course, the fact that most British funerals happen in winter, when our own garden is unlikely to be awash with colour, but this cannot explain the tradition, for high summer does not see its relaxation.

At one Australian crematorium funeral service, friends and relatives were invited not to send flowers, but to bring just one flower of their choice and place it on the coffin at a particular moment during the service. In that one, simple act, the service immediately became personal and real. At that funeral too, one child placed on the coffin his favourite toy; in life he could never be parted from it, but he wanted to give it to his favourite grandad; together with the flowers, it too was consumed by the flames.

At a funeral in the South West of England, the widow

asked everyone to bring just one red rose, her husband's favourite flower. The church was full of red roses. Nobody was in any doubt who they were saying goodbye to.

The day after the Hillsborough tragedy, there was a requiem mass at Liverpool's Catholic cathedral. The building full to overflowing, an impromptu second mass was arranged on the podium for the thousands left outside. Without anyone planning it, children started laying their club scarves, shirts and rosettes on the makeshift altar (Plate 6). At the same time, fans were tying scarves, ribbons, pennants and souvenirs to the gates of the club ground at Anfield (Plate 5). Later that day, the gates were opened, beginning the week-long pilgrimage of a million mourners, turning the pitch into a shrine of flowers (Plate 7).

The widow tending her husband's grave; the teenager at Anfield: we British know how to honour the dead through flowers. Why do we abandon that knowledge when we enter the crematorium?

The corpse as participant

I used to think that the point of the funeral is to enable the living to say their last farewell to the departed. It was only recently, when exploring the new forms of funeral being pioneered in London by people with AIDS, that I understood that it could also enable the departed to make a last farewell to the living.

Many British readers will have seen the BBC TV film *Remember Terry*, a documentary of the last months of a forty-one year old actor with AIDS. A larger than life character who always liked putting on a show, Terry went out in style, in a funeral he himself had orchestrated. As the coffin was brought into the crematorium, up struck a tape recording of 'There's No Business Like Show Business'. The BBC presenter Patty Coldwell said Terry had asked her to pop backstage behind the curtain and wave a black-gloved hand from behind the coffin as it was disappearing. 'Bridge Over Troubled Water' later reduced everyone to tears, which turned to laughter as the curtains closed to the tune of 'Come to the Cabaret'. This was Terry's last appearance, the Terry they all knew . . . and everyone clapped.

This film helped start a new funeral tradition among those in London's gay community with AIDS. Many of these men are not only in the full flush of young adulthood, but are creative people, used to being in control of their lives. The funeral has become, for them, a final statement that they do things their way, that they will be in control of their deaths just as they were in control of their lives. The AIDS funeral celebrates a life, refuting the popular image of AIDS as a punishment and the deceased as a victim. The funeral provides a final opportunity for the deceased to affirm – both to fellow gays and to a maybe perplexed family – what he believes. Within some pretty outrageous forms, these funerals display great integrity and honesty.

The idea of the deceased waving goodbye, or at least speaking to the congregation from the coffin, is not so original. It is there in the ancient Greek Orthodox service of burial, in which the choir sing the following words on behalf of the deceased, as the mourners come and give a final kiss:

> As ye behold me lie before you all speechless and bereft of breath, weep for me, O friends and brethren, O kinsfolk and acquaintance. For but yesterday I talked with you, and suddenly there came upon me the dread hour of death. But come, all ye who loved me, and kiss me with the last kiss . . .

Few go out in the theatrical style of an Orthodox believer, and few write the entire funeral script (as did Terry), but it is increasingly common for dying people to suggest a poem, reading or hymn they would like to share with those left behind. One thirty-three year old was thinking about his own funeral, with the help of a nun whose work is with people with AIDS. He decided on, for himself, Edith Piaf's 'No Regrets'; for his father, Kipling's poem 'If', which had been important to him as a soldier in the Second World War; and to his mother he offered the well-known words of Henry Scott Holland:

Death is nothing at all . . .
I have only slipped away into the next room . . .
I am I and you are you . . .
whatever we were to each other that we are still.
Call me by my old familiar name,
speak to me in the easy way you always used.
Put no difference into your tone;
wear no forced air of solemnity or sorrow.
Laugh as we always laughed at the little jokes we enjoyed
    together.
Play, smile, think of me, pray for me
Let my name be ever the household word it always was.
Let it be spoken without effect, without the trace of a
    shadow on it.
Life means all that it ever meant;
It is the same as it ever was; there is unbroken continuity.
Why should I be out of mind because I am out of sight?
I am waiting for you for an interval, somewhere very
    near – just around the corner . . . All is well.

The title of the book edited by Elisabeth Kübler-Ross,
Death – The Final Stage of Growth, hints at what is well
known in hospices. Far from just petering out, in their dying
weeks many people discover truths about themselves and
about life, for the grim reality of death can force us to break
through the façade behind which we have hidden not only
from others but also from ourselves. Sometimes the dying
person's becoming real to himself can re-establish real
communication with his family for the first time in decades.
Sometimes the dying discover what W. H. Vanstone calls 'the
stature of waiting': active, busy, independent men break
through the indignity of having to be cared for by others, to
discover the joy they can give by allowing others to care.

I do not want to romanticise death. Such breakthroughs
often do not happen. But when they do, is it not fitting that
they should be shared? If death has revealed to the dying
person something of the meaning of life, should she not share
this with those left behind? In her dying days, the person may
be too ill to be visited by many, but everyone comes to the
funeral. Is this not a time for sharing? And who better to
share but the deceased herself? A last letter, a poem she

discovered and took as her own in the final weeks, are these not utterly appropriate in the funeral?

A slightly different idea comes from David Ibry, an atheist who is an amateur video-maker. He made one or two videos for friends along the lines of the TV programme *This Is Your Life*, in which he interviewed the person, key friends, family and colleagues. It's the video equivalent of the family photo album; in years to come, the family can remember mum or grandad by watching the video. Then a relative of David's mentioned that when she dies she does not want a hypocritical religious funeral, or one in which an equally ill-informed secular celebrant spouts about her; so the idea emerged of making a video with her for the specific purpose of playing at her funeral. Not only would the video take the place of the funeral address, it would also act afterwards as a memorial – a rather more living memorial than a block of stone. David Ibry has now made half a dozen or so of these videos, which are accompanied by written suggestions by the individual as to the conduct of the funeral.

Participation or elaboration?

Participation need not mean elaborate ritual. It often means very simple, but telling, ritual.

When a Muslim dies, in Britain or elsewhere, the body has to be washed according to their religious rites. This is often done by the family – Muslim funeral directors invite their customers backstage to perform this religious ritual.

Jewish funerals are plain, simple, and short. The walk to the graveside, pausing several times as the rabbi speaks, with the men finally lowering the coffin into the grave and each throwing in clods of earth, speaks volumes. Movement and participation, not elaborate mumbo-jumbo, are what count. (No wonder some Jewish women feel deprived when they are not allowed to join in some of these rituals.)

When neighbours prepare the funeral tea on behalf of the family, their participation is not extraordinary; it is a simple act of service and love, and is deeply appreciated – only perhaps if they try to show off might it be resented.

When a little girl brings to the altar a flower she has picked as a last present for her granny, this is a simpler ritual than the florist – funeral director – crematorium sequence.

No, it is not ordinary folk, but the funeral business and priests, out to trade on vulnerable people's anxiety and guilt, who have invented elaborate rituals, and then persuaded us these rituals are 'traditional'.

This was something the Reformation – and more recently Jessica Mitford – understood. The mistake, though, was to throw out the baby of simple, meaningful, participatory ritual along with the bath-water of religious and commercial hocus-pocus. All I am saying is, remember the baby.

14

EATING, TALKING, SINGING

The funeral of George Glandish, of Ebony Court, Kent, in 1622, cost a total of £6 6s 5d. Of this sum, £5 1s 9d was spent on a feast at Ebony Court after the interment, for which the following items were bought: 2 sides of mutton, 6 bushels of wheat, 6 pounds of currants, half a pound of sugar, 1 ounce of cloves and mace, 1 ounce of cinnamon, butter, a fat calf, 12 pounds of bacon, 40½ pounds of cheese, a fat wether, 7 dozen and 2 loaves, 23 twopenny loaves and beer. The remaining £1 4s 8d was ample to provide a simple coffin and shroud and to pay the fees of minister, clerk sexton, bearers and bell-ringers, as well as any other incidental expenses.

Clare Gittings, *Death, Burial and the Individual in Early Modern England*

Eating

Scoffing and boozing are remarkably common at funerals, in all kinds of societies. Why?

Anthropology has an ingenious explanation. When we turn an ox into roast beef and two veg, we turn nature into culture; when we cook and eat, a part of nature nourishes the human being. When we die and are buried, the process is reversed: our body becomes food for the worms, food for nature, helping nourish soil and plants. This is made explicit in the words uttered after death in Crete: 'This very earth which nourished you will eat you as well.' Baking and eating, distilling and drinking, raise the very same puzzle as does death: our strange relation to nature.

A bit far fetched, you might think. But consider the

requiem mass, at the centre of which is the body and blood of Christ. As you go up to receive mass, you are conscious of performing both one of the most physical of human acts, eating, and one of the most spiritual. The mystical interplay between physical and spiritual is quite explicit in the mass. Death seems an appropriate time to be considering this interplay.

Of course, eating and drinking at the funeral play all kinds of functions. They can be an occasion for display. Alcohol can loosen the emotions after the stiffness of an English funeral. Eating – and talking about – the lovely ham gives embarrassed English people something to do. The post-funeral meal, the first time following the death that the family entertains visitors to a meal in the house, marks the end of the death-to-funeral limbo. Getting drunk at the pre-funeral wake, Irish style, expresses the inner chaos mourners feel.

But most of all, eating is something you do together, expressing human solidarity. In ordinary life the lonely person can find meals by herself the most lonely part of the day – there is something primeval about eating together. At no time is this more so than in the loneliness of bereavement. Eating together is the opposite of passing to the other side of the road as you see the bereaved person coming: it is an act of solidarity, even if there is little you can say.

The scale of funeral and feast have often been inversely related to each other: the bigger the one, the smaller the other. One London funeral director reckons that Irish corpses are no longer left in the home the night before the funeral but brought to the church, because priests are fed up with close relatives turning up sozzled, or even missing the funeral altogether. The priests attempt to reduce the drinking in order to maintain the religious ritual.

Clare Gittings suggests it is not just clergy, but undertakers too, who have opposed the natural human tendency to eat and drink together after a death. Sumptuous feasts, like Mr Glandish's, were ordered by ordinary people in the Puritan period to make up for the desperately thin funeral services. Far more was spent by Glandish's heirs on food than on the funeral itself. But then in the late seventeenth century undertakers arrived on the scene: they could not make any money out of beer and sandwiches, so they spent the next century inventing funeral paraphernalia which only they could sell.

The funeral feast withered. By 1800, one London burial club allocated no money for food, but contracted with an undertaker to supply:

> a strong elm coffin covered with superfine black and furnished with two rows all round, close drove, with best black japanned nails and adorned with rich ornamental drops, a handsome plate of inscription, angel above the plate, flower beneath, and four pair of handsome handles, with wrought grips; the coffin to be well-pitched, lined and ruffled with crape, a handsome crape shroud, cap and pillow. For use, a handsome velvet pall, three gentlemen's cloaks, three crape hatbands, three hoods and scarves, and six pairs of gloves, two porters equipped to attend the funeral, a man to attend the same with hat and gloves; also the burial fees paid if not exceeding one guinea.

The natural solidarity of eating together was undermined as not-so-wealthy people found themselves in hock to the undertaker and condemned to the isolation of Victorian mourning: 'A supportive, communal activity – the funeral meal – was being eroded by a competitive, isolating and individualistic element, the display of those material commodities in which undertakers specialised.' Gittings notes ironically that it is the successors of these very undertakers who are today in the vanguard of promoting 'grief therapy' for isolated mourners in the lonely modern city. Well, who isolated them in the first place?

Talking

When people eat together, they talk. They may not know what to say, they may be embarrassed, but they talk. About the funeral, about the departed. Through the polite formalities or the drunken laughter, the tut-tutting and the family in-fighting, people begin to renegotiate their relationships with one another, they reconsider their own mortality.

Weddings, funerals, christenings, coronations, all these rites of passage have a similar structure. Think of a coronation.

There is the *event*, a new queen. There is the *dramatisation* of that event, the coronation itself. And then there is the *incorporation* of the event into people's awareness and relationships, with the TV and the newspapers going over the highlights endlessly, people talking in the streets, memorial mugs and plates bought by the million. Without this talking, whether by press or people, the coronation would not register. It would be like swallowing without digesting.

So with a funeral. All over the world, people talk with each other. They talk about the one who has died, and about everything else under the sun.

In the Afro-Caribbean community in Britain the bereaved family is inundated with visitors long after the funeral. Orthodox Jews formalise this in the *shiveh*, when people come to visit. Geoffrey Gorer recalls the words of the wife of a businessman from the South East of England:

> It is amazing how these visits comfort you. They talk to you and start discussing the person you have lost; picture albums are brought out and everyone reminds you of little episodes in their lives. Suddenly one laughs and enjoys those memories. One's grief is lightened; it is a most healing and comforting week. Brothers and sisters who have drifted apart come together again and recall good memories. It is a comfort.

Some Hindus have an almost identical seven days (minimum) when the family sit on the floor at home and talk. No food is prepared in the house, but people come to the house to talk with you and feed you.

The Irish, like the Jews, are naturally good talkers, but after a death they too create a special time to talk: the pre-funeral wake, originally the time when you watched with the coffin the night before the funeral.

In the North of England people still set considerable store by the funeral meal. In South Wales men spend the rest of the day off work, drinking and talking in the pub. But in other parts of the country, where the ritual of the funeral itself has got thinner, there has not been any corresponding expansion of eating, drinking and talking.

A friend recalls going to a particularly tragic funeral following an accident. At the reception afterwards, everyone assiduously avoided mentioning the girl who had died. Everyone, that is, apart from her husband of three months, who, to everyone's embarrassment, kept on bringing out photos of her, commenting, 'She'd have loved this . . .', and generally mentioning her at every possible opportunity. This unplanned mix of hidden death and romantic death proved too uncomfortable for some.

Dr Colin Murray Parkes is concerned that even the Jewish *shiveh* is being subverted by English respectability and reserve. He has talked with a number of intelligent middle-class Jews who feel that in their circles, while the *shiveh* does succeed in drawing the family together, it tends to be used to distract from grief rather than express it. Conversation with the bereaved is often just neutral chat, and the 'successful' mourner is the one who shows a proper control of his feelings on all occasions. The *shiveh* becomes an ordeal, like the typical English funeral.

We white English must rediscover the art of calling the departed by their old familiar name, as Scott Holland's poem puts it (see p. 148). We must do this in everyday life; in eating and drinking; in writing and exchanging letters; and why not in the funeral itself? After all, Quakers do this.

And so do some others. When retired secretary and mother Mrs Chris Banks died in Canberra, the funeral service was enjoyably long. The church was modern, with the pews in a horseshoe: the family sat at one side, Chris's old workmates on the other, other friends in the middle. The hundred or so people present were invited to share their memories of her. After one of the adult children had mentioned some of her less than perfect traits, others felt free to be honest as well as affectionate in their remembrances, and it was forty minutes before everyone had said their piece. Word from several of those present got back to friends in England that this was far and away the best funeral they'd been to, and they'd really enjoyed it. They'd said goodbye to a real friend.

Maybe this frankness is a bit more than the reserved English would wish to inject into the funeral itself. But before one Scottish funeral, friends appreciated the revival of the pre-funeral wake when a member of the Iona community died on that remarkable Hebridean island. In a side chapel, around the open coffin, they came and stood around the body, sharing feelings and memories. As one of them said later, this was real sharing – unlike the conventional funeral where the minister says, 'We've come here to share our grief', but actually there is no sharing at all, just an embarrassed private snivelling into our hankies.

We can do without the make-up, the silk-lined coffins and the pseudo-classical funeral parlours of the United States, but perhaps we have something to learn after all from the American pre-funeral wake?

If we do not talk at the funeral because there is no opportunity; nor at the tea because we are embarrassed; nor at the pre-funeral wake because there is none; nor later because everyone else crosses to the other side of the road as they see us approaching – is it any wonder bereavement counselling, offering a chance to talk, is one of the growth industries of the twentieth century?

But there is much that can never be said. Certain cherished memories must remain private; the paradoxes of death cannot be comprehended by the human mind. A simple minute of silence during a short crematorium service acknowledges this, making the whole service both deeper and making it feel a decent length. As the philosopher Ludwig Wittgenstein, so keen to stop human beings talking twaddle, recommended: 'Whereof one cannot speak, thereof one must be silent.' This is where music comes in.

Sing the sorrow

Each of the Amsterdam crematorium's two funeral halls is dominated by a beautiful modern organ. In the funeral I attended of an eighty-five year old woman, the dozen or so mourners filed in, sat down, and listened to two pieces of music. The only person to speak was the funeral director; he thanked them for coming, and suggested that after the final, third, piece of music they filed around the coffin as they made their way out. This they did, one or two lingering a moment, touching the old lady's coffin. This funeral consisted of private memories, with a tear or two brought on by the music. If any of the pieces were known to have been particularly meaningful to the old lady, perhaps some of the silent memories would be shared memories.

When all else fails, there is music, for it can speak the unspeakable. At one cot death funeral, a friend – also a young parent – stood at the back of the little country church and began the proceedings with a solo on the flute. Peter's flute said what words could never say.

Words to the music are not necessary. But sung words can affirm faith, sum up the character of the deceased, or affirm that we will continue in our own lives what the deceased lived for. 'Make Me a Channel of Thy Peace' has been sung at more than a few funerals where the living have been inspired by the Christian love of the departed one. Or a song can simply bring back happy memories, with the old folk's club or rugby club choosing to sing together a lost member's favourite song. Communal singing can become both a cherished memory and an act of solidarity that unites living with living, living with dead.

Communal singing became the trademark of courage in the face of grief after the Hillsborough football stadium tragedy. Nothing could express the fans' feelings, save flowers and the song that had become the anthem of Liverpool Football Club, 'You'll Never Walk Alone'. Outsiders may have tired of it or found it sentimental, but in this one song was contained not only the grief but also the feeling of belonging to the club they loved and the spirit of camaraderie in adversity that permeates that troubled city. At every Liverpool match since, this has been sung not only as the traditional club anthem, but now also as a memorial.[1]

A surprising amount of classical music is about death. Not only committed Catholic composers like Bruckner, but also others like Brahms and Britten, have written powerful choral requiems which speak to both those with and those without Christian faith. '*In Paradisum*' from Fauré's *Requiem*, and

[1]It is a strange coincidence that, before being adopted by Liverpool fans twenty years prior to the Hillsborough disaster, the song had originally been written by Rodgers and Hammerstein for a scene in the musical *Carousel* – a scene following a death. By coincidence too, the Wembley Cup Final anthem 'Abide With Me' is a popular funeral hymn, which was not lost on fans, players or viewers at home when Liverpool played at Wembley later that year.

Andrew Lloyd Webber's '*Pie Jesu*' are popular and moving funeral pieces. In addition, much music – classical, folk and pop – is inspired by the parting of a loved one, from madrigals through Schubert *Lieder* to the Beatles' 'Yesterday'.

As the Church of Scotland minister and folk-singer Kathy Galloway says, 'sing the sorrow'. Many cultures have a folk tradition of mourning songs – the blues, Celtic folk-songs, the Scottish pibroch or funeral lament. The English, unfortunately, have lost their folk tradition of popular funeral songs, partly because of the reforming zeal of Victorian clerics who frowned on the songs' unorthodox theology.

This leaves us, usually, with hymns. Which is fine for the religious, but what about secular funerals? When younger people are involved, pop songs – such as 'Imagine' or 'A Whiter Shade of Pale' – can be used to great effect, though they are difficult for the congregation to sing together. One militant atheist complained to me that she can't stand secular funerals, because more than anything at a funeral she needs to sing; in many funerals, singing is the only thing the congregation does together, the only thing to express the shared nature of the occasion. Singing together is a balm for the loneliness of your grief, as with 'You'll Never Walk Alone'. It doesn't matter if it's corny or sentimental.

Nor do the songs need to be sorrowful. Many funeral hymns are hymns of thanks and praise. Kathy Galloway told me of the Zulu saying '*Unculo Uthokozisa Abadabukileyo* – Singing makes all the sad people happy because it is the voice of happiness.' They should know.

15

FITTING IT ALL TOGETHER

Many funerals today attempt to cram too much into too short a time. The traditional Jewish ceremony of burial may last only fifteen minutes, and is shorter and simpler than the typical English cremation service, but whereas the English cremation service is often the only ritual, the Jewish burial is part of a whole series of rituals. It is part of a flow that lasts from death to eternity.

After the burial, there is a meal at the house, initiating the week of *shiveh* – the week of being visited and fed. But a torn garment is worn for a month; and in synagogue every Sabbath for the next year, male mourners say together the *Kaddish* prayer of thanksgiving. After a year, it is assumed mourners have come to terms with the death, but they do not forget, nor will they ever. Every year on the anniversary, *Yahrzeit*, the family light a candle that burns for twenty-four hours, and they go to the synagogue to say the *Kaddish* prayer. You go on doing this for a parent, spouse, child, brother or sister every year until you yourself die. And every year, within a month of the most sacred day of the Jewish calendar, *Yom Kippur*, orthodox Jews make every effort to visit the grave of dead parents or children. If they visit a grave in another town, they place some stones on it to show that someone has visited.

The solidarity of the family, of the local Jewish community, of Jewish tradition lasting thousands of years, the incorporation into a predictable and secure sense of time moving on – all this is very different from the fragmented, isolating funeral service that many British people stoically endure.

Those of us who do not belong to traditional religious or ethnic groups, or to a community with a strong local tradition, do nevertheless have available a large number of possible rituals. Here is a list of some of those that fit white British culture – it would doubtless be somewhat different for other cultures. The point is not that you should indulge in every single available ritual. What matters is that the various rituals help the flow both into and out of social and emotional limbo (Chapter 12), that they are real to you (Chapter 13), and that they involve all those with an interest (Chapter 11).

Preparations

Preparations made before death can make things a lot easier in the rush after death. Many people with AIDS are writing into their wills not only what they would like done with their property, but also ideas for their funeral. Talk to others in the family, to a local funeral director, to clergy or a secular celebrant, or – if you want to conduct the service yourself – to the manager of the local crematorium or cemetery (Chapter 23). Find out what is possible, discuss what you want. Burial or cremation (Chapters 17 and 18)? Do you want a headstone or other memorial? What do you want to do with the ashes (Chapter 19)?

Following death

Following a death, do you want time with the body? Do you want to lay it out yourself? Do you want the body to stay at home, or to be looked after by a funeral director? Do you want friends to come to see and to talk?

Do allow family, friends and neighbours to do chores for you (Chapter 13). Remember the advice of the therapist Lily Pincus:

> For physical shock, rest and warmth are the recognised methods of treatment, yet the most frequent advice given for the emotional shock of grief is to 'keep going', 'get busy'. This 'remedy' may not only set the scene for a denial of loss and pain and subsequent pathological development, but it is likely to lead to all sorts of disasters.

In other words, you may not be in a fit state to make practical decisions with long-term consequences, so think about these things now, long before the event.

The funeral

Who is likely to turn up to the funeral, and can you cater for everyone in just one service (Chapter 11)? If not, have two ceremonies, a private one for the family, and a public one for everyone else. This could mean, for example, a private cremation or burial followed by a public memorial service, or a public funeral in church followed by a private cremation or burial.

Post-funeral

A ceremony of scattering or burying the ashes a few days or weeks after the funeral can be helpful.

One vicar offers to inter the ashes of local people in the churchyard on the Sunday following the cremation, and the family are told they will be mentioned during the evening service that Sunday. Many bereaved families take the opportunity to come – it's a bit like coming to hear your marriage banns read – and find it a comfort to know that people they

"It was his last request – he wanted his ashes thrown at the ref!"

may not even know are praying for them. I certainly found
it very helpful, on the Sunday following my totally non-
churchgoing father's death, to hear during Matins that
morning, 'We thank God for the life of Len Walter, and offer
to God's care his family and friends.' Like the Jews, I felt
reconnected, just a little.

Informal rituals

The post-funeral period will be marked by paperwork: not
just the administrative chores of wills, probate and insurance,
but also by the highly personal rituals of receiving and replying to letters. These can help focus your picture of the one
who has gone – something that is often surprisingly difficult
with someone you have lived with for decades. Ethnic
minority members will probably also receive lots of visitors.

Tending the grave

Tending the grave may be a private and personal act, though
on anniversaries you may well join with several other family
and friends. In some cultures, like Hong Kong and Mexico,
everyone does this on the same day, taking a picnic to the
grave and spending the day there: the hillside cemeteries
become alive with people, young and old, eating and talking,
laughing and crying.

The memorial service

In Britain today memorial services are increasingly popular.
Whereas the funeral ritually puts the person to death, as she is
committed to earth or flames (Chapter 12), a memorial
service has a different dynamic.

Sir Laurence Olivier's memorial service, some months
after his death and burial in 1989, began with a Westminster
Abbey full of mourners, all too aware they had lost a friend
and colleague. Then, slowly, Olivier walked through the
congregation. His Order of Merit, his Oscar, the crowns he
had worn in *King Lear* and *Richard III*, and other emblems of
the man and his achievements, were carried in by Douglas
Fairbanks, Jr., and leading British actors and actresses, down

the long, long aisle. The service went on to celebrate Olivier's contribution to the stage, and some of his triumphs, including a tape of his St Crispin Day speech from *Henry V*. This was no mere memory, but an acknowledgement of Olivier's lasting contribution: in film and recording, in the thousands he has inspired, he indeed lives on.

In several parts of the world, after the period of mourning comes a ceremony in which the spirit of the departed is woken up and invited back into the community. This recognises that the departed lives on in the lives she has been altering since the day she was born (Chapter 21). The modern memorial service recognises precisely this, whether or not the contribution is as obvious as was Olivier's.

Ideally, this acknowledgement of the continuing presence of the deceased should occur some months after the ritual putting-to-death in the crematorium or cemetery. For those friends who did not make it to the funeral, or if there is no funeral (as when the body is donated to medicine), the memorial service has to perform both functions: putting the person to death, and recognising their continuing life in us.

Ending mourning

Psychologically, it seems that a final ceremony after a few months, or a year, helps mark the end of mourning, and a readiness to move on and forward. Almost all traditional cultures have such a ceremony. In Theravada Buddhism, after one hundred days the mourner goes to the monastery to burn a token, such as a photo. In the West today, a memorial service, secular or religious, is the most obvious way of marking this stage in the proceedings.

Ongoing remembrance

Our family tries to get together on the anniversary of my father's death to have a meal together, rather like the Jewish *Yahrzeit* – though we're less talkative! Those who have lost family members in war may get together on the annual day of remembrance.

One example

One Anglican vicar, whose working-class Liverpool parish produces about 150 funerals a year, feels he should make available more rituals for the bereaved than just the funeral service.

On first visiting the family, he asks if they would like prayers in the house the night before the funeral. Nine out of ten say yes.

Once a month, at 7.30 p.m. on Wednesdays, he holds a Eucharist for those who have died that month, including a simple meditation. The families are invited, about half usually come, and the simple service is often quite tearful.

After the service, tea is provided. Here there is the chance to talk with other bereaved families, and with a group of parishioners who are committed to befriending the bereaved. Some of these counsellors remain in church in case help is needed by those who do not feel like socialising at the tea session. The names of those who have died are printed in the parish magazine, which that month is delivered to the bereaved families by members of the counselling group. In this close-knit working-class area, death is not yet privatised and most bereavement care is done by neighbours, so the task of the counselling group is to pick up those few who fall through the neighbourhood net. They hope to set up a local *Cruse* self-help group for the bereaved.

Once a year at Evensong, groups of laypeople name all those who have died in the past year. About three hundred people come to this service.

This is just one example of one man's, and one church's, attempt to create a flow of ritual that enables people to pray for and remember the dead, and enables them to move into and out of the limbo of bereavement. It unites communal religious ritual with individual friendship, neighbourhood networks with national bereavement care organisations like *Cruse*.

Another Anglican cleric visits all her bereaved families briefly in the week before Christmas, just to let them know she knows how they are feeling at that lonely time. Some crematoria invite the bereaved to monthly or annual memorial services. Families and individuals invent their own, more private, rituals. Nothing is impossible.

Plate 1 In the United Kingdom, the authorities frown on the use of photographs or other ways of personalising graves, but this is quite normal in Catholic and Orthodox countries. This photo shows an engraver by the grave of his own granddaughter, killed in the 1986 Armenian earthquake.
David Brinicombe/Hutchison Library

Death is an emotional, spiritual, social journey, in most cultures expressed by means of a physical journey.

Plate 2 In January 1958 two firemen lost their lives fighting a fire at London's Smithfield Market. Market workers stand in silent tribute as the funeral cortège passes. *The Hulton Picture Company*

Plate 3 In many societies, mourners help dispatch body and soul on their journey. In Bali the funeral tower is shaken and run around in circles to disorientate the deceased's spirit so that it cannot find its way home.
Michael Macintyre/Hutchison Library

Plate 4 The logo of St Christopher's Hospice, London: St Christopher carrying the Christ-child. Pictures of the living carrying those they love through death go back at least to ancient Egypt.

Grief, anger and love on Merseyside.

The Hillsborough disaster in April 1989 led to ninety-five football fans being crushed to death. The following week saw an entire city and an entire footballing community express its grief in spontaneous ritual. Liverpool's Anfield stadium and the Roman Catholic cathedral became places of pilgrimage where grief could be expressed and shared. *Liverpool Daily Post and Echo*

Plate 5 Some of the earliest messages to be attached to the Anfield gates. These came not only from Liverpool supporters, but also from rival teams.

Plate 6 At the requiem mass the day after, children spontaneously brought up scarves, shirts and rosettes to lay on the altar.

Plate 7 During the next week, one million people visited Anfield to lay flowers on the pitch.

How may those who have been cremated be memorialised? Plates 8, 9 and 10 show competition designs for memorials that are personal and tangible yet easy to manufacture and maintain. *Memorial Advisory Bureau*

Plate 8 The cubic column grows one cube at a time as each new set of ashes is buried around the base. Each cube could commemorate up to four people, with a short inscription on each side.

Plate 9 This memorial column is made from hollow sections which can each contain two sets of ashes. The columns would bear inscriptions, and can stand either singly or in groups.

Plate 10 This memorial gradually grows in height from a single kerb square to a complete pyramid as additional names are added with successive tiers. Ashes go inside or around the base.

Some memorials express not only individual loss, but also shared sorrow.

Plate 11 The view from the Amsterdam room in which Anne Frank and her family hid from 9 July 1942 until they were discovered on 4 August 1944 and sent to Belsen. The whole house is now a museum and memorial to all who have died as a result of racism. *Anne Frank Stichting*

Plate 12 The memorial garden in Amsterdam to the hundreds of tourists killed in the 1977 Tenerife aircrash. Around the simple circular table of granite are plaques bearing the names of those who died.

The Christian tradition is full of images of hope in suffering. Secular funeral settings must work at creating equally powerful symbols.

Plate 13 La Pietã
Michelangelo

Plate 14 Crematorium, Amsterdam. The modern design is light years away from the pseudo-comfort or churchiness of British crematoria. The broken column ascending to the ceiling holds the attention, expressing a life cut short yet hinting that life goes on beyond and above.

PART FOUR

PLACES

A funeral is a physical as well as an emotional event, spatial as well as spiritual. Part Four explores what we do to the corpse (burying or cremating it), where we do it, and how this affects the funeral.

16

JOURNEYING

And Joseph [of Arimathea] took the body, and wrapped it
in a clean linen shroud, and laid it in his own new tomb,
which he had hewn in the rock; and he rolled a great stone
to the door of the tomb, and departed. Mary Magdalene
and the other Mary were there, sitting opposite the
sepulchre.

St Matthew 27:59–61

Whatever else it does, a funeral has to dispose of a corpse. It is
not only an emotional, spiritual, social, and economic
business, it is also an irreducibly physical business. A corpse
has to be physically moved, and mourners have to follow it.
The funeral is enacted in place and space. Like it or not, the
physical aspects of a funeral, the wrapping in the shroud and
the rolling of the stone, the grinding of crematorium machinery and the getting stuck in a traffic jam, the crocuses and chill
wind at the graveside, are all part of the proceedings. Like it
or not, fire and smoke, earth and wind, become symbols of
emotional and spiritual states.

On the road again

The Chimanimani mountains of eastern Zimbabwe are for
me pretty close to paradise. I discovered them in late 1985,
climbing them on my own, enjoying the ethereal misty views,
and joining with local youngsters in sliding down waterfalls
into idyllic rock pools hidden in the mountainous jungle. At
the same time, and unknown to me, an old lady whom I had

never met was riding through the bush on her moped in search of the lone Englishman, with the news that his father was seriously ill. She found me surprisingly easily, and so I boarded the bus that twisted and turned, rocked and growled – with the indescribable beauty of Africa outside and the friendliness of Africa inside – slowly back to civilisation. I was met in the midday sun by my adopted black brother, who broke the news of my father's death. We wept together. He drove me speedily back to Harare; that night I was on the plane, and by eleven o'clock the next morning I joined my family in the cold grey drizzle of a Cotswold November.

I will never forget that journey in which I was loved home, by stranger and friend alike.

Here is another journey home. In their twenties Alison's maternal grandparents had moved forty miles from the little rural town of Fyvie to the big city of Aberdeen, where they raised a family and lived out their lives. In middle age they bought a plot in the Fyvie churchyard, to which – being natives of Fyvie – they were entitled. Gran outlived grandad by fifteen years, and Alison described to me her funeral in 1986, held in the Aberdeen church to which they had belonged. Then the funeral cortège of gran, family and friends, drove out to Fyvie – it was a beautiful day, and for Alison it felt like taking gran home. Gran had often talked of this her last journey to Fyvie, to join her husband. The church clock was striking eleven as Alison's husband and some of gran's nephews carried the coffin into the quiet churchyard.

Both Alison and I remember these journeys with affection. In each case the outward journey matched the inward journey – from vacation to bereavement, from life in the big city to reunion in the rural home. One was a downward journey into grief, the other an upward journey of comfort.

In New Orleans they make a habit of this. On the way to the grave, the procession is led by a jazz band playing, very slowly, 'Just a Closer Walk'. Then, as soon as the coffin is in the ground, the band strikes up smartly with 'When the Saints' and off they all go to the wake, to remember, to drink, to celebrate. Music, movement and emotion all change together, from sorrow to thanks, from grief to hope.

There is something very satisfying about the match of inner and outer movement. On pages 90–1 I wrote of how from time immemorial the spiritual, emotional, social passage that death involves has been reflected at the funeral in physical passage. Both death and bereavement seem like a journey, and at this time real physical journeys somehow feel appropriate (Plates 2–4).

Not always. If you are stuck in Sydney because it's Christmas and you can't get a flight in time to get to your brother's funeral in Southampton, and you arrive a day late, you feel doubly bereaved. If your car gets separated from the rest of the cortège in the traffic of the modern metropolis, a ritual journey turns into anxiety whether you will find the crematorium. And once there, nothing moves, save the lips of the anonymous clergyman.

How then to ensure that physical movement means something, given the conditions of the modern funeral? This is the concern of Part Four of the book. For now, I give just three examples: one a stubborn retention of an old custom, one a serendipitous revival, the third the invention of a new symbol.

Alf Smith, Funeral Directors, is a family firm going back four generations just up the road from London's Elephant and Castle. The funeral director always walks with his hearse for the first five or ten minutes, no matter that on the way they might have to crawl around a major roundabout on the A2, holding up all and sundry. A statement has been made, that the bustle of modern traffic should slow down for just a minute because something significant has happened – a local person has died. The cortège will often take a detour in order to pass a favourite pub, a former home, or a workplace, and again the director will walk with the hearse. The demands of efficiency and speed take second place when someone's final journey is made.

The tradition of people stopping and taking off their hats as a cortège passes has all but vanished in Britain – but it still happens at sea. The Britannia Shipping Company for Burial at Sea[1] has since 1986 been arranging burials and ash-sprinklings at sea, in which the family accompany the urn or flag-draped coffin a few miles out to sea for the ceremony

[1] Britannia House, High Street, Newton Poppleford, Sidmouth, Devon EX10 0EF (Tel. 0395 68652).

conducted by the company's chaplain. The journey over the water seems to calm the spirit in a way a modern road journey does not. A bonus is that as the funeral boat passes other vessels, their crew – not just professionals but also weekend leisure sailors – typically take off their hats, stand to attention, and dip the ensign. Families find this unasked-for respect a great comfort.

When St Christopher's Hospice was opened in the 1960s, they needed a logo (Plate 4). They decided on a simple representation of St Christopher, his back bent under the weight of the human child he is carrying over the river – a symbol of the journey of being loved over the river of death that all can understand.

The place of rest

In the compact little Dutch town of Edam, where the cheese comes from, the main Protestant church and its graveyard are at the very edge of the town, just inside the city wall. From the graveyard, you look out uninterrupted over the fertile green polder, and then the other way are the neat houses and streets of the town. The Protestant dead of Edam literally lie between the human world and the natural world, a fitting resting place for those who were human, but are now dust and earth. (Edam's unfortunate Catholics lie in what felt to me like no man's land, overlooked by the back wall of a factory.)

In rural North America and North-West Scotland, the cemetery is typically just a little way out of town. Not part of civilisation, yet not part of the great outdoors.

On Norway's Lofoten Islands, the village cemetery is often on the light sandy soil between the beach and the village – cosy homes on one side and the fury of the Atlantic on the other.

Three modern crematoria that immediately spring to my mind – in Bath, Aberdeen and Amsterdam – were built, and still are, on the very edge of town.

In ancient Rome, they often buried their dead on the road out of town. You can still see the tombs lining the Via Appia.

In Jerusalem, they took Jesus outside the city wall in order to crucify him, and they buried him nearby. Rejected by men, he was expelled by the city.

All these places of death are on the edge. They are, in Victor Turner's phrase 'betwixt and between', reflecting the betwixt and between state of the mourner, of the decaying body, of the soul (Chapter 12). All are in limbo between culture and nature. In the Edam cemetery, or at the Bath crematorium, you have a sense of being in two worlds at once, the world of the living and the world of the dead – reflecting the shock of bereavement, the confusion of the mourner. You are in danger of being absorbed by nature, yet the comfort of human society is not far away.

To get to any of these resting places, you have to make a journey. With the exception of the three crematoria, you can walk.

It is appropriate for cemeteries to be on the edge between culture and nature because death, like birth and sex, *is* the boundary between culture and nature. Death, like the Son of God, is something human society has difficulty handling, so is expelled to the edge. Doubtless cemeteries are often on the edge of town for the practical reason that this is the nearest piece of available land, but somehow these last resting places on the edge between the human and the natural world almost always feel, in a much deeper sense, right.

There are other satisfying places for the dead to rest. In the middle ages, the favoured resting place was as near as possible to the high altar of the church. The richer you were, or the more saintly, the more likely this ambition could be achieved, as a glance at the tombs in any pre-Reformation church will reveal. Here, then, you were on the edge between the city of man and the city of God. Next to the Holy Sacrament, yet visitable by human society. Though the church or cathedral containing such remains may physically be in the middle of the village or city, it is a mistake to see these tombs as in the middle of human society. That is how they appear to the modern, secular tourist, but to the medieval person they were on the edge between the physical world and the spiritual.

But the fact remains that many churchyards and cemeteries today *are* in the midst of where we live, and this can feel appropriate. The English village church and its graveyard may speak not so much of that awkward corner of reality that has to be pushed to the edge, but of the village itself, expressed through the tombs of the ancestors. Propose modernising or demolishing such a church, or flattening the tombstones, and there will be outcry; people who never darken the doors of the church will feel that the spirit of the village is about to be destroyed.

In industrial cities the crematorium grounds are valued by some as a garden of peace within the tumult of the city. Indeed, the urban park movement in the United States emerged out of the mid-Victorian habit of strolling at the weekends in the arcadian cemeteries that were fashionable at the time. For many, there is something satisfying about this reminder that, even within the city, there is something that speaks of other values.

So the cemetery or crematorium can be located successfully at the edge of town, or it can be the resting place of the ancestors in the midst of the village, or it can be an oasis within the city.

Unfortunately, fewer and fewer cemeteries and crematoria today are in such appropriate places.

Some were originally placed on the edge, but have since been surrounded by suburban development and are now neither on the edge nor in the middle. The cortège often has to drive from the family's suburb to another suburb with which they have no personal connection. Yet new, more local resting places for each suburb are not being developed; lots of little cemeteries would doubtless be too inconvenient for the municipality to maintain and would not make a private developer a profit. So the final, most personal journey gets lost in the nowhere-ness of a mediocre combination of suburbia and municipalisation.

Another problem is created by the modern European crematorium. To run at maximum efficiency, you need one crematorium for about every quarter of a million people. This is fine for a city like Aberdeen with a population of a quarter of a million. But in the Durham coalfield there are lots of little towns and villages, each with a strong sense of local identity, so where do you place the crematorium that serves them all? It is not so satisfying for natives of Chester-le-Street that they have to follow their departed to rival town Birtley for their last fond farewells. The missus spends her dying days in a strange hospital, her coffin is looked after by strange men, and eventually she is burned in a strange town.

There is the same kind of problem in London, where I grew up. I felt part of my suburb, one of a thousand, and very vaguely part of London, but I never felt part of the London Borough of Hillingdon – Hillingdon being the name of another suburb that my family never had any cause to visit. Goodness knows where Hillingdon's crematorium was, but I'm sure it was nowhere that meant anything to me.

Should we go along the American path, where some local funeral directors have their own cremator in the back garage? Those who work in the British cremation business are very worried about the technical standards of American practice, but the American approach does seem to get over the problem of the anonymous crematorium, on enemy territory even, that is all too common in British towns that don't just happen to contain the magic one quarter of a million souls. Whatever the case for more local crematoria, in Chapter 18 I will argue strongly that there is every opportunity just now to create more local cemeteries.

Symbols

A father commented to his children that there is more truth in most fairy stories than in the TV news. They were dumbfounded.

Ours is a scientific, literal age. We believe in clear facts. This is fine for dealing with technological problems, but not for the mysteries of life and death. Knowing certain facts is essential if you do not want to get pregnant, but poetry will serve you a lot better if you wish to express the pain of infertility or the joy of giving birth. Knowing certain medical facts is essential if we are to prolong life, but a silent holding of hands is better when you are with a sick person as she faces death.

The nearer we get to the imponderables of life and death, the more we need symbols that express what cannot be expressed in clear, logical prose. A symbol can mean many things, because its purpose is to help us explore the many angles on something that cannot be captured neatly in one snapshot. Unlike a fact, no symbol has a dictionary definition.

Take the symbol of clasped hands, common on nineteenth-century tombstones. When asked by Texan folklorist Carl Lindahl what this meant, one old man pondered: 'When do you shake hands? You shake hands to say "hello". You shake hands to say "goodbye". This is "goodbye" and "hello". "Goodbye, brother. Hello, God." I think that's what it means. I *hope* that's what it means, because it's tough to say goodbye.'

Younger respondents in the Houston cemetery, however, treated the clasped hands not as a symbol that explored something very complex, but as a sign with a definite meaning: 'Friends shaking hands'; 'Warm and friendly'; 'Friendship reaffirmed and a bargain sealed'; 'Goodbye to a good friend'; or 'It's hard to let go.' Almost all these younger individuals interpreted the clasped hands just one way, as either 'hello' *or* 'goodbye'.

At Undercliffe, a famous Victorian cemetery in Bradford, West Yorkshire, much work has been put in by volunteers to enable visitors to appreciate the place. Their attractively produced leaflet *Symbolism in Funeral Art* says curtly that clasped hands 'symbolise friendship'. Of the twenty symbols described, the leaflet hints at ambiguous meanings for only three. It is as though a trip around Undercliffe cemetery is not an aid to exploring the mystery of mortality, but an educational trip to learn historical and literary facts: see how many symbols you can find and whether you can work out the meaning of each. Unfortunately, this completely misses what symbolism, and cemeteries, are about.

If we are to be able to contemplate death – of ourselves or of others – we need symbols (Plates 4, 13, 14). But how are we to regain an appreciation of symbols in a world that believes only in literal facts?

The problem is not new. After the Reformation, zealots smashed all physical images of God and Christ, which they thought committed the sin of idolatry, and then tried to invent non-Catholic symbols to replace them. The trouble is that you can't invent a whole new stock of symbols just like that, and many of them didn't stick – symbols are a form of language, and they emerge only over time. Later, some Protestants came to distrust all symbolism, relying only on a literal reading of the Bible. (Incidentally, such Christians would be dismayed to realise that their literalism is the hallmark of the modern, scientific mind! A disproportionate number of them are, in fact, scientists.)

Architecture faces a similar problem. Architectural modernism was a kind of modern Puritanism, eschewing decoration, an attempt to get back to the bare bones of things. Nowadays people are rejecting the more spartan, inhuman forms of modernism, and they want to bring decoration and symbolism back into buildings. The Pompidou Centre in Paris, full of colour and movement; a butter factory in Wiltshire, shaped like a butter pat; houses everywhere with red and green-stained wood. A lot of people like all this, and the playful ambiguity of many post-modern buildings indeed recovers the ambiguity of symbolism. Many people like buildings which could be one thing, or could be something else; others, however, see this playfulness as tacky – decoration for its own sake, playing with styles and symbols in a way that undermines every style and every symbol.

One block of flats in Bath which I worked on when I was a builder's labourer was designed as an energy-efficient solar building, with one side expressing this by boldly facing the sun. Passers by, unfortunately, did not recognise this, and not one of them either liked or understood the building from this side. It was not that they gave it ambiguous meanings, they could see no meaning at all. We are all into energy conservation nowadays, but how do you *symbolise* energy conservation? By contrast, the other side – with arty-crafty porches that immediately read 'home' – was liked and understood by all.

After half a century of philistinism, there is little that can be taken off the peg as a thoroughly up-to-date replacement for the old architectural languages that everyone understands – classical and Gothic, Tudor and Jacobean. And if it is hard enough to introduce symbolism that makes sense in the late twentieth century in homes and offices, how on earth do you do it in crematoria and graveyards?

Those who have done most to reintroduce symbolism in architecture – the post-modernists – have a lot going for them. They know how to express irony and paradox, both of which are surely at the very heart of our human experience of death.

But things are tricky because post-modernist architects and artists are used to exploring irony and paradox in a playful way. Though death, like sex, has its funny side, you need something more than playfulness in a cemetery or crematorium.

Things are also tricky because religion is involved. In a society with every religion under the sun and none, how do you create symbols in crematoria and cemeteries that mean something to everyone? Barbara Smoker, the president of the National Secular Society, is rightly upset that 'Christians have taken the crematoriums to their bosom and are treating them as if they were their own – which they are not.' According to the *Guardian* newspaper, when conducting secular funerals at Honor Oak crematorium in South London, Miss Smoker is confronted by a Christ in Glory stained-glass window, religious embroideries, and a ceiling which lowers at the end of the service, covering the catafalque with a cross. Doubtless all this was designed to comfort people, but Hindus and Sikhs would find it as offensive as secularists. Must we then be limited to lightweight removable symbols that can be speedily changed as a party of Sikhs exit and a group of Catholics enter for the next performance?

If the problem nowadays is the offence of Christian symbols in a secular or multifaith society, the problem in the Victorian period was often the opposite. The private school educated élite's infatuation with Greece and Rome led to pagan symbols proliferating in a largely Christian country. The *Quarterly Review* for 1842 complains about the monuments to national heroes in Westminster Abbey and St Paul's Cathedral:

> When the government of a great and Christian nation could find no better mode of commemorating the dead than by re-erecting images of Neptune, and Mars, and Fame, and Victory, mixed up with dragoons and drummers, catapults and cannons, men without clothes in a field of battle, or English generals in Roman togas, and all the trash of the poorest pedant; and when a Christian church in a Christian metropolis is selected as the fittest depository for these outrages . . . there must have been something most unsound in the tone and manners of the age.

Are we then caught between the devil of an austere, comfortless, empty crematorium or funeral parlour, and the deep blue sea of symbols which comfort some but offend others? Or should such places just be warm, homely, and comforting? Unfortunately, a funeral parlour that feels like my living room, or a crematorium that feels like the lounge bar of the Rose and Crown, fails to address the mysteries of life and death. By being ordinary and cosy, they imply that nothing of significance has occurred. Well, it has, which is why such places need art.

Good art comes from good artists, unfettered by committee decisions and all-too-easily-offended public taste. Good art may offend and puzzle. Unfortunately, grieving people come to a funeral to be comforted, not to be offended or puzzled by art more than they already are by death. So are we inevitably stuck with effete art if we are going to have art in and around the funeral?

St Christopher bearing the human child, Bath crematorium's glass wall overlooking the peaceful Somerset countryside (p. 184), and other gorgeous symbolism that works for everyone (Plate 14), these encourage me to believe we are not. But I hope by now you see that getting the physical and symbolic side of the funeral right needs to be thought out carefully. (The next three chapters explore this in more detail.)

Nor do I believe all this can be left to the experts, those 'who understand these things'. In Britain funeral buildings are largely in the hands of local authority Environmental Health or Leisure committees who do not understand these things. Only when the public demands something better will we get anything better.

17

THE CREMATORIUM

> The central question becomes: what can crematorium design express?
>
> Jeremy Barton, 'An Architecture of Hypocrisy', 1981

In South Bristol crematorium, opened in 1971, you have to look hard to find the coffin, tucked away in the far right-hand corner. There is only a very limited opportunity for mourners to touch the coffin, and none at all to circle around it. The interior is clad with warm wood of quality, the furnishings are comfortable, and all is light and airy, but apart from the flower display on the way out, nothing refers to death, nor even to life. Just cosy comfort. The building first hides the fact of death, and then cossets you so that you don't notice. People rather like it, I suppose because it helps them get through the funeral without too much pain. The cremation industry is also rather proud of the building.

There are other ways the building is symptomatic of most modern crematoria in Britain. It is not designed to enable people to mark a life and a death, but to get one party in and out without bumping into the previous and following parties. From the outside, the 'works' are hidden around the back; the chimney is not prominent; and you might be forgiven for thinking the building is a small branch library or school dining-hall. You approach it through a new and windswept park in which, unfortunately, there has been difficulty getting the trees established.

The building's chief assets, shared with many other modern crematoria in Britain, are a splendid location and ample foyers for gathering before and after the service. The exit foyer is filled with the colour and fragrance of potted plants, labelled with touching anniversary notes from mourners to their departed.

Cremation in the West was introduced in the late nineteenth century as an efficient, technological solution to the disposal of bodies (Chapter 4), and to express the secular view that nothing remains after death (Chapter 8). These two original motives still dominate both crematorium design and the experience of a cremation service. This leads to two intractable problems.

One is that where religious symbols are required, they have to be grafted on, and the graft does not always take too well. Unlike a Catholic church designed for celebrating the mass, or a Protestant church designed for hearing the Word of God, a crematorium is designed to burn bodies. Religious symbols, Christian or other, have to be added.

The problem is not inherent in cremation. In Thailand, where cremation is based not on utilitarian convenience but on Buddhist philosophy, there is no problem with designing crematoria, which look much like any Thai Buddhist temple. Our problem is not cremation *per se*, but what cremation means in the West.

The second problem is that we do not like to think too closely about the details of cremation: in the arithmetic of a Christian or post-Christian society, *burning + death = hell*. For secularists, burning a dead body is simply a practical form of disposal. None of us finds it very nice, none of us finds it comforting. There is no crematorical equivalent of the honest-to-goodness phrase 'dead and buried'. ('Dead and burnt'?!) So crematoria interiors end up with a pseudo-gentility that tries to hide the facts of the matter. This is what Jeremy Barton calls 'an architecture of hypocrisy'.

How can the modern crematorium get over these problems? Can it transcend the faith in technology, the pseudo-professionalism, the secularism, and the individualism that Part Two suggested are underlying problems of the modern funeral, and that seem to be woven into the very fabric of the crematorium?

Participation

Very few Western people wish to see the coffin actually slide into the flames, so this is hidden. And from this stem most of the problems of the Western crematorium.

The sliding into the flames, like the burial of the coffin, is a second death (Chapter 12), painfully dramatising what happened a few days before. It is a symbol of death. Unfortunately, few of us in the West can cope with this particular form of second death. The symbol is too violent.

So instead, we have to rely on a symbol of a symbol: the closing of the curtains symbolises cremation, which in turn symbolises death. Or even a symbol of a symbol of a symbol – the lowering of the coffin into the floor symbolises burial, which in turn symbolises the actual cremation, which in turn symbolises death. All this is just too far removed to work well. It may work in hiding death, in reducing the shock, but it does not work as a dramatisation of death. If it is painful, it is often not so much because it reminds us of death, as because it is eerie.

Given our modern sensibilities, the desire to protect mourners from the facts of cremation is necessary. What is not necessary is to extend this protection to every aspect of the service. The building not only hides the coffin as it slides into the flames, but all too often separates mourners from the coffin during the service itself, in ways quite unknown in a church or at the graveside.

In Marylebone crematorium the catafalque on which the coffin rests is raised up, so the congregation can see it. This, however, also turns the congregation into an audience, turning participation into passivity. It prevents people, especially little children, from coming and touching the coffin, or laying a flower on it, or peering into it.

In South Bristol crematorium the catafalque – although nearer the floor – is in a corner, so you cannot stand around the coffin.

In every crematorium I have visited the coffin is removed by the touch of a button. There is no equivalent of mourners lowering the coffin into the grave themselves. There is no way mourners can themselves, physically, participate in removing the coffin from their view. Technology has removed all human effort. A mourner could press the button, but this is usually at the lectern where the minister stands and/or at the back where a crematorium attendant can press it; neither location is where mourners would want to be at that moment.

Things do not have to be like this. The earliest modern cremations, for example the poet Shelley's on an Italian beach, were like Hindu cremations, with everyone standing around the funeral pyre. A German design of the 1870s had the mourners standing around the coffin, just as at a burial, themselves lowering it with cords to the 'works' below. It is only subsequently that mourners have been protected from participating in the destruction of the corpse.

Siemens' Cremation Apparatus, 1874
(From the collection of Prof. James Stevens Curl)

If mourners are not willing symbolically to put the coffin to death, the culmination of the service must at least be a symbolic farewell. To this end, something must *move*: either the coffin sliding behind curtains or into the floor, or curtains sliding in front of the coffin, or the mourners processing around or past the coffin to say farewell. It is all right at the end of the service to leave the coffin in view so long as it is somewhere mourners can file past to say their goodbyes on their way out (see Figure 3b). It is not all right to leave it up on a podium, in view but out of reach.

Possibilities

If only the mourners were able to interact with the coffin, as they do in Catholic and Orthodox funerals and as they did in nineteenth-century cremations, the final committal might be more real and less eerie. Even within existing crematoria, fortunately, there are many ways in which this can be done.

I have already mentioned the Amsterdam crematorium, where the coffin is in the middle, at the front, almost at floor level. The family can choose whether to leave the coffin there or have it lowered; there are also possibilities of touching, kissing, walking around the coffin on entry or exit, or standing around it at the committal. In the crematorium at Canberra I have stood around a coffin as it descended, holding hands in a circle with the few other mourners; it was one of the simplest and best funerals I have been to. (I describe it in detail on pp. 243–4.)

The leader of the funeral can do much to help focus attention on the coffin, or on some symbol of hope if the crematorium is lucky enough to offer one. Even if the mourners do not touch the coffin, the minister can. One Anglican cleric greatly appreciates the facility in his local crematorium for the button to be pushed by an attendant at the back; at the committal, this clergyman leaves his lectern and goes over to the coffin, touching it as he speaks the committal prayer. This human touch prevents the eeriness that so often accompanies this moment.

(If you lead such a funeral, though, do ensure the attendant knows when to push the button. One Nonconformist minister

I know does fewer funerals than her Anglican counterparts, so she doesn't know the crematorium staff so well, nor are they so familiar with her non-Anglican liturgy. Once, she was horrified to observe the coffin sliding away prematurely, out of reach and out of view!)

Part Two documented how the focus at funerals has shifted over time from helping the dead on their way, to comforting the living. Burials are conducted 'in the round', expressing our togetherness at this awesome moment, and some early crematorium designs were arranged as mock burials. Since Vatican II and the advent of the charismatic movement, many churches are organised in the round, yet every modern crematorium I have visited is arranged like the old front-facing church, or indeed like a cinema. If we gain comfort from the presence of our friends and family, why do we not express this in how we sit in the crematorium? Chapter 14 described one funeral in a modern church, with seating in a horseshoe, which facilitated sharing of memories and thanks during the service (p. 155). When a similar sharing was attempted at the funeral of another member of this family in the local crematorium, they had to twist around in their seats as they talked.

To sum up. Crematorium design should enable people to interact with the coffin and with each other, should they so desire. Those conducting funerals should, within the limitations of the particular crematorium, be open to the possibilities of this kind of interaction. Then the remoteness of people from what is going on, and from one another, can be mitigated.

Maybe the majority of people wish to remain remote. Fair enough, but this is no justification for their remoteness to be set in concrete, in an architecture that obstructs those who wish to turn remoteness into real sorrow, real thanks, and real joy.

Natural symbols

The crematorium at Bath, built in 1961, is on the very edge of the city. The entire far wall of glass looks out on to the most idyllic English countryside, speaking peace to Christian and atheist alike. The first time I entered the

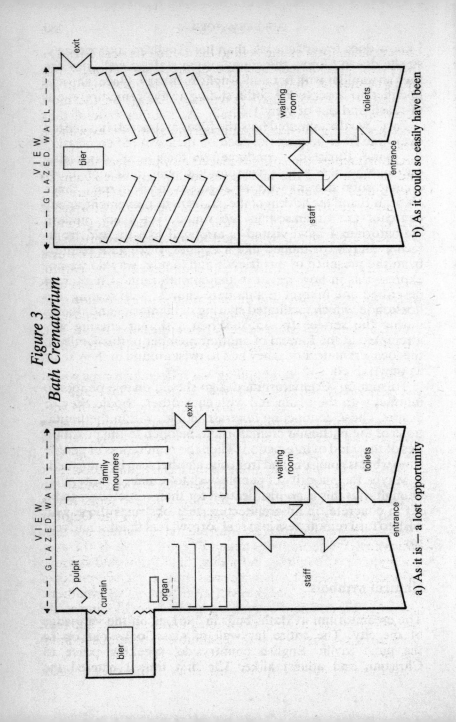

Figure 3
Bath Crematorium

VIEW
GLAZED WALL

pulpit
curtain
bier
organ
family mourners
exit
waiting room
toilets
staff
entrance

a) As it is — a lost opportunity

VIEW
GLAZED WALL

bier
exit
waiting room
toilets
staff
entrance

b) As it could so easily have been

crematorium, processing behind the coffin of a dear friend as the priest proclaimed the hope of the resurrection, I was overwhelmed at finding myself seemingly outdoors in an arcadian paradise. Friends have said it must be the most beautiful crematorium in Britain. At another funeral they were harvesting outside, an appropriate symbol if ever there was one.

Unfortunately the coffin is placed nowhere near the view, and the pulpit for the minister is somewhere else again, so once seated the family don't know where to look (Figure 3a). The other mourners enjoy the view, in the middle of which is the family, their grief on full view; meanwhile, family members are tempted by the view to look right away from the coffin. It is all a dreadful muddle, in which wonderful natural symbolism vies with, rather than complements, the painful reality of the coffin. Instead, we should all face the view, with the coffin in our midst and the celebrant standing beside it; at the end of the funeral, either mourners could file out past the coffin, or the coffin could descend below the floor (Figure 3b). This building could so easily have been a model for the whole country.

The one occasion this building was redeemed for me was at the funeral of Cyril. Cyril was a staunch lover of the countryside; each week he was out repairing footpaths with the conservation volunteers; he gave prize-winning slide lectures and was well known. He died unexpectedly, and the crematorium was full to overflowing.

The minister wisely abandoned the lectern, and stood right in the middle of the view, close to those Cyril loved and to the countryside he cared for. We all knew where to look. It was the day in February 1988 in which a repeat of the October 1987 hurricane was forecast – fortunately it turned out only storm-force. The minister talked of Cyril's love of the very countryside we could see before us; that Cyril would approve of today's weather; that he was not a picture-postcard country-lover, and had himself been out in all weathers, looking after and helping create what we were looking at. As the storm gathered force, the whole building shook; and then for a moment, just before the committal, a glint of sun lit up the view.

And so to the point of this story. One of the most

comforting, though not always comfortable, things about burial is that it is outdoors: you are surrounded by the symbolism of nature, of autumn and spring, death and new life. But go indoors, into a crematorium, and you have lost all this. The best you can have is a picture window, as at Bath. Or paintings, or potted plants.

At the same time, you are protected from the wind and rain. The very discomfort of wind and rain and mud at a burial reminds us that the nature of burial is not picture-book nature. The weeds and uncut grass in the country churchyard contrast with the mown sections, unkempt nature threatening human tidiness. Death is not pretty. You miss all this in the centrally heated crematorium, where even the grounds outside are neatly manicured. I think we all appreciated at Cyril's funeral the centrally heated and modern building shuddering in the storm; for once, we had not got nature quite so neatly packaged.

The four elements

Apart from the symbolism of decay leading to growth, nature offers other symbols: the four traditional elements of earth, water, wind and fire. The great advantage of natural symbols is that they can be interpreted in more than one way. Every human culture has given each natural element both positive and negative meanings. For example, in the Judaeo-Christian tradition:

Earth is the dust out of which God made us, and the land promised to the children of Israel. But it is also what eventually will consume our bodies, as Job knew well.

Water is full of symbolic significance. Though it was created by God and declares his handiwork, the Hebrews feared the sea, which enters the biblical story mainly as a danger. Jonah, Christ and St Paul all had adventures in boats on stormy seas. Yet water also quenches the thirst of the desert traveller – from Rebecca offering a drink to Jacob, to Jesus promising living water to the woman at the well in Samaria. Much later, in *The Pilgrim's Progress*, the Puritan John

Bunyan adapted the Roman idea of death as a river to be crossed.

Wind can be either the refreshing breeze of the Holy Spirit, or the wind of destruction.

Fire can be either the fire of hell, or the fire of persecution that purifies the Christian.

The great thing about these natural symbols is that they can express both sorrow and joy, fear and hope. As the funeral party gathers around the grave, one person will see the fallen leaves, while another will see the crocuses. One will feel in contact with nature through the breeze, another will be just cold and miserable. Natural symbols express what people feel, rather than force them to feel what some human committee of designers intends them to feel.

But go inside the crematorium, and what are you left with? You are detached from the earth. Apart from the exceptional day of hurricane, you are not aware of the wind. Most of us do not like to contemplate the fire into which granny will soon be slid, while outside, the chimney is usually hidden or, with modern technology, eliminated entirely.

All Western attempts to symbolise the fire of cremation have failed. The Phoenix, that fabulous Arabian bird that burned itself every five hundred years or so and rose rejuvenated from its ashes, is not one most of us would immediately be able to distinguish from any other bird portrayed in stone, metal or paint. In Australia, efforts have been made by funeral liturgists to use the new ecological understanding of bush fires (essential for some seeds to open and take root) as a symbol of purification and growth, but unfortunately, for every Aussie who appreciates the ecological function of a bush fire, there are probably ten who are petrified it will destroy their property. Not a comforting symbol.

So in the modern crematorium, earth, wind and fire are out of bounds. Which leaves us with water. Is this why crematoria throughout the Western world are awash with pools, streams and fountains? Anyway, people seem to find them peaceful.

Although the possibilities are very limited, crematoria can

nevertheless use natural symbols creatively. A plate-glass window does not need a glorious view to be effective. On a small suburban lot in Melbourne, the six yards between the picture window and a neighbouring fence in one funeral parlour are richly planted. Since Australian trees remain green all year, at all times you feel almost as though you are in the midst of a lush Australian forest.

The walk from the car to the crematorium, and back again, is crucial. This can provide the sense of passage that otherwise can be so badly lacking, and there are examples of this having been well handled. The walk need not be through a manicured park, one of the more successful alternatives being a short but symbolic walk through forest or bush; this solution works particularly well in Scandinavia, North America and Australia, where virgin forest is a national symbol of a life-giving nature.

A significant place

Recently I went to the service of blessing following a wedding between a pregnant non-churchgoing divorcee and someone who had hitherto seemed a committed bachelor. It was a super occasion. The soaring Gothic arches of the Victorian church pointed to a transcendent reality, something stronger than the happy couple, that might sustain them; the whole building was one where life and death have been celebrated through the generations, where life and love can be given greater significance, even for those who are not sure they believe; and the whole Christian tradition spoke of forgiveness, of a new start, of hope.

It struck me how important this building was for giving significance to these human lives, and how difficult it is for a crematorium to do this. If a crematorium pretends not to be what it is, how can it attain any deep significance? It is like asking a church to pretend not to be about the worship of God, and then expecting it to confer transcendent significance on a wedding.

One of the good things about a church is that, apart from the daily or weekly worship of God, it sees baptisms, weddings and funerals. It is not defined by death, for all of life is there. One problem of the crematorium is that it is used just for death: by excluding life and birth, by excluding the ongoing life of the local community, major sources of comfort and hope are excluded. No wonder the poor clergyman has his work cut out to comfort a distressed congregation all by himself and in sixteen minutes flat.

The recently opened Centennial Park crematorium in Adelaide is apparently of such high quality that people are actually asking to be married as well as burned there. The original Forest Lawns cemetery in Los Angeles also attracts weddings. This is one road to go down – to make the crematorium of such high priority and quality that it transcends its natural limitations.

Where else?

The other road is to reduce the crematorium to its essential task of burning human corpses, and hold all ceremonies elsewhere.

This is typically the pattern of cremation in the United States, where the service is completed in a church or funeral parlour, or there is no funeral service, simply a later memorial service. The European concept of a funeral service in the crematorium simply does not exist in America.

There are problems, however, with a funeral service in a funeral parlour. This practice developed in the United States partly because there were, and still are, too many funeral directors. The only way small operators can make a decent profit is to add value to what they can offer – so they build beautiful funeral parlours, shut the clergy out of the act as far as possible, offer an elaborate performance around a dolled-up corpse on their own premises, and charge for it all.

The trouble with the American way is that, once funeral directors have borrowed millions of dollars to build a beautiful parlour, they have a direct financial interest in selling you as long a ceremony as possible. In large measure, economics drives, prolongs and elaborates the American funeral.

In Britain, the reverse operates. Ninety per cent of Britain's 224 crematoria are owned by local municipalities, and although they typically make a profit, crematoria do not have a high priority for the committees that run them. There are no votes in death; certainly more votes are to be gained by refurbishing the leisure centre than by upgrading the crematorium. (This comparison is not artificial, for often these two facilities are controlled by the same committee.) Worse, the 1980s have seen restricted investment throughout the public sector, with the result that crematoria are run on tight budgets, with little of the American entrepreneurial attitude looking to add value. So the aim becomes to get a funeral party in and out as quickly as possible, a slim and slick operation with slots of only twenty or thirty minutes.

So, if in the United States there is an economic pressure to make funerals as long and elaborate as possible, in the United Kingdom there is bureaucratic pressure to make them as slim and short as possible. This is where a church building scores. Unlike the American funeral parlour, its capital cost does not have to be recouped out of funerals; unlike the British crematorium, it is available for use most weekdays for as long or as short a time as the family wishes. It doesn't matter whether the funeral takes fifteen minutes or an hour and a half. Neither economic nor bureaucratic pressures distort the prime purpose of marking the human life that has passed.

We should therefore be exploring other venues for funerals. These venues should a) already have their capital costs met through other means, and b) be meaningful to the mourners. Fortunately these two conditions go together, for a building that is meaningful (home, church, local pub) will not be looking to funerals to repay capital costs.

So what are the possibilities?

The church

(temple, synagogue) is the most obvious. If people who do not go to church can get married in church, because it is more meaningful, why can't they have their funerals in church? I'm not sure who got the idea around that it's not done, especially as more people seem to want a religious funeral than want a religious wedding. Nor am I sure the present situation is what people want. The Harrogate crematorium, built in 1936, was shut for six months in 1972 for major repairs and renovation.

For these six months, they borrowed a neighbouring Method-
ist church for funeral services, and folk liked this so much that
even now a third of Harrogate cremations have the service of
committal in the nearby church.

The funeral parlour

is a very common location for the funeral in North America
and Australia. This is not always a good deal for the consumer
if the motive is simply to reap more income for the funeral
director. In small communities, however, where the funeral
director is known and trusted, and where there is no local
crematorium, the local funeral parlour could be a better
location than the ninety-minute drive to an alien crematorium.

The family home

used to be a common place for the funeral service. It still
happens in Wales, the North-East of England, Northern
Ireland, and some other parts of the United Kingdom. If your
home is not big enough to hold everybody, perhaps you could
use a friend's home? One middle-class southerner who did
this was afterwards thanked by her previously doubting
friends, who said it was 'the most wonderful celebration'.

A local community building

of importance to the deceased is a distinct possibility. If the
deceased belonged to a working men's club, sports club, or
drank regularly in the local pub, why not hold the funeral
there?

A residential home or hospice

is another possible venue. The person may have spent the
past few years in a hospital, an elderly persons' home, or a
mental hospital; or even just the last few, but life-transforming,
days in a hospice. Why not hold the funeral there? Other
residents or patients may be deeply upset at losing a friend,
yet be unable to travel to a church, crematorium or funeral

parlour. Rather than efficient nurses sweeping their loss
under the carpet, could they not say goodbye together, on the
premises?

The only such place I have discovered that is set up to do
this is the London Lighthouse, a centre for people with AIDS
that opened in 1988. Their meeting room was designed,
among other things, to accommodate funerals.

Other hospices are reluctant to hold funerals in their own
chapel, lest it become associated too strongly with death. At
St Christopher's Hospice, the nurses say commendatory
prayers around the bed immediately after the person has
died, including in this little ceremony any other patients who
wish to join in, and a table with a bunch of flowers is left for
twenty-four hours in place of the absent bed. In many homes,
hospitals and hospices, mention will be made in weekly
religious services of those who have died recently. One
progressive elderly persons' home in Lambeth does what
most families do, inviting the funeral party to return home for
liquid refreshment. This home encourages residents to go out
to funerals, and collections are taken to buy some item as a
memorial for the house or garden.

But in general, old-fashioned hospitals and old folk's
homes continue to sweep the death of a patient or resident
under the carpet, simply filling the bed as soon as possible;
and progressive institutions tend to deal with bereavement
through one-to-one conversation rather than communal
ritual, stretching only to the mini rituals I have described. It
seems it is only the gay community, facing up to AIDS, who
have reclaimed not only dying and bereavement, but the
funeral too.

Least imaginative of all is the Church of England (of which
I am myself a member). Though lay as well as ordained
people may read the Anglican funeral service, they may read
it only in an authorised place – a church, chapel, crematorium
or cemetery (and presumably aboard ship). If you wish to
hold the funeral elsewhere, you will either have to find a
Nonconformist minister or a secular celebrant, or an Anglican cleric who is not too fussy about the rules. It is most
peculiar that the Church of England is happy to perform
funerals in faceless crematoria inspired by a philosophy of
secular utilitarianism, yet may not perform the complete

funeral service in a person's own home (or pub or funeral parlour). At this point it seems that the established church is more concerned with ecclesiastical dogma than with meeting bereaved people in their need, on their terms. I really do not see why the bereaved family should not choose a better place for their last farewells than the municipal crematorium, nor why – if the family should ask her for her services – the established church should not oblige.

18

THE BURIAL GROUND

Never build massive cemeteries. Instead, allocate pieces
of land throughout the community as grave sites – corners
of parks, sections of paths, gardens, beside gateways –
where memorials to people who have died can be ritually
placed with inscriptions and mementoes which celebrate
their life. Give each grave site an edge, a path, and a quiet
corner where people can sit. By custom, this is hallowed
land.

Christopher Alexander, *et al.*, *A Pattern Language:
Towns, Buildings, Construction*, 1977

The way cemeteries are run can be a touchy issue. The *Daily
Mirror* reports: 'A mother is facing a new heartbreak over her
dead daughter. She has been ordered to remove a portrait of
her daughter from the young girl's grave. If she refuses, the
local council have threatened to chisel it off themselves . . .'
The *Coventry Evening Telegraph* laments: 'A widow has been
asked to remove a headstone from her husband's grave . . .
because of wrong-coloured lettering . . .' Similar problems
are recorded in Blackpool: 'A father is fighting for the right to
plant flowers on his son's grave . . .'

At the same time, many British (and some Australian)
graveyards are suffering from an almost total lack of public
interest. Memorials by the thousand in vast Victorian
cemeteries are unsafe because the descendants of those
commemorated are no longer interested in maintaining them.
The cemeteries are full, so there is no income coming in from
new purchasers of graves. Maintaining these old cemeteries
has to be subsidised out of cremation fees, but the public

resents being charged to maintain other people's memorials.

Yet suggest that one of these Victorian junk-yards be levelled off and made into a lawn cemetery, and out of the woodwork there immediately emerges the local historical society, whipping up public indignation over this desecration of valuable historical monuments. Or suggest that the bones be dug up and the area used again, and a peculiar British folk religion obsessed with 'disturbing the dead' is roused from sleep.

The state of hostilities occasionally flares up into an active skirmish between the public and the graveyard's administrators – religious or secular. As far as the recently bereaved are concerned, the authorities are heartless bureaucrats who are more concerned with regulations and ease of mowing than with the feelings of the bereaved. Yet these same authorities are tearing their hair out, not knowing what to do with old graves in which the public is no longer interested – unless, that is, the authorities are unwise enough to propose some change to the derelict status quo, in which case a furore is likely. The bureaucrats are plagued with headaches, the bereaved with heartache, and the historical societies with paranoia.

How did we get into this no-win situation? It does not exist in some European countries, and is not inevitable.

Shrine or dodo?

It all goes back to the individualism explored in Chapter 6. The little churchyard of my parish church, St Thomas in Widcombe, now a suburb of Bath, has been receiving bodies for burial ever since the founding of the church in the ninth century. Records at St Thomas' date from the 1580s, and in the following century about two thousand people were buried, and there is no reason to suppose that numbers were not of a similar order in previous centuries. Yet you will find tombstones only from the late 1600s to the early 1800s. You will find the same in many old English churchyards that are now within city boundaries. Rural churchyards typically contain stones up to the present and may still have room for burials, but none have stones earlier than the mid 1600s.

What happened to the millions of graves from the dark ages

to Charles II? And why virtually no burials at St Thomas' over
the last hundred and fifty years? The answer is surprisingly
simple.

Throughout the middle ages, most people were buried in
unmarked or crudely marked graves, either in the churchyard
or under the church floor. Only the very powerful or the very
holy would have a grand tomb, of the kind unfailingly
described today by church and cathedral guidebooks. The
others may have had some simple marker – initials in the
flagstone floor, or a wooden cross outside. Whenever gravediggers discovered old bones, they would put them in the
communal ossuary or bone house. In appropriate soil conditions, it takes only five or ten years for flesh to decompose, so
it was quite possible to reuse a fairly small plot of land
indefinitely, so long as there was not the kind of population
explosion experienced in the new industrial towns of the
nineteenth century.

By the sixteenth century, however, a substantial middle
class had developed. These upwardly mobile heirs to the
Renaissance liked to record in stone the achievements of the
paterfamilias, and at least the individual existence of mum
and kids. They held a very high view of their right to hold
property, and the grave too came to be seen as family
property. Enter the idea of the perpetual grave as the
inalienable right of the property owning Englishman.

This was all very delightful for a hundred years or so,
especially as the eighteenth century with its Georgian
architecture was one (as we now judge it) of widespread good
taste. Hence all the tasteful Georgian tombs.

But judgement came in the nineteenth century. First there
was the Romantic movement. The simple Renaissance
memorial turned into over-the-top sentimentality, with elaborate tombs and top-heavy memorials. As Philippe Ariès
said of this period in the more secular, but equally romantic,
France: 'When God is dead, the cult of the dead may become
the only authentic religion.' It is one thing today to have a
simple Georgian headstone or a well-constructed table tomb
gently weathering in a country churchyard, it is something
else to have a municipal cemetery stuffed with tottering
Victorian sentimentality in which the once so affected heirs
have long since lost interest.

There was also the population explosion of the nineteenth century. Decaying flesh frequently began to accompany pure white bones in the gravedigger's spoil heap; the stench under some church floors became unbearable. A more rational approach was urgently required, and John Claudius Loudon led the way with his influential book of instructions *On the Laying Out, Planting, and Managing of Cemeteries and on the Improvement of Churchyards*. The perpetual grave became the norm for all but the pauper, thus ensuring that putrid matter would never be disturbed. Vast cemeteries – first private and then municipal – were laid out, which eventually, of course, all filled up (little churchyards like St Thomas' having long since filled up).

So this explains a) the problem of the decaying Victorian cemeteries, many of which went bankrupt when they ran out of land to sell, and were taken over by local authorities who now have to maintain them at public expense; b) the use of vast tracts of valuable urban land for now unwanted cemeteries; and c) the rise of the cremation movement, with its motto: 'Leave the land for the living!'

But what about the crass bureaucratic rules that so upset some of the bereaved today? The utilitarian, rational approach to organising the Victorian cemetery is still alive today. So too is romanticism, into which it so often collides.

Mourners often want an individualised grave. In her adult education class one mother made and inscribed a pottery teddy bear which she took to the cemetery to install as the headstone for Luke, her little cot death baby. 'It's made with love, whereas granite is made for profit,' she said. Pictures of the bear, and of her regular visits to it with her two other children, must have won many hearts when shown on BBC television in 1987 (see also Plate 1).

Edward Bailey, the rector of the village church in Winterbourne, estimates that as many villagers come to tend graves, or sit by them, or even discuss everyday problems with their occupants, as come to worship inside his by no means ill-frequented parish church. Most of the time, someone is by a Winterbourne grave. Three to four hundred come in the week before Mothering Sunday, performing their own private rituals. Writing in 1982, Rev. Bailey recalls that 'the grave of a man who died in 1970 has had flowers placed on it every Sunday since; the grave of a woman who died in 1975 has been visited by her husband every day since; the grave of a teenaged boy, killed in 1981, has been visited daily by his father'. He concludes: 'The real purpose, or use, of the churchyard, today if not in the past, is to serve as a place that is set aside for the erection of private shrines.' Those who work in municipal cemeteries observe similar behaviour. Privately run Highgate Cemetery encourages it; other cemeteries obstruct it. In the United States, by contrast, having paid for 'perpetual care' relatives are absolved from having to visit to tend the grave.

Frances Clegg, a psychologist who has interviewed visitors to graves at Chanterlands Crematorium and Cemetery, Hull, stresses that visiting is far from passive. Mourners actively interact with the grave and its occupant. I recall one Jewish mourner arguing vehemently with the air for fifteen minutes before finally leaving the grave, apparently much restored in spirit. Others housekeep for their dead, lovingly continuing their care even after death by looking after the grave and its flowers.

Unlike colleagues who only see bereaved people with problems of delayed or unresolved grief, for whom grave-visiting may be pathological, Dr Clegg suspects this kind of visiting can be helpful to the bereaved. Grief can be focused at the graveside, instead of dominating the whole of life.

She also notes that visiting the grave declines dramatically after ten to fifteen years. Of the sixty graveside and columbaria visitors she interviewed, only six had been bereaved fifteen or more years. This is very much what you would expect: widows and widowers die, children move away, grandchildren lose interest – at least, the active interest of the kind Dr Clegg and Rev. Bailey describe.

Ten to fifteen years is also the time by which we can be pretty sure there are only bones left. The flesh of the deceased and the feelings of the living decay in uncanny harmony (see pp. 90–1).

Reusing graves

There is much to be said, therefore, for reusing graves, as

they do in much of Europe, once flesh and feelings have disappeared.

In the cemetery at Wommelgem, a Belgian village of some five thousand souls, I found how reuse works there from Edward Thilemans, who lives just over the road where he makes gravestones and sells flowers. You used to be able to buy a plot in perpetuity, but that changed in 1971. The citizens could see that their cemetery was getting full, so the village council determined – and now regularly reviews – the length of time for which you can rent, not buy, a grave.

Say it is ten years. Tending the grave is your responsibility. If after ten years, you or other relatives are still tending the grave, you can pay for another ten years, and so on, until interest wanes. If after any ten-year period you do not reapply, a notice is pinned to the grave, giving you a year's notice. If you still do not reapply, the grave is available to be used again. This way, money is always coming in to maintain the cemetery, and there are always relatives willing and able to maintain individual graves.

The result is typical of cemeteries in the Low Countries: small, local, beautifully kept, and a blaze of colour. Such cemeteries are the well-cared for home of the ancestors that everyone knows, not – as in Britain – a decrepit historical document recording people whose names none now recognise. (I have yet to see a derelict tombstone in the Low Countries.) If people declare an interest in a Belgian grave, they back up that interest by paying rent; nobody complains about their grave, thinking some remote authority ought to be looking after it. The only price the community pays is that it loses the visible historical record that the tombstone provides.

In this book I have been rather indebted to historians, and on occasion critical of psychologists and psychiatrists; certainly much modern psychology of grief displays an extraordinary lack of awareness of the extent to which our emotions are specific to our own era. In the matter of cemeteries, however, I think we British are obsessed with graves as historical monuments, and run roughshod over the psychological needs of the bereaved. For once, the historians should listen to the psychologists.

One historian, however, James Stevens Curl, argues for

reusable graves in his classic book on mortuary architecture, *A Celebration of Death*. He gives four reasons.

1. Maintenance is guaranteed.

2. Vandalism is virtually unknown. There is always someone around with an interest in the graveyard, automatically deterring would-be vandals; indeed, in Wommelgem I cannot imagine anyone wanting to vandalise the tomb of one of his own neighbours.

3. Reusing graves is ecological. Crematoria create ongoing problems for the neighbours, problems not only of sentiment but also of the chemical composition of chimney emissions. What could be more natural than organic matter being restored to the soil?

4. Small local cemeteries will thrive. This to my mind is the most important benefit. Since we British have not reused graves, our small local churchyards and cemeteries have filled up. So vast cemeteries on the outskirts of town were created, to be succeeded by mass-throughput crematoria. Hence the tragedy of the crematorium rose, of a life spent in search of individuality ending in the grip of well-meaning but soul-destroying municipality. Personally, I would rather have the opportunity to be buried in St Thomas' churchyard for ten years, knowing local folk have been buried there since AD 800, than have a perpetual – or even a hundred-year – grave in a vast anonymous cemetery.

In life, people struggle to find something beyond the impersonality of the mass society and the isolation of the private family. They move to villages and small towns in search of community, they join local community associations, and for a generation or more 'community' has been an 'in' word. Yet in death, we abandon community, we abandon the individual to the mass society. We come to dread crematoria and cemeteries, abandoning responsibility for them to a few unfortunate civic officials, even at a time when we are reclaiming everything else – schools, hospitals, roads, shops – as local community resources. We fight to save the local post office or school, yet let the local cemetery or churchyard fill up and shut up without so much as a bleat.

In my own local suburb of Widcombe there are nine little cemeteries dating mainly from the nineteenth century. Only one, the Catholic cemetery, is still in use for burial. Of the others, two have had bungalows built on them, two are virtually unknown and unused wildernesses, one has become a rather unused and wild part of a community centre garden, one is almost full, and one (St Thomas') is closed for ordinary burial, though it has a section where ashes can be interred. But one is a creative gem. Here, the Quakers have put the gravestones along one wall, turning it into the most delightful walled garden; the names of cremated Quakers may be inscribed on one large stone; and the garden is regularly used by local Quakers for annual picnics and the like. It is once more a communal place of green and rest, where living and dead commune, where another time, another place, another spirit offer an oasis in the city.

Unless you are Catholic, you can no longer be buried in Widcombe, even though the suburb contains derelict and once-charming little cemeteries, and even though the Quakers have shown us what can be done with them. So meanwhile, we get disposed of two miles away by the municipality; and the local community association and local churches continue to promote community in every area bar death.

But if graves were to be reused, small local cemeteries could continue. There would then be a real alternative to, on the one hand, impersonal cremation in an impersonal and distant crematorium and, on the other hand, burial in a vast and almost as distant municipal cemetery.

All change?

What I am suggesting may not yet have occurred to the good people of Widcombe, and may well seem offensive to many British people. There is a long-standing British tradition against reusing graves. Loudon in his influential book of 1843 continually inveighs against this disgusting and European habit which offends against 'Christian [= English?] decency and propriety'. When in 1875 a certain Mr Haden proposed in the letters column of *The Times* an eminently practical and ecological system for a shallow and coffinless burial and a subsequent and speedy reuse of the grave, he was howled down by a worried undertaking profession and an ill-informed medical profession.

But things have begun to change. Though privately owned cemeteries can still sell plots outright, publicly owned cemeteries cannot: since 1974 they have had to offer graves for a hundred years or less, and some now offer graves for as few as twenty-five years. Cemetery managers now understand we cannot carpet the whole of our green and pleasant land with decaying tombs that posterity is not allowed to touch. What is not clear to me, however, is what our public cemeteries intend to do after their twenty-five, fifty, seventy-five or hundred-year period. Reuse the ground for more burials? I suspect not. More likely the headstone will be removed, and a park created.

In Anglican churchyards the situation is different. There has never been a legal right of perpetual ownership of a churchyard grave, and the incumbent has considerable power to do what he wants, but it appears that since 1964 he has not been able to offer rights in a grave for more than a hundred years.

But this still strikes me as a typically British fudge, the recognisable offspring of a public lack of interest and a municipal or ecclesiastical paternalism. It still seems that the length of time the grave is to be occupied is decided by the municipality or church authority rather than, as in Belgium, the family. And without a regular income from the tenant, maintenance will continue to be a headache.

How will people react if they find out that granny's bones may be dug up in a few decades' time? To date, the evidence is heartening.

A number of Anglican vicars who are running out of space have decided to reuse some of their ground – just as their forebears did centuries ago. When reuse occurs in a small community where the vicar is known and trusted, there is not the outcry readers might expect. British people take quite happily to old bones being dug up if the alternative is their losing the right to a local place in which to be buried. In rural communities the alternative is by no means local – the nearest crematorium may be twenty-five miles away, and who wants a grave in someone else's town? I have talked with the vicar of one Yorkshire village, and another vicar in the Forest of Dean, both of whom have started reusing their churchyards with no great difficulty. If the local historical society is contacted right at the beginning of proceedings, its members can photograph and record all the tombstone inscriptions and become partners in caring for the recent dead as well as the long dead.

The problems come when the chief actors are not local. In the late 1980s there was an outcry in Bath when an old graveyard was emptied of bones by a housing association prior to building a block of flats. There was even more outcry when Westminster City Council sold off three of its old cemeteries for five pence each to private developers.

Though the law has now ended the creation of perpetual graves in all but private cemeteries, and though there are heartening examples of cemeteries being reused, I would estimate that each year still sees many more burial grounds being closed than reused.

What does 'closing' a burial ground mean? When a parish church's burial ground is full, it may legally 'close' it, meaning that the local authority now has responsibility to maintain it. This is an attractive option for a church struggling to keep the fabric of its worship building in good order, let alone looking after the crumbling graves of long-dead parishioners. It is a fair deal for a church that for centuries has had the responsibility of burying churchgoer and non-churchgoer alike.

Unfortunately, we shouldn't be closing small local burial grounds, we should be reopening them. There should be some law offering a financial incentive to churches to keep their burial grounds open, not as at present to close them. Otherwise, on present trends, we will end up with thirty-year leases at vast anonymous municipal cemeteries, while parish churchyards become fossilised (like the churches they surround) into tourist attractions, their vicars meanwhile badgering an unwilling and impecunious local council to live up to its responsibility to fix the tottering churchyard wall. Really, even we unimaginative British should be able to do better.

19

MEMORIALS

'. . . Another kind of memorial to Phoebe is our pig collection.' This is a mother writing about her baby who died four months before, aged thirty minutes. She continues:

> During the pregnancy we adopted the highly unoriginal term 'The Little Pig' to describe the baby, on the basis that a foetus is not unlike a piglet. Because of this, we were given lots of piggy things – from ornaments to pencil holders – and we now have quite a collection.
>
> I have a number of sweet little pig badges/brooches and people often comment on them when I wear one. If it's someone who knows all about Phoebe, I explain why I'm wearing it – I don't lumber strangers with the story – which, of course, is a way of talking about her and remembering her. I find people are quite relieved that I obviously want to be reminded; so often, people are terrified of mentioning someone who has died in case it upsets the relatives, and this helps our family and friends to know that we want to be reminded and don't want them to forget either.

People are much more inventive about creating memorials than you might think from the rows of rose bushes at the crematorium or the thousands of identical niches in the columbarium.

Many memorials that are personally meaningful arise naturally out of inheritances. When my grandfather died, I was able to choose one item to remember him by. I will surely never forget who the elegant but temperamental turn-of-the-century clock on my mantelpiece came from, nor the effort it took to clean it of the oil that motor mechanic grandad had coated it in to stop it rusting, and that had succeeded in well and truly gumming up the works!

Nor will I forget the origin of the little coffee table in my living-room, coming as it did from a neighbour whom I and other neighbours helped look after as she was dying of cancer.

Since my father's death, I have worn many of his clothes – which fit perfectly. When someone comments on the jacket I am wearing and how it suits me, it feels good to reply, 'Yes, it was my father's!' Particularly fun are the blue coolie trousers I sometimes use for dirty jobs – he bought them in Shanghai in 1912 while in the merchant navy.

Without our houses or our bodies becoming museums of memorials, these artefacts help us remember the ancestors. Without mummifying the ancestors, we can make them a natural part of everyday life.

Gifts

Some memorials are given by the survivor to others, specifically as memorials. In Dr Frances Clegg's research (see p. 198), recently bereaved churchgoers had donated imaginative and practical items as memorials to their late husbands: a telescope to a local Wildlife Trust; a new bugle for the local Boys' Brigade; a stained-glass window for the church; starting a fund to renew the church's electrical wiring. These women considered their memorials helpful, rather like my dad's sports jacket, as a reminder and focus.

One woman bought a minibus for the church. Dr Clegg speculates 'whether such a mobile memorial might prove to be troublesome in that it may be encountered unexpectedly, and perhaps at unwelcome times and places. All the other unusual memorials were static ones.' Grief must proceed at the mourner's own pace, and that means her having some control over when and how to be reminded of her loss.

These churchgoers were more imaginative in the memorials they chose than were others questioned by Dr Clegg. I suspect that you need to be part of a living community for there to be somewhere permanent to house a memorial. A picture for the old folk's home, a bed for the hospice, a new sign for your local pub, new netting for the soccer club's goal nets,

an endowment for a school, a seat for the village green, are
all possibilities for those who were associated with such
groups.

Some memorials, like the Belgian graves in the previous
chapter and the minibus in this, are appreciated for only a few
years, and this is appropriate if the period matches the period
of grief. Too many stained-glass windows for forgotten
ancestors, like too many forgotten graves, can become a
headache to future generations.

If a common way of instituting a memorial is for the
deceased or the family to give something to some individual
or group, another possibility is for others to give something
to the bereaved. The Rev. Wesley Carr describes a touching
example:

> A man comes to the cathedral dressed in motor-cycling
> gear. From his leathers he produces a delicate gold cross,
> not a cheap one, and asks me to bless it. It is to be given to a
> girl – not his girlfriend – as a memento of her boyfriend,
> who was killed in a crash. When we talk – inevitably briefly
> – many issues arise: genuine affection for the dead friend,
> whom he can now only contact through the man's closest
> friend, the girl; a concern for the girl, lest she should feel
> that no one cares; some vague feeling in himself of the need
> to express the worth of his own life; and against all these the
> pervasive background of the nearness of death, even of a
> young man in his twenties.

In the grounds of another of England's cathedrals, Wells,
was a neglected corner containing a small medieval ruin
which the Dean, who looks after the cathedral and grounds,
was considering what to do with. Meanwhile, his wife, who
loved gardens and flowers, was dying of cancer, and a friend
broached the idea of a memorial. After Mary died, her many
friends raised a subscription to create and maintain, in this
cathedral thronged with tourists, a quiet garden of peace
around the evocative ruin.

Too often we wait like vultures to hear what we are to
receive from the will. Perhaps we might think, too, of what we
could give to the dying, and to the bereaved – or what we
could give, with the dying, to the bereaved.

But most memorials will remain private, known to only a

few. When staying in Bangkok, my Thai host took me to visit her sister, and in the course of the visit we went upstairs to the special room containing the family Buddhist shrine with its usual offerings. In the corner of the room was another smaller shrine with a baby doll in place of the Buddha, and all around the various things a baby needs: baby powder, toilet paper, toys. This was the shrine to the woman's baby, premature and dead these four years; as the child grew older, so its mother presented it with new things it would need. I hunted in my bag for something for a four year old.

All this we did for the dead child. But the child could do much for its mother. As it died so young, she believed it died in a state of some perfection and therefore took on some of the character of the Buddha. She would pray to the child for help and assistance, and I was told I could pray to it for safety on my travels. With us was her next son, handicapped and now two, and together they prayed, her hands folding his in devotion.

Some Western psychologists might diagnose all this as mummification, a refusal to accept the baby's death. I am not so sure. It could also be a healthy way in which the ancestors are recognised, dead or alive. The living child will grow up seeing its older brother as a natural member of the family – unlike myself, whose step-brother died when I was a toddler and who was hardly ever mentioned by the family.

The mother's sister, my hostess, had trained in the United States as a psychologist, and indeed thought the veneration a bit excessive, but was very happy to go along with it. To have one baby die, and then give birth to a handicapped child, is traumatic even for a Buddhist, and this shrine helps the mother deal with this very personal problem of suffering. Buddhism, of course, considers suffering to be the basic human condition; far from running away from it, a whole philosophy is built on its reality.

Few of us will go to such lengths, but many of us make mini shrines: not just the grave, if there is one, but also the photograph on the mantelpiece, or the collage of family photos framed on the wall. Where young children are grieving the loss of a brother or sister, a small display of some of the dead child's toys and possessions could form a very helpful focus.

Memorials in stone

Recently I visited the annual exhibition of the (UK) National Association of Monumental Masons. I was struck by the difference between the rows and rows of traditional neo-Gothic headstones on display by the masons, and the display in one corner by sculpture students at the local art school. Their work was so avant-garde I had difficulty knowing how to respond.

This is a symptom of the problem of art in the United Kingdom. On the one hand there is a *very* conservative general public who buy Constable and Rowland Hilder prints from Woolworths and order neo-Gothic headstones for their loved ones, and on the other hand a tiny art-buying public who buy avant-garde paintings and probably get cremated. This is very different from continental Europe and Australia, where there is a large market both for comprehensible but thoroughly modern works of art and for comprehensible but thoroughly modern gravestones.

It is also very different from Victorian Britain, where every latest fashion would be incorporated into memorials. If ancient Egypt was the flavour of the decade, then the middle classes would order Egyptian tombs; if Rome was the flavour, they would order a niche in a catacomb – just take a tour around Highgate Cemetery to see the Victorian relish of fashion. Somehow, between then and now, this playful, adventurous commissioning of architectural style for the dead has decayed into the most unthinking conservatism.

Every year, Britain's Memorial Advisory Bureau[1] sponsors the Phoenix Awards for innovative memorial and cemetery design. When it comes to the cemetery awards, the verdict of MAB's Sam Weller is that the landscape architects to whom cemetery managers turn for ways of making cemeteries more attractive 'don't even understand the questions'. When it comes to stone memorials, for both graves and cremated remains (Plates 8-10), some of the competition entries are excellent, but all too often are never actually put into production. Yet such designs are the common currency of European cemeteries and columbaria.

[1] 139 Kensington High Street, London W8 6SX (Tel. 071-937 0052).

Part of the problem in the United Kingdom is the way gravestones are manufactured. The local monumental mason from whom you will order your gravestone will get his stone from one or two of the couple of dozen wholesale suppliers. They offer him a range of 'blanks' – cut headstones of maybe a dozen or so shapes, in maybe four different materials (e.g., grey granite, black granite, sandstone, York stone). This sounds like a reasonable range of choice ($4 \times 12 = 48$ possibilities), until you realise that the authorities locally (civil or ecclesiastical) often prefer just one type of stone – in order that a yellow limestone church will not be surrounded by pink sandstone or black granite gravestones. Moreover, only a few of the dozen designs may be in the popular price range, with the result that often only three or four basic types of headstone predominate in a cemetery. The locally cut lettering may be much more varied, but the overall impression comes from the lack of variety in material and shape.

Growing

If some memorials are in stone, and some are living memorials, others are growing memorials. Many people like to plant a tree or bush, especially one that flowers or produces fruit yearly – helping mourners review how things are now that their husband or son is one more year gone. The deep but simple symbolism of this kind of memorial is described by Steven Levine in his book *Who Dies*:

> Often, in the back country of Montana, a hole will be dug and the body, in a plain pine coffin or perhaps just wrapped in a tie-dyed cloth, will be lowered into the ground. Instead of a tomb stone, a fruit tree is planted over the body. The roots nourished by the return of that body into the earth from which it was sustained. And in years to follow, eating the fruit from that tree will be like partaking in that loved one. It touches on the ritual of the Eucharist.

Talking (and walking!)

Not all memorials are places or things. Perhaps the main way we remember, apart from our private memories, is by talking with others: 'Let my name be ever the household word it always was.'

Talking can be helpfully ritualised, not just at and around the funeral, but later. Only this week I read in the local paper:

A weekend street party held in memory of the 20-year-old who drowned last month while returning home from a city nightclub, attracted hundreds of people from all over Bath. In his memory, one of his friends arranged the street party outside their council flat. A collection at the party also raised £75 for the family. Most of the residents supported the party with two supplying the disco with electricity from extension cables through their windows.

A woman in her twenties who died of cancer was remembered six months later through a sponsored walk to raise money for cancer research. Not only did this give her friends an opportunity to meet again and talk, it was also a much more personal way of raising money than the usual 'No flowers. Donations to . . .' notice in the local paper. With lunch at a pub *en route*, where they were joined by friends unable to take part in the walk, it was simple to organise.

The deputy director of the research institute I used to work for was commemorated by a day seminar, enabling ex-staff from around the country not only to meet and debate but also to symbolise their continuing the work Gordon had started. It was a remarkably enjoyable day, commemorating a life rather than mourning a loss.

The most common form of talking memorial is surely the memorial service or thanksgiving service. This can be particularly useful following the death of someone whose friends and acquaintances are not only many and varied, but also scattered around the country or even around the world. A time of thanksgiving some months after the death enables people to get together who may have taken some time to hear about the death, and it comes at a time when the initial shock is past and thanksgiving can be the keynote.

And as I have already mentioned, there are those religious groups that meet yearly to eat and talk about the departed, from the Jews with their meal around the family candle, to the Chinese thronging the hillsides of Hong Kong once a year to visit the family grave (Chapter 14).

Communal memorials

However much we may try to privatise death, death on occasion forces us together. When over three hundred Dutch holidaymakers died together in the KLM plane crash at Tenerife, some were buried in already established family plots. But most of the identified bodies, or their cremated remains, were buried together in a specially created garden in Amsterdam, as though these people, strangers to each other in life, shared in death something deeper even than family ties. At the centre of the garden is one vast circular table of granite, while on the ground around it are the 130-plus names of those whose charred bodies could not be identified (Plate 12).

The Jewish Funeral Directors of America have established a programme of planting trees in the Negev Desert, as a memorial to American Jews. One group of trees is for the thirty-five students from the foreign studies program of Syracuse University, and the husband and wife from the Syracuse suburb of Clay, who, returning home for Christmas, perished in the crash of PanAmerican flight 103 at Lockerbie. A few weeks later, everything in the city shut down as fifteen thousand people attended the memorial service for the students at the University's Carrier Dome stadium.

War memorials

The Cenotaph, London's permanent memorial to the un-known warrior, was not planned by some high-up committee, but forced on the authorities by spontaneous public senti-ment. Originally, the architect Sir Edwin Lutyens was asked to design a temporary wood and plaster shrine. When unveiled in July 1919, pictures of the saluting generals appeared in newspapers throughout the land, and in the days that followed wreath after wreath appeared at the base of the plaster shrine. No such response had been anticipated. Only eleven days later the Cabinet agreed to replace it with an identical and permanent structure.

I grew up in a London suburb created around the Metropol-itan railway station and having no natural focus like a village green or old parish church. With the suburb only a couple of

decades old, the memorial to those who died in the First
World War became the focal point. Likewise in town after
town in Australia, where often more than a quarter of those
who went to fight the mother country's war did not return, it is
the war memorial that has become the town's focal point. In
this federal nation where loyalty to the local state or city is
intense, the one building that symbolises the entire nation of
Australia is the War Memorial in Canberra.

But war memorials need not be grand. I recall driving west
out of one old Australian gold-mining town; for mile after
mile the road was an avenue of trees, all the same height,
all planted at the same time. I did not understand why the
avenue was so long until we stopped the car, and I could see
that each tree had a name attached. There must have been
several thousand in all. For the remaining few minutes as we
completed the tree-lined section, a vacation to the bush
turned into a pilgrimage.

I also recall walking across the Mall, that lovely two miles
of grass down the middle of Washington DC, when a middle-
aged man asked me the way to the Vietnam memorial. He
was in town on business, but twenty years ago in South East
Asia he had lost a buddy.

Later I arrived at the memorial myself, designed by Yale
student Maya Ying Lin and dedicated in 1982. Unlike so
many war memorials that rise in triumph high above the
ground, the Vietnam memorial is sunk into the ground. As
you walk down below the grass of the mall, you pass the
names of the 57,692 Americans who died, each carved into a
low 492-foot long wall of black marble, while in the polished
stone you see the pale reflections of mourners. At places at
the foot of the wall, in varying states of health, are potted
plants. One or two people lean over the top, pressing crayon
on paper to get a tracing of the name they have been looking
for.

Unlike the Canberra memorial, where each name is listed
in alphabetical order and by battalion, at Washington the
names are simply in chronological order of death. There is no
regimental pride here, just 57,692 sets of individual pain.
Seekers after a name are told which section theirs is in, and
then they have to seek among the dead to find their man. My
path again crossed that of the middle-aged businessman. I

too, a foreign tourist, had come to feel the universal sorrow of war.

Tourists by the million become pilgrims in such places. It happens in the concentration camp at Dachau; in Amsterdam's Anne Frank house (Plate 11); at Jerusalem's Yad Vashem memorial to the Holocaust. In such places, the chattering children and the clicking cameras fall silent.

PART FIVE

ISSUES

Part Five looks at some current issues such as do-it-yourself funerals, secular funerals and funerals for babies, and at developments in the funeral industry.

20

SECULAR FUNERALS
OR LIFE-CENTRED FUNERALS?

Ladies and Gentlemen,
We have come here today, as an expression of our regard
for the life of a beloved human being . . .
Funeral ceremony, Adelaide, 1987

It was much less depressing. Instead of all this stuff about
going off to heaven, it centred on our son-in-law's personality. Instead of praying for his soul, we celebrated his life.
The Independent, 25 September 1989

People are beginning to realise, by word of mouth mainly,
that they have a choice. They really can have the kind of
service they want.
Maeve Denby, British Humanist Association, 1989

Australia: The life-centred funeral

Brian McInerny lives in Melbourne and is now in his late
fifties. He worked for thirty years as a journalist, but was
retired on health grounds ten years ago. Since then, he has
conducted two thousand funerals. He has become a funeral
celebrant.

Until the mid 1970s almost all Australian funerals were
conducted by clergy, but now in Melbourne one in eight are
conducted by life-centred celebrants, and the proportion is
increasing in other Australian cities too. Unlike their counterparts in Britain, the life-centred option is routinely offered by
Australian funeral directors, and not just humanists and
secularists opt for it. How did this change come about, and
what does it signify?

217

In the early 1970s, after fierce opposition from the church, the office of Marriage Celebrant was instituted, and the kind of wedding these marriage celebrants offered quickly became popular. Within a few years some marriage celebrants found themselves being asked to perform a funeral for someone they had recently married. They soon found themselves inundated with requests to do funerals, and to their surprise they found this work extraordinarily satisfying. They conduct what has come to be called the life-centred funeral.

These funerals are not anti-religious. Brian, for example, was raised a Catholic, but has since followed his own inner light and now describes himself as a gnostic Christian. The funerals he and other Australian funeral celebrants conduct focus neither on God, nor on secular philosophy, but on the life, character and relationships of the one who has died.

When the family approach the funeral director, they are routinely asked if they want a clergyman or a funeral celebrant. If they opt for a funeral celebrant, the various celebrants available are discussed, and the family choose one. A day or two later, the celebrant visits the family.

I joined Brian the day he visited Pete and Jenny. Pete's dad had died. We sat around the kitchen table, and Brian explained he wanted to give a clear picture of Pete's dad at the funeral, and that picture could come only from them: 'We've only got one shot at it, and we've got to get it right.' Stories, a few tears and a few more smiles flowed easily for an hour or so. Their two little children sat and drew quietly.

This talking together is part of the ritual: it encourages the sharing of feelings and memories that should be going on within the family anyway, but often isn't. The children's drawings became part of the conversation as it became clear that their drawings pictured their own feelings about their grandad.

Brian then found a quiet corner of the house, and wrote what was to be the centrepiece of the funeral – a thousand-word, ten-minute eulogy capturing Pete's dad and his life. He returned to the kitchen to read the eulogy to Pete and Jenny for them to edit, stressing that it was *their* eulogy, and he was simply their servant. The aim was to create a shared picture of Pete's dad, to include all his significant relationships and all those at the funeral who cherished his company the most.

They then discussed the possibility of poems, readings, songs, prayers or other items for the funeral, and whether anyone in addition to Brian was to participate in reading any of this material.

A couple of days later the funeral was held in the local funeral parlour. It took about fifteen minutes, with just a short introduction before and after the eulogy.

Brian described conducting funerals to me as 'The best work I've ever done. I felt that with my first funeral, and the feeling's never left me.' Rick, another celebrant, described how, almost without fail, someone would come up to him afterwards with the uncanny words, 'You know, you brought him to life. Thank you.' Rick particularly values the approval of skinhead types who come up to him afterwards, stick up their thumb, and simply say: 'Top job, mate!'

Both celebrants stressed to me that they are not bereavement counsellors, but specialists in ritual. Both are exceptionally well qualified for this. As a former journalist Brian has had thirty years' experience of going out to get a story, getting to the human heart of it, including all the significant people in his story, and writing it up for three o'clock that afternoon. Rick has been Mayor of his local town and a JP, so – even in this land of informality – he understands the value of formal ritual. He used to work in the garment trade and has made his own celebrant's robe, which he insists on wearing at each and every funeral. It proclaims that this is a special occasion.

Self-fulfilment and death

The life-centred funeral is a secular version of the Protestant funeral. Protestants have generally perceived the purpose of the funeral as threefold: warning against damnation, proclaiming the Christian hope, and thanking God for the life of the deceased. Warnings against damnation more or less ceased around the turn of this century, and nowadays secularisation has removed God and the Christian hope too, so what we are left with in the life-centred funeral is giving thanks (to one another rather than to God) for the life of the individual.

If the life-centred funeral in part secularises the Protestant funeral, it also in part reacts against it. Each death is both unique and a universal human experience, and a good funeral reflects this. Religious liturgy is good at expressing universal truths about death, but does not always express the unique-ness of this particular death. The 1662 Prayer Book burial service, anxious to avoid Catholic concern with the departed soul, doesn't require the name of the deceased to be mentioned. In the United Kingdom today, religious funerals for non-churchgoers in crematoria will, one hopes, mention the deceased's name, but all too often they lack the personal touch.

It is largely because of dissatisfaction with such impersonal funerals that many Australians are opting for the personal touch provided by the life-centred celebrant.

There is, however, more to the life-centred funeral. It expresses what might be termed a secular religion of self-fulfilment – the notion that a full human life is one in which the person's full potential is attained. The funeral's job is to state what that uniquely fulfilled potential was: the last thing we can do for her, or him, is to make a final statement of who she, or he, was. Without a statement of who the person was, his or her project of self-actualisation is incomplete.

In Chapter 8 we identified a fundamental dilemma in the modern funeral. In virtually all traditional societies the purpose of funeral ritual is to help the departed on their journey into the next life, which involves the mourners in various ritual acts, which in turn may help them through their grief. But with Protestantism, and even more with secular-ism, there seems to be nothing we can do for the departed. What then is the funeral's job?

In modern post-Protestant countries the purpose of the funeral has become what had previously been hidden: helping the bereaved. How, though, can ritual be developed for the sake of the bereaved rather than for the departed? I do not believe it can. It would not be ritual, but a mass self-help therapy session.

Until I visited Australia I could not see how non-religious funerals could do anything for the departed. But with a secular religion of self-fulfilment there *is* something we can do for the departed: we can round off their process of self-actualisation by stating what that actualisation entailed. In other words, we can pay them our respects. As I see it, this is the major strength of the Australian life-centred funeral: although celebrants may tell visiting sociologists that they are helping the bereaved, the bereaved themselves see it as doing one last thing for the departed.

This life-centred funeral involves a philosophy similar to that of hospices like St Christopher's. Its founder, Dame Cicely Saunders, enjoys saying of a patient that 'he was himself', that to the end he displayed that fondness for whisky, that sense of humour, which made him himself. The St Christopher's patient who comes in as an agnostic, making wry comments about God to the end, is treasured by this hospice's Christian staff as much as the one who in the last days begins to see something of God.

One of the tragedies of some strokes, unlike cancer, is that overnight they can totally change a person's personality; he is no longer himself. This is surely why the anonymous or hypocritical funeral is so ghastly – like a stroke, it distorts and destroys the person we knew and loved.

For Cicely Saunders, the good death is one where the patient remains him or herself to the end. The good death – and the good life-centred funeral – validates the person's individuality. This is very different from the good death believed in by Christians a hundred and fifty years ago, in which, far from displaying individuality, you displayed piety and conformity to the dictates of religion. For better or for worse, even among Christians individual integrity has replaced piety.

Britain: The ideological secular funeral

Many of the lives lived in some Melbourne suburbs are completed by a life-centred funeral. There is no equivalent on regular offer in the United Kingdom; instead, a tiny minority of funerals are led by an avowedly secular celebrant on behalf of committed humanists and secularists.

The aim of the Australian life-centred funeral is to capture the uniqueness of this one individual, in terms of the values of that individual. Unlike religious funerals, the celebrant does not stipulate the dogma or ideology that will govern the ceremony, other than the implicit dogma of individual self-fulfilment. The secular funeral as known in Britain, however, has traditionally aimed to interpret a life through an explicitly secular philosophy. The aim is not only to mark the passing of a life, but also to affirm an atheist, agnostic or humanist philosophy at this particular moment when everything is in danger of collapsing. Interpreting death through this philosophy reassures secular believers that their philosophy can cope with everything, even death. This is, of course, precisely what the religious funeral does for the religious believer.

If in Australia the main aim in opting for a funeral celebrant is to avoid impersonality, in Britain the aim in contacting a secular celebrant has until recently been to avoid hypocrisy. As with a priest, you know what kind of line will be peddled; and as with a priest, the extent to which the funeral is personalised varies enormously. Some have complained that a secular celebrant who has come from fifty miles away has been as impersonal and ill-informed as any rota priest.

Things may be about to change, however. In the West Midlands and in Central Scotland several funeral directors are now offering information about secular funerals to their customers, and the late 1980s have seen in quality dailies such as *The Independent* a minor flurry of articles by satisfied customers recommending secular and do-it-yourself funerals.[1] Jane Wynne Willson, a funeral celebrant in the West Midlands, has recently written an excellent guide to non-religious funerals, called *Funerals Without God*, published by the British Humanist Association. Her book expresses something like the Australian life-centred approach, in which 'our ceremonies are by their very nature personal celebrations of an individual's life'.

Barbara Smoker, a likeable, jolly woman very different from the stereotype of the intellectual humanist, takes great care to personalise the funerals she conducts. Since she covers a wide area, she often has to talk with the family over the

---

[1] Secular funerals may be arranged in the United Kingdom through the British Humanist Association, 13 Prince of Wales Terrace, London W8 (Tel. 071-937 2341), and the National Secular Society, 702 Holloway Road, London N19 (Tel. 071-272 1266).

phone, but still tries to talk with at least two family members and one colleague so she can get a rounded picture of the person and guard against the prejudiced or idealised view that next of kin can sometimes have. Like Australian celebrants, she keeps going until she feels she knows the person, and begins herself to feel the loss of this valued human being.

But for these celebrants there is a bottom line: if someone asks her to include a prayer or hymn, she will stick to her secular principles. As Jane Wynne Willson writes:

> You could make it clear that, while you yourself cannot include something specifically religious, if someone wishes to contribute something on a personal basis, then you would be prepared to accept that, so long as no general act of worship resulted. Or you might prefer to dissuade them.

Likewise, Barbara Smoker could not do what Brian McInerny often does – co-operate with the local priest in co-leading funerals for nominal Catholics. As one who has firmly rejected her Catholic upbringing and is now President of the National Secular Society, the bottom line must be the integrity of her own, as well as the deceased's beliefs.

So the recent modest expansion in non-religious funerals in the United Kingdom still leaves out of the reckoning the kind of person catered for by the Australian secular funeral: someone who wants a personal, life-centred funeral and is not particularly religious, but who may well want the Lord's Prayer or 'The Lord is my Shepherd' thrown in for good measure. In Britain at present, such folk are all too often stuck with the choice between a possibly impersonal religious funeral and a personal but strictly non-religious one – that's if they are aware of the secular option; otherwise they have no option but the religious one.

Neither priest nor secular celebrant in Britain seems to know what to do with those by no means few people who combine practical secularism with a small dose of folk religion. Here, surely, is a market waiting to be tapped by celebrants whose respect for the life they are publicly celebrating is not limited by the belief or unbelief of the celebrant.

Secular funerals, Soviet style

In the USSR since the 1950s there have been official attempts to replace the traditional religious funeral with a socialist funeral. Like the church funeral, the socialist funeral proclaims 'This is what we believe . . .'; at a time when for the bereaved everything seems to be falling apart, the funeral holds things together by reaffirming the social and political order. According to Sovietologist Christel Lane, the aim is to help integrate people into communist ideology. The state simply takes over from the church: 'The Citizen of the Russian Soviet Federative Socialist Republic (full name) has concluded his (her) life's journey. The Motherland takes leave of her son (daughter). May a good memory of him (her) eternally be preserved in our hearts.'

One can but admire the openness with which socialist funerals approach death. Such funerals are not hidden and private. Celebrants try to make the family's loss a responsibility for the whole community; friends and colleagues are actively involved in preparing and performing the funeral. Once buried, the dead are not forgotten, but are remembered in annual remembrance ceremonies; the living are linked to the dead as cemeteries are changed from places of gloom-laden neglect into 'Parks of Good Memories'.

However, socialist funerals have been a lot less popular with Soviet people than secular weddings (now almost universal) and secular ceremonies marking the birth of a child. Even by the late 1970s, before *glasnost*, socialist funerals were criticised officially – for impersonality and uniformity, for being overladen with speeches, and for lack of symbolism. They seem to have combined the worst aspects of the traditional religious funeral (impersonality and lack of individuality) with the problems inherent in any secular funeral (lack of time-worn symbols and language, resulting sometimes in wordy and abstract speechifying).

Socialist funerals have become most common in areas such as Latvia and Estonia where the traditional religion is Lutheranism rather than the more resilient Russian Orthodoxy or Islam.

Holland: The absent celebrant

The Netherlands is another country where non-religious funerals are common.

There has long been a tradition within some Dutch Protestant funerals of people being invited to say a few words about the deceased, rather like Quaker funerals in the United Kingdom. When the religious content of the funeral is removed, what remains are the speeches made by those present. There is no equivalent of the Australian funeral celebrant, so if nobody feels moved or confident enough to speak, then nobody says anything.

Without a celebrant to orchestrate events or to speak the feelings of those who do not feel able to speak, and without a priest to speak of more universal truths, all one is left with are private feelings and private memories. This is the ultimate private funeral. Unlike a Christian service, the death is not related to all those others who have died, nor are memories shared. Doubtless they are shared afterwards over coffee and cake, but during the funeral itself there is just private grief (see pp. 156–7 for an account of one such Dutch funeral).

The Australian system understands something that is lacking in the Dutch. At a time of grief, even if people do not want a priest, they do need someone to orchestrate proceedings, to act as a competent master or mistress of ceremonies who can enable those present to regress safely into their emotions and safely out again.

National differences

Although Australia is heavily influenced by British ways, and though the Netherlands and the United Kingdom are European and historically Protestant, secularisation has taken different paths in these three countries. This helps explain the different form and development of secular funerals in these countries.

Although more individuals attend church in Australia than in Britain, Australia is a more secular place. Popular folk culture is anti-authority, with national myth recalling how early convict settlers were abused by the governors, guards and chaplains who were white Australia's first rulers. Today, politicians, police and clergy win no automatic respect, and each one has to prove him or herself. Australians are therefore less willing than the British to put up with impersonal, hypocritical clergy-led funerals, and more willing to experiment. Clergy have learned to recognise the strengths of secular celebrants, and sometimes to work with them; for example, nominal Catholics may have a secular celebrant give a eulogy and a priest perform the committal.

In the Netherlands there is religious pluralism. The respective jobs of church and state are clearly defined and separated, so if you have a church wedding you must still go to the town hall for the state registry of the marriage; the priest cannot do the job of wedding registrar, as in the United Kingdom. Religious groups, including humanists, are free to work out their faith in their own way, through their own schools, clubs, trade unions, radio stations, and so on. In a climate of religious tolerance where there is no expectation that clerics should do the state's work for it, secular funerals are a natural development.

In England, though people are often distressed by impersonal funerals, there is a long tradition that clergy are the natural people to officiate at funerals. This has to do with the legacy of Henry VIII, of four hundred years of the church performing various jobs on behalf of the state. Also, the ancient language of 1662 imparts a sense of occasion to a funeral; even if the congregation is too distressed to hear the actual words, traditional ritual means much at a time of loss and change.

At the same time, Britain has a small élite of intellectual humanists who have developed explicitly secular funerals. Down under, they are more concerned about having lost a mate than with philosophy and Bertrand Russell.

Life-centred funerals: Weaknesses

The strengths of the life-centred funeral are clear, and substantial. Such funerals are more personal, enabling the bereaved to focus their grief on a real person. All the life-centred celebrants I have talked with have said that they have wept with their clients; few clergy have said this to me. In completing the person's life story the life-centred funeral provides (unlike the Protestant funeral) something for the bereaved to do *for* the deceased. And it can accurately and without hypocrisy express the beliefs and values of the person who has died.

The weaknesses are less obvious, but doggedly intractable. The most obvious is language. Compare the opening words of one traditional religious funeral service, full of poetic resonance, with those of one Australian life-centred funeral service, full of stodgy abstract prose:

> I am the resurrection and the life, saith the Lord: he that believeth in me, though he were dead, yet shall he live: and whosoever liveth and believeth in me shall never die.

> We brought nothing into this world, and it is certain we can carry nothing out. The Lord gave, and the Lord hath taken away; blessed be the Name of the Lord.
>
> (1662 Book of Common Prayer)

> Throughout the history and cultural heritage of every single recorded society, there lies the ever-persistent belief in the continuation of a consciousness, and an existence, in another reality, after death.

> This belief, shared by those untold millions of people, of every thinkable philosophy or religious belief, persists to this day, and it is shared by some of the world's greatest intellects. The durability and strength of this belief, power to influence the affairs of men, and its ability to give a meaning and purpose to our existence, should be a consolation to us all . . .
>
> (Funeral ceremony, Adelaide 1987)

If you want the spoken word to communicate, fill it with personal pronouns. The 1662 Prayer Book introduction is full of them: I, he, me, he, he, me, we, we; but we have to wait until the last line of the Adelaide quote before we come to a personal pronoun. If you want the spoken word not to communicate, stuff it full of abstract nouns. The Adelaide service has them in abundance: history, heritage, society, continuation, consciousness, existence, reality, death, belief, philosophy, belief, durability, strength, belief, affairs, ability, meaning, purpose, existence, consolation; the 1662 Prayer Book extract has but two: resurrection, and life.

When people attend a funeral they are often in great pain and are unable to take in every word, or even one word. All that may register is the ring of language which *sounds* significant; there is comfort in time-worn phrases remembered from the funerals of forebears immemorial. The trouble with most of the life-centred funerals I have been to is that the bit before and after the eulogy is too prosaic to meet people who are in grief – in stark contrast to the eulogy, which is easily heard and meets mourners precisely where they are. The Adelaide example's intellectual dissertation on the meaning of death simply will not be heard by nine out of ten of those present.

It is not just language. The problem goes deeper, and is well described by Australian authors Des Tobin and Graeme Griffin:

> It has proved extraordinarily difficult in practice to frame rites which say something worth saying and which are not just imitations of church liturgies. The mystery of death calls for a response at depth. Secular liturgies have little to fall back upon for that depth when the transcendental is excluded by definition. Unfortunately it is just as easy in a non-religious funeral as in a religious one to substitute sentimentality for meaning, and triteness for truth.

This is a valid criticism of the Australian life-centred funeral, which is excellent at capturing the uniqueness of *this* death, but not good at pondering the universal questions raised. Its spokesman could have been André Malraux: 'There is . . . no death . . . There is only . . . *me* . . . *me* . . . *who is going to die*.'

Funerals organised by the National Secular Society or the British Humanist Association, however, *do* address the universal question of death. They draw on a philosophy that is capable of considering the perplexity of death – not just this death, but death as a universal human experience. The sprinkling of quotes from Bernard Shaw, Bertrand Russell or Boris Pasternak is not superficial, for such authors have wrestled as hard as any Job or any gospel writer with the mysteries of life and death. But they may mean even less to the ordinary person off the street.

The eulogy that without a word of abstract philosophy truly goes to the heart of a person's life can be very challenging. In revealing what that person lived and perhaps died for, the eulogy challenges me to ask what the purpose of my own life is. It needs a skilful (and sometimes a brave) celebrant to do this.

Another problem is caused by the modern religion of happiness. Many of us believe in happiness as a human goal. Unfortunately, happiness and death are incompatible. The temptation facing the eulogy writer is to avoid the bad times: he or she is effectively censored by the 'religions' of happiness and of family life, and ends up affirming the cosy 'truths' of these false religions.

Finally, there is an insuperable problem with guilt, with the unfinished business between living and dead, for there is no God to forgive either ourselves or the deceased. Psychiatrists tell us that guilt is one of the most common aspects of bereavement, yet in most life-centred funerals guilt and forgiveness are ignored. The ways in which the deceased may have hurt us are assiduously avoided. It is dangerous to raise the reality of sin if there is no way it can be dealt with, in which case guilt may have to wait for resolution later in the privacy of the therapist's consulting room. (The potential of the funeral to become a vehicle for forgiveness is explored in Chapter 22.)

The church's response

In some parts of Australia religious and life-centred funerals compete harmoniously. Life-centred celebrants are challenged by the church's ability to articulate both despair and hope, to express through symbol and song the dilemmas death presents to the human being. In turn, clergy are challenged by the life-centred funeral's ability to capture the essence of this particular life, this particular death. Each is kept up to the mark by the other.

Some British clergy claim that a residual folk religion is what stops large numbers of British people demanding life-centred funerals, but I suspect that the main barrier is that there is no one ready to hand to conduct such funerals.

Secular celebrants are few and far between, and in any case
secular dogma rather than individuality is their bottom line.
But were non-dogmatic life-centred funerals to become more
easily available, I predict a demand would quickly material-
ise. The British, like the Australians, are not at heart
ideologues.

Should such a move gather momentum, I believe the
church would be foolish to resist it. Many clergy might at first
feel threatened, especially if the celebrants did their job well,
but the long-term reaction – especially in busy parishes –
could well be relief. The church should accept its inability to
provide good funerals for the entire population. As in
Australia, clergy should seek to co-operate with secular
celebrants, learn from them, and rejoice that those who ask
them to conduct funerals will in future do so because they
want the Christian faith to be expressed, not because they
have no other option.

As one who believes that the local parish church is there to
serve the local community, not to be a private club for
believers, I hope and pray that the role of the church in
helping local people at a time of grief will not only continue,
but be done better. But I do not see how this aim is served by
the vicar having a virtual monopoly on funerals – this just
leads to vicars becoming either complacent or burned-out, or
both.

Nor is there any reason why life-centred funerals should
not be conducted by Christians. Though the dogmatic secular
funeral and the religious funeral are not compatible, the
life-centred funeral and religious faith are, just as the modern
concept of self-fulfilment and Christian faith go hand in hand
at St Christopher's Hospice.

Many clergy are now individualising their funerals, within a
broadly Christian format. One Anglican clergyman described
how at the centre of his funerals is a silence, in which he asks
each person to concentrate on just one memory; and a long
prayer of thanksgiving, whose aim is to invoke memories and
has the effect of a eulogy:

> We remember with sadness the pain Freda had to endure in
> her last years . . . We are thankful for her ever-present
> sense of humour . . . We are thankful for the patience that

her past pupils remember as her hallmark as a teacher . . .
We remember the joy she felt in nature, and her lovely
garden . . .

You might call this a religious life-centred funeral.

A funeral director in the South of England who is also a
practising Anglican told me how for his non-believing clients
he offers to conduct the ceremony himself, along life-centred
lines. One English friend of mine, an evangelical Christian,
herself arranged – with total integrity – a do-it-yourself life-
centred funeral for her unbelieving father, which she and her
family found most rewarding. My own father's memorial
service was similar. I also know a hospital chaplain and a
Baptist minister who, on request from families with no
religious faith, have conducted life-centred funerals.

These clergy and other Christians are making their funerals
more life-centred; and secular and humanist celebrants in the
United Kingdom are subtly changing their promotions pitch
from secular to life-centred. We are in fact moving rapidly
towards the life-centred funeral, but nobody in the United
Kingdom has yet been willing publicly to admit that this, not
religion *or* secularism, is what many people really want.

21

THE AFTERLIFE

I think that I go to a wonderful tea party in the sky, set in an
English garden, and alternately set in other beautiful places
– with excellent company and very good cream cakes.
Michael Winner, film director

What do I believe happens when I die? To tell the truth this
is something I think about hardly at all.
Mrs Mary Whitehouse, campaigner for Christian morality

There seems to be a basic disbelief in many human beings that
they totally cease to exist after death – they find it difficult to
imagine themselves not existing. It is perhaps easier to
believe in an afterlife than not; and it certainly would be nice
to know that spirit triumphs over matter, or that our frail
earthly bodies could be transformed into some perfect
heavenly body, or that the one we have loved does not
disappear entirely with death. But *is* there an afterlife?

Many human cultures have, like the Greek Stoics, managed
perfectly well without any such belief. My own father, for
example, got through ninety years, with their fair share of joy
and sorrow, without any belief in God or an afterlife. We
humans can only believe, half-believe, not believe, or simply
not know.

Before this century, when you and your loved ones were
likely to die well before your 'three score years and ten',
death destroyed life in its fullness. It left the most terrible gap,
and the wish to believe in a substantial and continuing
existence may therefore have been greater than today. Today
a vaguely continuing ethereal soul seems an appropriate

future existence for an aged aunt who has long since already been dismissed from the real world into a geriatric ward. If we have already put her to death socially by our passionate belief in the younger generation, maybe we do not need to believe she continues in any very tangible form?

According to Gallup Polls, those who believed in life after death declined from fifty-three per cent of the British population in 1963 to thirty-nine per cent in 1974. The European Values Survey conducted in the early 1980s put it slightly higher:

		Great Britain	European Average
		%	%
Believe in:	God	76	73
	personal God	31	32
	spirit or life force	39	36
	sin	60	57
	soul	59	57
	heaven	57	40
	life after death	45	43
	hell	27	23

We cannot infer from this, however, that those who believe in an afterlife necessarily believe in a Christian afterlife. In Geoffrey Gorer's 1963 study of bereavement, only eleven of his 359 respondents held orthodox Christian beliefs about the last judgement, and only another fifteen referred to God or Jesus. High levels (seventy-six per cent) of belief in God do not mean high levels of belief in an afterlife, and belief in an afterlife does not mean belief in an orthodox Christian afterlife.

Even for believing Christians like Mrs Mary Whitehouse, the afterlife simply is not salient. To quote her more fully: 'What do I believe happens when I die? To tell the truth this is something I think about hardly at all. I just feel content to leave it all in His hands and try to make the most of being alive!' I would say something very similar for myself.

Mrs Whitehouse and I are laypeople. Maybe the clergy know what they believe about the afterlife? I suspect they do not. I have already mentioned that when I ask my evangelical theological students what their college teaches about death they refer to lectures on the pastoral care of the bereaved, not on the doctrine of the resurrection. When, after they leave college, their first parishioner asks them, 'Reverend, where is my husband now?', they are shocked to discover they are totally unprepared for this question.

In the nineteenth century theologians continually debated the nature of the afterlife. But not today – neither in the theological colleges nor in the churches. What *is* debated today in Britain, following the Bishop of Durham's publicising of views commonly held among academic theologians, is not what will happen to us, but what happened to Jesus. Many Christians have been alarmed at what they see as the Bishop's woolly view of the bodily nature of Christ's resurrection, but these same Christians hold equally woolly notions of their own future resurrection. Those who live in glass houses shouldn't throw stones.

At the same time as (and perhaps because of) the church's silence on what happens to us after death, spiritualism and the New Age movement are sprouting vision after vision of the afterlife. Here are just a few, currently in the bookshops: Annie Besant, *Death and After* (1906); Anthony Borgia, *Life in the World Unseen* (a former priest's findings as a medium, 1970); Arthur Ford, *Unknown but Known*, and *The Life Beyond Death* (1969); Jane Sherwood, *Post-mortem Journal* (communications from T. E. Lawrence, 1964); M. H. Tester, *The Bewildered Man's Guide to Death* (a statement of spiritualist beliefs, 1970); and Bardo Thodol, *The Tibetan Book of the Dead* (a guide to states of consciousness after death). Clearly, Christians are missing a trick if they think people are no longer interested in the afterlife. The only Christian book you could add to this list is C. S. Lewis' fantasy on life in heaven, *The Great Divorce*, written nearly forty-five years ago.

What then do people today believe about life after death? What is it possible to believe? What do Christians believe?

You cannot conduct a funeral with integrity without first having thought through such questions, even if your congregation has not. And if they take various words you may use about the afterlife to mean something different from you, you ought to know this before you start using such words in a public funeral.

'His soul goes marching on'

'John Brown's body lies a'mouldering in his grave, but his soul goes marching on' sums up what many of us believe today. We believe not in the bodily resurrection of which St Paul wrote, but in some vague continuing essence. John Brown did not die in his entirety, nor is he due for resurrection in his entirety; instead, his body died for ever, while his soul somehow goes marching on without ever dying. A large number of people today have a similar view, not of resurrection, but of the survival of a part of the person called 'the soul'.

With this loss of belief in bodily resurrection has come the increasing popularity of cremation. When John Brown dies in old age (as he usually does these days), with the body already half-shrivelled up, few mourn the body and few want it resurrected. More like 'John Brown's shell has been disposed of by the local authority refuse service – thank goodness – but his soul goes marching on.'

This notion of a soul that survives one's physical death is a version of what many ancient Greeks believed. The philosopher Plato split the human person into body and soul, claiming the soul to be the person's real essence, the body a mere shell; if there is any post-mortem existence for Platonists, it is a continuation of the person's essence or soul. The elevation of soul and mind over body was also reflected in everyday Greek city life, with citizens engaged in political and philosophical debate, and menial manual labour left to non-citizens – slaves and women.

The Hebrews had a more material and integrated view of the human person. If the person went anywhere after death, it was the whole human person that went, not some disembodied part called a 'soul'. For the earlier Hebrew writers, such as King David, the person descended after death to Sheol – a dull and unexciting place of bare semi-existence. Sheol was a sort of half-life for the whole person. Isaiah contrasts this pathetic state with the vibrancy of life:

> For Sheol cannot thank thee,
>   death cannot praise thee;

> those who go down to the pit cannot hope
>   for thy faithfulness.
> The living, the living, he thanks thee,
>   as I do this day.
>
> (Isaiah 38:18–19)

In the centuries before Christ some rabbis developed a more robust idea of a post-mortem existence. This was then developed by the early Christians – in, for example, St John's vivid dream of the last judgement or in St Paul's teaching of a bodily and imminent resurrection. In all the various biblical portraits of life after death it is the whole person that is involved.

Those of us who today think about life after death assume we are going to heaven rather than hell, yet our picture of heaven is much woollier than that of hell, and has been since the middle ages. Whereas the Book of Revelation paints solid and dramatic pictures of both hell and heaven, medieval and later Christian art depicts a hell of real fire engulfing real human beings in real agony, and heaven as a rather ethereal, cloudy kind of place, inhabited not by humans but by cherubs and disembodied souls. As the eighteenth-century Japanese saying goes:

> Judging by pictures
> Hell looks more interesting
> Than the other place.

Today's green movement rejects neo-Platonism, for it proclaims the importance, the desperate importance, of the material world. We have ignored and misused the world, thinking the human spirit would ever triumph; and soon matter will wreak a dreadful revenge on human civilisation. If civilisation is to survive, we must reintegrate body and soul, humanity and the natural world. Perhaps the Jews of old were on to something after all.

Quite what revamped view of life after death the green movement will come up with is not yet clear. Its reverence for matter certainly seems at odds with the esoteric spiritualism of the New Age movement. Surely there must be trees in heaven?

Gone before

Many people today have a clear idea of heaven: it is where they will be reunited with loved ones. Just look at the '*In Memoriam*' column of the local newspaper in certain towns and count the number of notices which add 'Gone ahead' or 'Gone before'.

Chapter 6 recounted how we are heirs of the Victorian obsession with the death of the loved one, so death today equals bereavement – in the theological colleges as well as in the social services departments. Heaven is where the pain of bereavement is healed, in spiritual reunion – not a bodily reunion, but the spiritual reunion of thwarted romantic love.

In the West today the private family performs the same kind of job once performed by traditional religion. A person's ultimate commitments can be discovered by asking questions such as 'Who or what could you least do without?'; 'Who or what is most valuable for you?'; 'Who or what would you die for?' Overwhelmingly, the answers – from churchgoer and non-churchgoer alike – are 'My partner', 'My children', 'My parents'. Family life provides many people in our society with meaning and purpose.

In 1646 the Westminster Confession of Faith declared the chief purpose of man to be 'to glorify God and to enjoy him for ever'. Authoritative pronouncements today come from the pop music industry, telling young people that the meaning of life is to be found in romantic love, and from the advertising industry, telling adults that the purpose of life is to care for their families and to enjoy them for ever.

Just as the sacred family governs our ethics in life, so it governs our view of heaven.

Christian hope

When the priest proclaims 'I am the resurrection and the life . . .', over half of those who believe these words are not thinking what he is thinking. They are thinking of a spiritual reunion with their loved ones. But what does the priest believe?

The New Testament does not teach a vaguely continuing

Platonic soul that never dies: if anything is a denial of death, a continuing essence is. Instead, the New Testament teaches that the human being, the whole human being, really does die; and is really resurrected by the power of God. Its resurrected form is physical – the New Testament talks not of resurrected souls but of resurrected bodies. It talks not of heaven as an ethereal place in the sky, but of God transforming the earth. With this language the New Testament draws on the very concrete and material visions that inspired so many of the Old Testament prophets:

> . . . and many nations shall come, and say:
> 'Come, let us go up to the mountain of the Lord,
>   to the house of the God of Jacob;
> that he may teach us his ways
>   and we may walk in his paths.'
> For out of Zion shall go forth the law,
>   and the word of the Lord from Jerusalem.
> He shall judge between many peoples,
>   and shall decide for strong nations afar off;
> and they shall beat their swords into ploughshares,
>   and their spears into pruning hooks;
> nation shall not lift up sword against nation,
>   neither shall they learn war any more;
> but they shall sit every man under his vine and under
>   his fig tree,
>   and none shall make them afraid;
>   for the mouth of the Lord of hosts has spoken.
>
> (Micah 4:2–4)

Christ used similar language to describe heaven:

> He has sent me to bring the good news to the poor,
> to proclaim liberty to captives
> and to the blind new sight,
> to set the downtrodden free,
> to proclaim the Lord's year of favour.
>
> (Luke 4:18–19)

Perhaps one reason so many Christians today have abolished the afterlife and a future hope is that they have written off most of the relevant texts as 'political'. They are then left with a very weak image of heaven.

In the view of Christ and the prophets, heaven is a transformed earth where justice is done, gifts and abilities used, and peace is everlasting: 'They shall hunger no more, neither thirst any more . . . and God will wipe away every tear from their eyes' (Revelation 7:16–17). It is a time and a place where everything will be straightened out, for heaven is not a passive place of comfort but an active completion of all we had hoped for.

This hope for restored relationships is more widespread than Gorer and other researchers have realised. Richard Hoggart, in his book *The Uses of Literacy* (1957), describes a popular working-class view of heaven in which personal tragedy in the family – induced by war, industrial injury and domestic drudgery – will be straightened out. It may not use words like 'salvation' or 'Christ', but it is very much like the biblical view, mixed with the hope of being reunited with loved ones.

For Hoggart's working-class mother

Life in Heaven . . . is envisaged as a re-creation of the happier side of family life, with God as an extension of her own father (if he was 'a good dad'), and one much more able to straighten things out, not harassed by powers outside the family which he cannot control. Heaven will be, above all, the place for 'straightening out', and for comforting. Things will be easier there; there will be time to sit, to get a good rest. There will be a moderate and understanding 'jacket-straightening' for the 'bad 'uns' who led her such a dance. There will be a reunion with those who have gone before and have since been so much missed; with the lively-spirited young sister whom T.B., aggravated by the mill, took away; with the rickety bright son who went off at nineteen.

Written over thirty years ago, this neo-biblical neo-socialist hope may not characterise the mums who people Thatcher's Britain, but it does describe the grandmums who people Thatcher's crematoria.

However clear or vague our view of heaven – and mine is vague – heaven must remain a mystery; to pretend we know what it all means is distinctly unhelpful. I asked one evangelical hospice chaplain what he believed about the afterlife. He paused before saying, 'You know, the longer I'm in this job, I know less, but believe more.'

This man is returning to the hope of the early Christians. They followed the Scriptures in being rather vague about the details of what happens after death. Not only this, but the Scriptures seem to show considerable development – from the shady Sheol of the earlier writers, through the very earthly hope of some of the prophets, to Paul's bodily resurrection of those with faith and St John's vision of the triumph of the elect. A lot of questions are begged. Only in the later middle ages did scholastics try to fill in all the gaps, resulting in a complicated theology of the afterlife, the multiplication of indulgences and masses for the dead, and the ringing of church bells to call people to pray for the deliverance of the dead from purgatory.

Perhaps all the Christian minister or priest can say with certainty is that God is looking after the one who has died. We cannot use earthly experiences of time or place to describe that care, except as metaphor. In particular, we cannot state the destination of any particular individual. Some Protestants, like some Catholics, are far too ready to praise God that this sister is now with the Lord, or to condemn that man to hell. But it is surely not up to us to decide who is and who is not on good terms with God, for if anything saves us it is surely God's grace, not our love or our spirituality. All we can do is entrust the dead to the love of God.

The chaplain I talked with, like most Christians who work in hospices, has been too challenged by religious people dying badly and atheists dying well to be dogmatic about who ends up where. He has come to believe that the biblical teaching that God has a 'preferential option for the poor' means, among other things, that he has a special love for the dying. Who can tell what goes on in the spirit of the dying? Nor can this man ignore near-death experiences. He cannot ignore the patient who showed no interest in religion, went into what was expected to be a terminal coma, only to come out of it saying he was now a believer in Jesus. This chaplain can only make a charitable assumption as to the eternal destiny of anyone whose funeral he conducts.

Fortunately, this honest doubt about what we do and do not know, do and do not believe, matches most people's faith:

most people, and especially the bereaved, both believe and don't believe. Only sectarians and atheists claim to know with certainty what happens when we die.

One wise Anglican deacon I know never says at a funeral 'This is what I believe . . .', or 'This is what we believe . . .', but 'This is the Christian belief . . .' Her own faith is challenged by death and is not strong enough for the pain facing her; she understands that it is not her own faith that carries the congregation, but the faith of the church. She understands that at this point she is playing not herself but the role of the priest representing the Christian faith. (Though of course at other points in the service she does play herself, sharing the pain of the mourners.)

The living dead

What about those who have no religious faith? Can they live on beyond the grave?

Yes, they can. It was with this news that my African friend comforted those gathered at my father's memorial service (p. 3). He explained how many Africans talk of 'the living dead'. Once born, you live and love, work and hate, and nothing is the same again; this doesn't change when your body dies, for in part others are as they are because you have lived. This is well expressed in a passage from Boris Pasternak's *Doctor Zhivago*, often read at secular funerals. Yura tells Anna on her death bed:

> You are anxious about whether you will rise from the dead, but you have risen already – you rose from the dead when you were born, and you didn't notice it . . . However far back you go in your memory, it is always in some external, active manifestation of yourself that you come across your identity – in the work of your hands, in your family, in other people . . . This is what you are. This is what your consciousness has breathed and lived on and enjoyed throughout your life. Your soul, your immortality, your life in others. And what now? You have always been in others and you will remain in others. And what does it matter to you if later on it is called your memory? This will be you – the real you that enters the future and becomes a part of it.

In our individualistic way of thinking, we all too easily lose sight of this truth. We imagine ourselves to exist as some inner set of feelings, considering the inner me to be the real me, denigrating our effects on others as mere role-playing. When we say things like, 'I'm only playing a role – it's not the real me,' we reveal that we see the real me in inner consciousness, not in external behaviour.

Unfortunately, inner consciousness dies. Fortunately, the effects of behaviour, of mere role-playing, do not. I'm playing the role of author as I write this book, which is – in Pasternak's phrase – an external manifestation of me. Should I die tomorrow, it is such external manifestations that will live on – not only the book (I hope!), but also the conversations I had with many people while preparing it and the myriad minor ways in which these conversations became a part of their lives. It takes less individualistic peoples like Russians, less subjective peoples like Africans, peoples who do not denigrate role-playing, to see this.

Our subjective culture often thinks that what lives on are the bereaved's subjective memories. These do indeed live. But I am saying more than this, for the dead live on objectively, in the form of changed, altered lives, as well as in the inner memories of those who survive. How we have affected others, the things we have made, the people we have helped shape, do truly continue to exist. The dead do live on.

22

FUNERALS AND FORGIVENESS

Grace was not an appropriate name for Rob's aunt. She had
been neither his, nor anybody's favourite person. With some
apprehension, Rob and his family had arranged for Grace to
move four hundred miles to an elderly persons' home in
Canberra, close to them and Rob's brother – her nearest
surviving relatives. They visited her, dutifully, and it was with
a mixture of relief and guilt that one day they heard from the
nursing home that she had died.

Rob was a founder member of the basic Christian community movement, or home church movement, in Canberra,
where they are used to doing things themselves, so it was
natural for him and his brother to lead the service for the
dozen or so who gathered at the Canberra crematorium. The
group comprised Rob and his wife and teenage children,
Rob's brother and wife and teenage children, and one or two
others, including 'the researcher from England'. This little
band had somehow to mark the life and death of one of the
less lovable of God's children.

Somewhat disillusioned with funerals where nice eulogies
are dispensed and everyone is very polite until they go off to
the funeral tea and bitch about the real person, Rob aimed to
bring the funeral and the talking together. He invited us to
share our memories, our feelings, about Grace.

The mums and dads, being true Aussies, pulled no punches
and admitted Grace had not been easy to live with. As
Christians, they were not proud they had found her so
difficult. One of the teenagers piped up: 'I know that's how
you feel, Mum, but when I was little I rather liked Aunty
Grace,' while another recounted happy memories of childhood; the grown-ups admitted she was good with little

children. They also recognised that in the past year or two she had found some faith in God, which had mellowed her.

After ten minutes or so, Rob prayed. He prayed for forgiveness for Grace, he prayed for forgiveness for us and how we had responded to her, he thanked God for her. Then we went up on to the podium at the front, and stood around the coffin, holding hands. An attendant pressed the button and someone read a prayer as we watched Grace's coffin descend below, out of sight.

Anger and guilt

Anger and guilt are two of the most common emotions after someone dies. Some of the anger is irrational: 'Why did he have to die on me just now, when the kids so need a father?'; 'Why didn't the hospital do more?' (when everyone knows he went into hospital to die). Some of the guilt is irrational: 'If only I hadn't gone out today, I'd have got the doctor sooner and he wouldn't have died' (after months of devoted care by the wife of a terminally ill husband). Friends can help by accepting these emotions and by reassuring the bereaved that there is nothing more that they or the hospital could have done.

But much of the anger is reasonable. People do die because of incompetent doctors and because of cuts in hospital financing. People do die in football stadiums because of incompetent stewarding and policing.

Much of the guilt is reasonable too. When someone dies suddenly, the statement 'I could have done more' is probably an honest assessment. With the wisdom of hindsight we see that we wasted a tragic amount of time on trivialities, time which could have been spent in cementing and enjoying a precious relationship. Few of us relate to our parents, our partners, our children as though this day were the last: 'If we knew that life would end tomorrow, would we still waste today on our quarrels?' Too often, we forget to reach out and tell those we do that we love them; and then, suddenly, it is too late.

Those who loved the most are not always those who grieve the hardest. It is not the quality but the intensity of the relationship with the deceased that is crucial, and the hardest grief can be for those close family members with whom you did not get on. Or with the ones you both loved and hated.

Death can be harder than divorce. Listen to therapist Lily Pincus:

> I have heard separated people say, 'It would all be so much easier if he (she) were dead, then I would know where I am.' If she or he were dead, however, it would be much more difficult to acknowledge or express the hate and anger, the recriminations and self-justifications which in divorce or separation can serve as a vent to let out the bad air.

With luck, we can even shake hands with our ex, say thanks for the good times and sorry for the bad, and go our separate ways. But once the person has died it is too late to say sorry, too late to forgive them, too late to change your own behaviour. No wonder, after death, that anger, guilt and regret can linger on for months or years. No wonder, if the funeral is all sweetness and light, that the funeral tea will be all recrimination and spite. No one wants to speak ill of the dead; and when we do, we feel guilty.

Simply giving vent to anger doesn't necessarily release it; it may make us feel guilty, or it may give us satisfaction and a thirst for more venting. Talking about guilt to a friend or a therapist doesn't get rid of it if you truly have wronged someone – though it may help resolve irrational guilt feelings.

Rob understood both the necessity for forgiveness and the value of asking for forgiveness together. He also understood that you can neither forgive until you have first faced up to how you have been wronged, nor ask for forgiveness until you have first understood how you have wronged. So, before we could pray for forgiveness, we had to admit truthfully how Grace had been and how we had been.

A Quaker friend told me enthusiastically that Quaker funerals are always positive, with only the good things about a person remembered. Tolerance is the key. If the person was a bit crochety, a bit of an Aunt Grace, someone would mention that she'd had a lot to put up with in life, struggling through difficult times valiantly and in her own way.

The Quaker approach obviously has its merits. It assures us

that the person is worth mourning. It assures us that we will not be spoken ill of at our own funeral (surely a major reason for the injunction not to speak ill of the dead). It can prevent irrational guilt and anger from spilling over and hurting others.

But what about reasonable guilt, reasonable anger? Things have *not* been perfect, and we have *not* yet made amends. Until we face up to the truth of our, and her, failings, we cannot seek forgiveness, for ourselves or for her. If we do not face up to this together in the safety of funeral ritual, it may come out under the influence of alcohol an hour or two later, or under the influence of psychotherapy a decade or two later. The drink can loosen our tongues in quite hurtful ways, the therapy can be a ridiculous waste of resources as several mourners go off individually to their therapists, each coping separately with their own negative emotions about the deceased. You have loneliness enough when bereaved, there's no need to add to it.

Secularism is incapable of resolving real guilt once someone is dead. Christianity, on the other hand, can explore the real guilt of both living and dead, and offer forgiveness; so for those mourners whose only religious contact is at the funeral, this ceremony provides a unique opportunity.

When the person has been dying slowly there may be no need for all this. When I know you are dying we each have to live in the light of our mortality, and it may be the first time you and I have truly been honest with each other. Partners often report that their marriage became completed in its dying days, the first time they have lived within the truth that neither partner, nor the marriage itself, is immortal. Homosexual men with AIDS may for the first time discuss being gay with their parents, and mutual understanding may develop; for the first time, the parents may meet and accept the man's partner. When you know you're going to die this kind of miracle can and does happen. But all too often it does not. The church may even compound things, adding to guilt and disillusion, rejecting the dying person with AIDS.

In Chapter 11 I said that funerals belong not just to individuals but also to groups. Just as individuals use funerals to mourn, so groups use funerals to affirm their values, and the most common group to control the funeral is the family.

Fortunately, forgiveness is one of the key values of living together in families, so it may be possible openly to seek and find forgiveness as part of a family funeral like Aunt Grace's.

Forgiveness, the chance to start again after failure, is also inherent in education. At the funeral of one school teacher who died in harness, the head teacher began his address by calling him by his nickname, which alluded to the fearsome persona he put on when patrolling the corridors. This allowed the children to mourn the man they knew, and to forgive him.

I suspect it is also possible publicly to face up to forgiveness in the funerals of political figures. Politics is the art of accepting that no one is perfect, and together we will talk a way through things; it is about compromise, about men with

"He's just been doing the revised Stalin period at school."

feet of clay. War, on the other hand, is about pretending we are always right, about pretending God and righteousness are on our side only. The theologian Haddon Willmer sees politics as a structure of forgiveness, a way in which we accept the mess we and others have got ourselves into and together work out how to patch things up. I can imagine the indiscretions of a politician being alluded to at his or her funeral, and forgiveness emerging, for politics, after all, is all about making the best of a bad job.

But there are groups where forgiveness is not part of the group ethos. There is no forgiveness for an Edward VIII; no forgiveness in the army for the soldier who is a coward, a traitor, or who becomes a pacifist; no forgiveness in the police force for the officer who is exposed as crooked. Edward did not receive a state funeral. The cowardly soldier is unlikely to receive a full military funeral.

So, *some* funerals provide an opportunity, a structure, for the communal seeking and finding of forgiveness – when relationships were intense but bad, when the death is sudden, and when family or perhaps political values dominate the funeral. But guilt and forgiveness cannot usually be addressed as directly as they were for Aunt Grace, and this is because of the vexed question of *who* is offering forgiveness. Forgiveness does not come cheaply.

Cheap grace

In the winter of 1988 Emperor Hirohito of Japan died, and it was announced that the Duke of Edinburgh would attend the funeral on behalf of the Queen. The Duke had himself served in the Far East during the war, and his attendance could in part become an act of reconciliation.

A furore followed. The Burma Star organisation of veterans who had served in the Far East in the Second World War were outraged. How could this mass murderer, on a par with Hitler, be honoured by heads of state attending his funeral? How could there be reconciliation for such atrocities? It was bad enough when in the 1970s the Emperor had visited the United Kingdom as Japan's head of state – though that was perhaps acceptable since he was indeed head of state.

Attendance at the funeral, however, implied respect for him as a man.

On BBC Radio's *Thought for the Day* the Bishop of Oxford clarified things. The only people who can forgive are those who have been wronged. The Duke could not go on their behalf and offer a forgiveness they were not able to give. This was cheap forgiveness, cheap grace.

The problem is not confined to the funerals of emperors. Few funerals are like Aunt Grace's, conducted by one who has hurt or been hurt. Most are conducted by a priest or celebrant who is neither guilty nor angry about the deceased. How can he or she offer forgiveness on behalf of the congregation? Indeed, how can he or she even think to raise the matter? Colin Murray Parkes rightly warns that to speak ill of the dead is to increase the risk that the so-called minister will be rejected by the bereaved; the would-be comforter will become the offender against all decency.

This is where liturgy comes in.

Liturgy and forgiveness

If the priest or celebrant is prevented from naming the sins of either living or dead, he or she can include readings and prayers addressing the problems of anger, guilt and forgiveness in a more general way. Those who feel angry or guilty can plug into this; those who do not will ignore it.

The Bible is full of passages expressing anger at God. Job and the Psalmist knew what it meant to pass through the dark night of the soul, to 'Rage, rage against the dying of the light' as Dylan Thomas put it. Job is there in the traditional Catholic office of Matins for the dead:

> My soul is weary of life,
>   I will speak in the bitterness of my soul,
> I will say to God do not condemn me,
>   show me wherefore thou contendest with me.
> Is it good unto thee that thou shouldst oppress me,
>   that thou shouldst despise the work of thine hands?
> Thine hands have made me
>   and fashioned me together round about,
> Yet thou dost destroy me.

Even Christ on the cross cried out: 'My God, my God, why hast thou forsaken me?'

For millennia the Greek Orthodox funeral has included prayers of forgiveness. As the whole community shares the *koliva* bread, the symbol of resurrection, you say 'May God forgive him', as you hand the bread on to the next person. Now the cord of life has been cut, everyone must forgive and forget.

The revised Scottish Episcopal funeral rite of 1987 includes these two optional prayers:

> Forgiving God,
> In the face of death we discover
> how many things are still undone,
> how much might have been done otherwise.
> Redeem our failure.
> Bind up the wounds of past mistakes.
> Transform our guilt to active love,
> and by your forgiveness make us whole.
> > Lord, in your mercy
> > Hear our prayer

> God our Redeemer,
> you love all that you have made,
> you are merciful beyond our deserving.
> Pardon your servant's sins,
> acknowledged or unperceived.
> Help us also to forgive as we pray to be forgiven,
> through him who on the cross
> asked forgiveness for those who wounded him.
> > Lord, in your mercy
> > Hear our prayer

The Scottish Episcopal church is rediscovering the ancient need for both the living and the dead to be forgiven.

But many other churches are abandoning such prayers of forgiveness, such readings of pain. The Church of England has never been good at this. In the middle ages the Catholic church taught that all the dead faced a common purging and that all the living could help them through it. As the Catholic scholar Eamon Duffy stresses, death was something we all faced together, binding us together in one great communion transcending earthly divisions between serf, clergy and lord. But for Thomas Cranmer, the architect of the Church of England Prayer Book, who was influenced by the doctrine of predestination that divided the elect from the damned, there was no need to seek forgiveness for the sins of those elected to salvation, and no point in seeking forgiveness for the sins of those predestined to damnation. Sin was simply a condition of the world, out of which the elect are thankfully removed. Dealing with sin could no longer be an active ingredient in the funeral, as this prayer from the Prayer Book funeral service makes clear:

Almighty God . . . We give thee hearty thanks, for that it hath pleased thee to deliver this our brother [sister] out of the miseries of this sinful world; beseeching thee, that it may please thee, of thy gracious goodness, shortly to accomplish the number of thine elect, and to hasten thy kingdom . . .

The 1980 revision of the Prayer Book – the Alternative Service Book – passed up the opportunity to include prayers of the kind the Scottish Episcopals introduced later in the decade. Perhaps this is because the ASB is a product of the late 1960s and 1970s, dominated by a liberal theology in which the love of God (rightly) came to be stressed, but to the exclusion of sin. An affluent, never-had-it-so-good 1960s could perhaps believe such a theology, but post-Vietnam, post-Watergate, post-Ethiopia, post-Chernobyl it has come to look somewhat inadequate. God is a God of love, but has a world of sin to deal with.

The American Methodists revised their funeral service back in 1916. In the very midst of the horrors of the Great War, they omitted the traditional quotations from Job, and edited Psalm 90 to omit all reference to God's wrath!

Eamon Duffy is worried by recent changes in the Catholic rite which leave out that tremendous and terrifying hymn of judgement, the *Dies Irae*. The requiem mass, whose object is to pray for the soul of the deceased, is back-pedalling on judgement, with hope and comfort squeezing out the reality of sin. Duffy's criticism could just as well have applied to the American Methodists of seventy years earlier:

It is characteristic of a post-Enlightenment bourgeois culture that it was the . . . psychological effect of the *Dies Irae* which led to its banishment. Its universal scope, its admittedly formidable yet deeply scriptural association of this death, and the moral worth of this life, with the universal, with justice and human destiny on the grandest scale, have been too lightly sacrificed.

The modern Christian funeral has become two-dimensional, fitting the liturgy

for the use of those for whom death is the seemly affair of geriatric decay in hygienic hospital seclusion which our society has elected as its model of the ideal death . . . Sudden death, violent death, unjust death, cruel death: these find little voice in the new liturgy.

Worse, those who grieve a peaceful death are not helped to identify with the universal suffering of those, from South Africa to Armenia to China, who mourn the sudden deaths of famine and injustice. We have locked ourselves within 'a provincial and unrepresentative cultural experience of death'. We collude to pretend that death is not an injustice, not an offence.

Our post-Enlightenment bourgeois culture, intending to comfort the bereaved, obsessed with assuaging the pain of grief, has done the very thing that makes some grief impossible to come to terms with. It has eradicated the possibility of mourners at the funeral, communally and before God, sorting out the sin that has marred their relationship with the deceased and with their Maker. You don't have to go to a *secular* funeral to seek in vain for sin; and without sin, there is no forgiveness.

23

DOING IT YOURSELF

'I'd like to buy a coffin.'

'You mean you'd like me to arrange a funeral?'

'No, I'd like to buy a coffin – 5′5″ and as plain as possible.'

'You don't want me to arrange the funeral?'

'No, I want to do it myself.'

'Well . . . I suppose it's all right.'

'Oh, yes, I know it is – I've done it before.'

Such was the encounter between Jane Warman and the funeral director when she went to buy a coffin for her mother. Why did she want to arrange the funeral herself?

Recently she had helped with the funeral of a close friend who had died of cancer; he and his wife had decided that he should die at home, and that a few people close to him should do as much for him as possible – even after he died. Jane wrote afterwards:

I felt privileged to have been part of this; it made a bond between the four of us who helped and I believe that knowing that we personally did everything we could has made it easier to grieve . . . This certainly was the feeling after arranging my mother's funeral a few months later. The previous experience made it possible for me to carry out her funeral. I knew much more what was possible; but also what changes I could make in the arrangements. Before she died, my mother and I discussed much of what should be done.

For many people, the physical action of placing a loved person in the coffin and closing the lid is inconceivable, but there are usually others, perhaps friends or relations, who could and would like to help. Also many people think that there is a lot to be done in preparing the body – in fact, usually very little needs to be done and there is usually someone, perhaps a district nurse, who could help if necessary.

Several people helped with the funeral arrangements. Rather than hold the main ceremony in the crematorium, a friend offered their nearby large house in the countryside. About fifty people came. Jane's two little daughters took part – the nine year old accompanied a professional singer on the recorder, and the seven year old read a poem she had chosen. There was no master or mistress of ceremonies, but a printed programme told each participant when to come in. Afterwards, the close family went to the crematorium for a short committal ceremony, which also had a printed programme. The funeral had great dignity, yet was intimate and personal.

For many of those present this was the first do-it-yourself funeral they'd been too. Several said afterwards that it was the most wonderful funeral they'd ever been to, a real celebration of a life. I have yet to come across anyone who arranged a funeral themselves and then regretted it. If minor things do not go to plan, you can have a laugh about it afterwards – but if the funeral director makes a mistake, you may feel very bitter.

Reasons for doing it yourself

It is not unusual for people, after caring for their loved ones during a terminal illness, to want to continue this care after death. Why should they hand everything over after death to a funeral director, when they have rejected handing everything over before death to high-tech hospitalised medicine? Why should care suddenly be handed over to strangers just because the moment of death has been reached?

Others are unwilling to pay what they see as exorbitant sums to a funeral director.

These are the two most common reasons in the United Kingdom, Australia and the United States for people wanting to organise the funeral themselves.

It is of course entirely a matter of choice. As Jane Warman writes:

For some, the greatest way of showing their love, respect and grief is to have the ritual of an arranged funeral, and that is right for them, but for others perhaps the knowledge that one can do it extremely simply, personally and cheaply may be of benefit.

Some facts

There is no law in the United Kingdom that says you must:

1. Use the services of a funeral director.
2. Use a coffin (though there may be local bye-laws or regulations).
3. Have a funeral.
4. Hold the funeral in a licensed building (unless you want the funeral conducted in England according to the Anglican religious rite).
5. Have a clergyman or other official preside at the funeral.
6. Be buried or cremated in an official cemetery or crematorium.

Contrary to popular belief, you have enormous scope to do things your way.

However, the next of kin are responsible for procuring a death certificate (two certificates for cremation), registering the death, and disposing of the body in accordance with public health regulations. Moreover, individual cemeteries and crematoria have regulations that go beyond what the law insists on, and public health regulations limit how and where you can dispose of a body. All this means that organising a funeral is not something that can be mugged up overnight, especially when you are in a state of shock. You need either time and ample preparation, or to belong to a group that regularly arranges its own funerals.

There are three kinds of do-it-yourself funeral:

1. Doing without a funeral director.
2. Doing without clergy or other professional celebrants.
3. Doing without a licensed crematorium or cemetery in which to hold the ceremony, or in which to dispose of the body.

The simplest way of doing without all of these is to donate

your body to the nearest medical school. The body will be used either for research or for teaching anatomy, and when they have finished with it after a few months they will arrange for it to be cremated. If you are interested in such a donation, you should contact the hospital and make arrangements; but do discuss this with the rest of your family, and ascertain from the hospital under which circumstances they will not want your body. Families have discovered to their dismay only after death that the hospital did not want a corpse riddled with cancer, and have hurriedly had to make other arrangements for disposing of it.

Doing without a funeral director

Many of us today who are seeking alternatives to the mass-produced consumer society are learning how to do things for ourselves that professionals used to do for us: some of us convey our own houses, or teach our own children at home, or learn complementary medicine.

However, organising a funeral is not always easy; it may come at an unexpected time, and can't always be organised months in advance like a wedding. Dispensing with funeral directors and arranging the funeral yourself is perhaps easiest when – as with Jane's mother – the death is predicted, there is a good relationship both between the dying person and the next of kin and between the next of kin and other close family, and together they can arrange the funeral in advance as a mutual act of love.

Do make sure you discuss things with other close family. One man, an engineer, decided to make coffins for himself and his wife and do the funeral their own way – a down-to-earth, no-nonsense fellow, he found funerals impersonal and a rip off. He forgot, however, to consult with his children, who of course would most likely have to arrange at least one of the funerals! Do-it-yourself funerals work only as a *shared* act of love.

Laying out the body

Apart from acting as a carrier, the main job of a funeral director is to look after the body, so you must be prepared to do this or arrange for someone else to do it. If the person dies at home, you could ask the community nurse to complete the last offices, or you may wish to do this yourself. Lay the body on the back with the hands at the sides, close the eyes (placing coins or cotton wool on the eyelids will help), support the jaw with a pillow, and plug all the natural outlets of the body with cotton wool. After the doctor has certified the cause of death, wash the body, brush the hair and dress in whatever clothes you desire. All this should be done fairly soon, before rigor mortis sets in. (Details from the Age Concern Fact Sheet, listed at the end of this book in Appendix III, 'Further Reading'.)

If you are going to keep the body in the house until the funeral, choose a north-facing room that you can keep cool. The body may begin to show some signs of decay after a few days, though any offence will be to personal sensibility rather than to hygiene. Some people have said that to witness the changes to the body as day succeeds day has actually helped them come to terms with the death.

Visiting the crematorium

Before the death, arrange to visit the crematorium or cemetery where you wish the body to go, and ask to see the manager. He (it usually is a he) may be a little surprised to see you if he hasn't before come across people wanting to do their own funerals, but he'll probably be extremely helpful. Crematoria managers rarely meet their customers face to face, so it can be a treat for them to meet you; they will tell you about procedures and what forms to fill in, and advise you what is and is not feasible. Typically, they will offer you far more options than will a funeral director.

After the death, you will have to return to the crematorium office with the relevant documentation and fill in the forms giving permission to cremate (which would otherwise be filled in on your behalf by the funeral director). This can be a helpful ritual in itself. Since you do not have to find a time for the funeral that suits both a funeral director and clergy, as well as the crematorium, you may well be able to book a slot at the crematorium or cemetery somewhat sooner (or at a time more convenient for you) than had you gone through a funeral director.

Coffins

In practice, though not in law, you will need a coffin – a crematorium or cemetery is a public place which at any one time will have a range of visitors, and it is reasonable that the feelings of both the visitors and the staff are not offended. Brookwood Cemetery, near Woking, is to my knowledge the only cemetery in London that will allow coffin-less burials: it is popular with Muslims who, strictly, should be buried in a shroud. There may be one or two other such cemeteries in other parts of the country.

So long as it will not collapse, the coffin does not have to be elaborate; handles are purely for decoration and you can do without them. There should be some way of sealing the coffin against leakage – the crematorium manager will advise on such practicalities. You may make your own coffin, or get a local joiner to do it.

To my knowledge, there is only one retail outlet currently selling coffins to the British public. This is Sepulti Cash-&-Carry Coffins, Timberman DIY, 106 Church St, Gainsborough, Lincs DN21 2JU (Tel. 0427 810121). In 1989 a good quality basic coffin there cost £56, plus carriage if you wanted it delivered. No manufacturer has yet developed a mail-order self-assembly coffin, which obviously would ease storage problems between the time of purchase and the time of use. People can be quite creative at storing their coffins, using them in the meantime as coffee tables and bookcases – and as topics of conversation!

You will be able to buy a coffin, at rather greater cost, from some local funeral directors. Those belonging to bigger chains may not be willing to sell you one, but small independent firms are more likely to.

Transport

To transport the coffin, you will need an estate car, a Dormobile, or a small van, and four to six people.

Individual or group?

Although the most newsworthy do-it-yourselfers tend to be individuals, the majority of home-grown funerals are actually organised not by individuals or individual families, but by groups. Some stable communities (religious, occupational or residential) have worked out how to do their own. The group has a member or two who know how to lay out a body, another who can instruct relatives on how to carry a coffin, and so on. The group hires a funeral director only for those aspects of the funeral that the group cannot master for itself – procuring a coffin perhaps, or transport and storage in the event of a member dying abroad.

The only groups I have encountered that regularly do this are religious groups – Orthodox Jews, Muslims, and certain house churches – and traditional communities on some of the more isolated Hebridean islands off the West Coast of Scotland. However, I see no reason why a social group such as a Working Men's Club or a local Women's Institute, an occupational group such as a trade union, or a residential group such as a commune, an old folks' home or a hospice could not arrange its own funerals. The London Lighthouse shows it can be done; this new centre for people with AIDS has its own mortuary, viewing room, and a room designed to accommodate funerals, and is certainly in a position to do the whole thing itself, should anyone want.

Effectively, such groups act like local communities of old, reducing the funeral director back to someone who undertakes to provide a few specified goods or services. Funeral directors will usually co-operate, since a) they get a long-term contract to supply coffins to the group and b) even though they make less money than if they arranged the whole funeral themselves, this is better than losing the trade altogether. Also, selling a coffin without other services is an easy way to make a profit.

(Even if you do not belong to a group that arranges its own funerals, and you do not feel like doing it all yourself, there are many small ways in which you can make a funeral more personal. These are outlined in Chapter 13.)

Doing without clergy or secular celebrants

If you do not want to pay a stranger to conduct the funeral ceremony, who is to lead it?

It can be entirely appropriate for individuals taking small parts, like reading a poem, to be seen to struggle with the lump in their throats, but the congregation must feel secure that the overall leader will not break down and will remain sensitively in control. Though close relatives may well contribute to the ceremony in important ways, only rarely will one of them be the right person to be the master or mistress of ceremonies.

The key to organising an alternative funeral ceremony is therefore to find an MC who knows both the deceased and the bereaved, but not so well as to have a major need to grieve themselves. (Which, of course, is why a conscientious vicar can often do the job rather well.)

Quaker funerals do not have an MC, but Quakers are used to MC-less meetings. So I strongly recommend that you find someone to hold things together. *What* is held together can vary, from spontaneous tributes from the floor to prearranged readings. One solution is to do what Jane and her family did: print a detailed programme, so every participant knows their cue.

If you are organising the service yourself, do go through it first with the crematorium or cemetery officials at which the ceremony is to take place. It is no good arriving with a tape of the deceased's favourite music, only to find that the crematorium has no tape equipment; or planning on everyone placing flowers on the coffin, if the catafalque is out of reach.

What to consider in preparing for the ceremony is covered in Part Three of this book, but do bear in mind the following:

1. Death is a contradiction. It is natural, yet an obscenity. It demonstrates the final triumph of our bodily nature, yet raises the most spiritual of questions. It is universal, happening to us all, yet each death is a unique experience. It can evoke both sadness and thankfulness.

Ordinary language is poor at capturing these paradoxes. By contrast, poetry, songs, art, silence, can begin to express the inexpressible. Symbolism is what it is all about.

2. When someone dies, anger and guilt are common emotions as well as sadness and thankfulness. A funeral that does not recognise these emotions will not be real to some of those present. If you ditch religious language, you will have to think hard about how to enable people to acknowledge such feelings.

3. Death is a transition. Most cultures express this in physical movement or procession: walking behind the coffin, throwing earth on to the coffin. Modern crematoria and modern city traffic are rarely conducive to this kind of symbolic physical movement, so you will have to be creative!

4. It is rare to be able to pack everything into the funeral itself. Feel free to have other rituals, perhaps sharing memories at home before or after the funeral, or a time for recollection and moving on a year later.

Doing without a cemetery or crematorium

One reason for wanting to do it yourself is that you have found cemeteries and crematoria distressing or offensive places. One possible solution, increasingly common in California, is to have the body cremated with no ceremony at all, to be followed some weeks later by a memorial ceremony in a place of your own choosing – perhaps your own home, the pub, the local park, a mountain or a forest. An increasing number of secular memorial services are held in the United Kingdom usually for public figures whose friends and relations in the arts, education and politics are used to public speaking.

I would not encourage omitting the body from the funeral, unless this is unavoidable (or because you wish to donate the body to medicine), but there are all kinds of places where a funeral can be held. The public funeral for Jane's mother was held in their friend's house; this worked well because the place was homely, beautiful, meant something to the family, and was large enough. Pubs and clubs, the sort of place you might have your wedding reception, are also possibilities.

It is all right if you want to hold the main ceremony somewhere other than a cemetery or crematorium, but what if you want to bury the body yourself, on your own territory?

In the United Kingdom, you have to get the permission of the local authority environmental health officer. You are unlikely to get permission for burial in a suburban garden (registered cemeteries have to be a hundred yards from the walls of the nearest dwelling, according to the 1956 and 1906 Burial Acts), but what if you should wish to have the burial in the

wood at the back of your garden or in your favourite
meadow? The local council will be concerned about the same
dangers as if you were digging a latrine, which like a grave
contains decaying human matter: they will need to be assured
that the site is not near a water course, and that the body will
be properly wrapped.

In practice this is a matter of public decency more than
physical health. After all, you can bury a pet in the garden,
and there are many suburban gardens which could accommodate a single human grave without any danger to physical
health. But the feelings of your neighbours are important, as
indeed are the feelings of anyone to whom you may in future
want to sell your house and garden. But it is possible: one
owner of a medieval manor house recently got permission to
reinstate the house's private chapel, which is physically a part
of the house, and to be interred therein in due course.

The steps you should take are these:

1. In good time, contact your local funeral director in order
to check the local situation, what to do, and who in the council
to see. The funeral director may even offer to do this for you,
or put you in touch with someone else locally who has done a
home burial. Other funeral directors may be less co-operative,
in which case, ring around and find one who will tell you what
you need to know.

2. See the environmental health officer of your local
council, and discuss the particular site you are considering.

3. If you get the okay, put it in your will.

Be prepared for officials who may be less than helpful or
unclear about the law. The law in Scotland on home burials is
more obscure than in England, but the above steps are still
the ones to take.

Should you want to *cremate* on your own property, in law it
is still a matter of environmental health, but this will be
interpreted by the authorities much more strictly, and I know
of no such private cremation in Britain in the twentieth
century. Perhaps if you are a Scottish laird, owning miles
and miles of deserted grouse moor, there might be no
objection?

Finally

The deceased, the next of kin, other relatives and friends may not each want the same kind of funeral or disposal, and this can be the cause of considerable friction. There are two points to bear in mind:

1. The next of kin, not the deceased, has the right in law to determine the form of disposal (including donation to a medical school) and the type of funeral. You can state in your will, with all the force of the law, the disposal of your possessions, but you can state only a preference when it comes to the disposal of your own body.

2. Nevertheless, the next of kin would be wise to bear in mind the deceased's wishes, along with the wishes of other friends and relatives, and weigh these along with his or her own wishes. The next of kin is not the only person who is bereaved.

24

THE FUNERAL TRADE

The funeral-directing trade is often in the press; this was particularly true in Britain in the late 1980s while I was researching this book. As well as the continuing concern about the cost of funerals (Chapter 7), there is another reason for media coverage – the decision of one particular funeral director, Howard Hodgson, to abandon the usual attitude of 'the less news about funeral directors the better', and positively to sell himself, his business and his views through the news media. The press are delighted to respond to the overtures of this flamboyant character.

With or without Mr Hodgson, however, there are two current causes for public concern: take-overs, and pre-need selling.

Take-overs

Until a decade ago most funeral directors were small family firms, with the large Co-op chain the only exception of any size – though there has been a steady reduction in the number of firms since the Victorian days when British towns were grossly overstocked with undertakers. The 1980s have seen dramatic changes, with groups such as Hodgson Holdings and Kenyon Securities (which merged in 1989 and then became part of the French firm Pompes Funèbres Générales) and the Great Southern Group, buying up small family firms. Often the small firm cannot find another family member to take on the business – it can be a twenty-four hour on-call and not particularly glamorous business – or high interest rates may prevent it from investing in updated equipment. Usually the deal includes retaining the employees and the old firm's name, a valuable asset if well-trusted locally. The new owner will retain the old business as a shop-front and selling-point, but centralise into regional offices other facets of the business such as vehicle maintenance and embalming.

These ever-expanding firms claim that this kind of rationalisation is more efficient, and will result in better value for the customer. But according to the 1989 survey of funeral costs by the Odd Fellows Manchester Unity Friendly Society, the cost of a basic funeral is now £736, up £200 or thirty-seven per cent from 1986; and according to the 1989 Office of Fair Trading report, funeral prices since 1975 have risen by twenty-eight per cent above the rate of inflation. So perhaps this 'rationalisation' is not reducing but adding to costs, as bodies and staff are trundled around from one specialist office to another. Or is it perhaps that the new corporate owners are extracting a higher profit?

The policy of the big new chains is to buy a lot of firms in any one area, so that the chain has enough turnover and enough premises to permit rationalisation and specialisation. In some towns such as Aberdeen this has led to a local monopoly or near-monopoly, which obviously not only reduces consumer choice but could also lead to higher prices.

One problem the bereaved have experienced, according to the Office of Fair Trading report, is that many funeral directors do not abide by their own code of practice in providing customers with written estimates and fully itemised bills, though the evidence for this is disputed by the National Association of Funeral Directors. Firms continue to slap around three hundred per cent on to the wholesale price of the coffin to cover sundry expenses, with the result that the customer does not know what she is paying for. It may well prove easier for consumer organisations and the National Association of Funeral Directors to get a few big and well-organised chains to put their house in order than it has been to raise standards among hundreds of old-fashioned family firms which are reluctant to change the generations-old practices of their forefathers.

What other effects might result from small family firms being absorbed by large national, or even international, conglomerates? From the point of view of the customer, the strength of the family funeral directors is that they can deal with their customers more personally, rather like the local grocer; the weakness is that they are less likely to have any formal training (though they have often learned a lot in the school of life). The strength of the larger firms is that their employees are more likely to be formally trained, but this educated professionalism may be at the expense of rootedness in a local community and responsiveness to individual customers.

Bereaved families who have arranged do-it-yourself funerals have found it easier to obtain a coffin from a small family funeral director than from one of the major chains. This suggests to me that the commercial power and professionalism of the bigger chains reduces their responsiveness to customers who do not want the whole package and who wish to use the undertaker as the supplier of certain goods and services rather than as the provider of a take-it-or-leave-it package. The big chains are more than happy to accede to customers' requests, however idiosyncratic (pink coffins, horse-drawn hearses), that add to the standard package, but definitely not to requests for something less than the package. The manager in the local office of a big chain will be unwilling to set precedents such as selling a coffin to a do-it-yourselfer for fear of a reprimand from head office. It is the small owner-manager who can say to the customer, 'Well, I don't see why not,' and pocket the modest but tangible profit.

This then is my main concern about take-overs – that they impose even more of a standardised product on the consumer, a product their research department has advised them is in their own commercial interest and in the customers' emotional interest. Grass-roots innovation from the consumer will consequently find a less willing response from the funeral trade.

I do not propose to discuss the much-publicised take-overs further, because there is nothing the ordinary reader can do about them, and the purpose of this book is to enable you to see and do things differently, if you should choose. There is, however, one feature of the big chains that does give you a new choice: they offer you the option to buy your funeral in advance, or 'pre-need'.

Pre-need selling

I am often asked what I think of pre-need selling. It has existed in America for decades, but is only now coming to Britain.

The funeral business is steady, but difficult to expand. The size of the market is determined by the death rate, and no amount of advertising will increase that. It is a unique business.

Those funeral directors who enjoy the business side of things typically like to expand. There are only two ways to do this. One is to add value to your services, to elaborate the funeral so that it costs more and profits are higher. The other is to get to your customers before your competitors do, which is what pre-need selling is basically about.

Undertakers

The funeral chain sells pre-need, at a guaranteed price, to the healthy middle aged. When they come to die, they are guaranteed a funeral of the quality paid for. The funeral director normally does a deal with an insurance company to finance the scheme, though the customer deals only with the funeral director.

So there's a lot in it for the funeral director. But what about the customers? Well, there's a lot in it for them too.

Normally people do not buy a funeral until the time comes. They are upset and in a hurry, so they hardly ever shop around. They are vulnerable to being exploited, and buying the funeral is an extra chore and worry at a time when there are worries enough already. Paying pre-need changes all this: you can shop around and take time to consider the options. Once the funeral has been bought, the family can be at ease, no longer worrying about the future cost of the funeral to a frail and grieving elderly spouse, as inflation cuts into savings. Everything is sorted out in the clear-headedness of healthy middle age.

People typically want a simpler funeral for themselves than for someone else: 'Oh, don't bother about me. Just tip me in the ground, and have a drink on me.' In pre-need selling the customer is not the bereaved, but the not-yet-deceased, who is likely to opt for a relatively cheap funeral.

Although the price you pay pre-need is usually slightly higher than your family would pay today for an equivalent funeral, it can still make financial sense. More and more as a society, we buy now and pay later, crippling ourselves with exorbitant interest charges, but with the pre-need funeral you pay now and buy later. I strongly suspect that when you work out the interest rates it is not at all a bad deal.

Age Concern and Help the Aged, the two main organisations for the elderly, have each co-sponsored the pre-need deals offered by the United Kingdom's two biggest funeral chains, so I am not alone in giving pre-need my vote of approval.

So much for the advantages. But are there snags?

The funeral-directing industry must be pretty desperate to get into pre-need. Though selling pre-need may increase one firm's share of the market, the likelihood of people buying cheaper funerals pre-need than they would at-need will reduce the overall value of the total market. This might mean more small firms going out of business, and more take-overs.

That apart, once we have all been mopped up pre-need, the industry will be back at square one, with a finite market incapable of expansion. It will find that adding value pre-need is a lot more difficult than in the guilt and shock of immediate bereavement. This is another reason why the end result of pre-need selling has to be some funeral directors going bust.

There is also a potential snag for the general public. Funeral directors do not need to advertise funerals at the point of need. The bereaved come to you, and quick. But you do have to advertise if they are to come to you pre-need, which raises the whole issue of funereal advertising – something Australia has on TV – which may offend public taste, especially if the adverts come in the middle of dinner or while you are escaping contentedly into your favourite soap opera or movie.

One Florida magazine reveals how pre-need enables American funeral directors to engage in all the usual high-pressure sales techniques that had previously been unavailable to them: blitz ad campaigns, telephone sales, special discounts. It also gives them 'a real two-fisted concept: Responsibility and Guilt. Responsibility? There are big savings for those who buy now and die later. Guilt? Those who fail to pre-arrange their funeral leave the "burden" to their children.' British funeral chains are less up-front about all this, but they too use the emotional impact of responsibility and guilt.

Finally, purchasers of the pre-need funeral are stuck with it. They can upgrade the quality, if required; and if they move to another area another funeral-directing firm will honour the deal. But what if, maybe decades later, attitudes change and purchasers want to join a burial society or even do the funeral themselves?

This is not so very unlikely. Many purchasers will attain in retirement a degree of economic stability unknown during an upwardly mobile working life, or at least their children will feel more secure, and it is these higher economic classes that tend to be more interested in simpler and even do-it-yourself funerals. If society continues to want to abandon both the isolation of the individual and the impersonality of bureauc-racy, and move towards a more green, participatory, com-munity-centred society, then attitudes may well change towards more participatory funerals. In which case, those who purchased pre-need funerals in the 1980s and 1990s may face a dilemma as they grow old in the 2020s – whether to continue with the archaic twentieth-century funeral they have already purchased, or to lose their money.

Consumer choice

So far, I have been concerned with funeral directors not offering enough choices to consumers. But neither does the church, and here the funeral director may well be on the consumer's side.

Until a decade or two ago the non-churchgoing non-atheist (probably eighty per cent of the population) who was cremated would be dispatched by an Anglican cleric who was on duty at the crematorium that week. His having to do up to a dozen funerals a day was a major reason for the 'production-line' feeling of such cremations.

This system has been superseded in many areas by one in which the funeral director arranges for the funeral to be conducted by the family's local vicar. This is more hassle for the funeral director, for good vicars are usually out visiting, not waiting by the telephone, and it is difficult to fix a slot that suits the crematorium, the funeral director and the vicar if you can't get hold of the vicar. But the new parish-based system should have provided more personal funerals, the credit for which would in some measure go to the funeral director. (If a family suffers an impersonal rota cleric, the person they blame for not finding someone better is the funeral director.)

Unfortunately, funeral directors are now reporting that the local vicar often isn't much better. Funeral directors nowadays would love to have a free choice as to which cleric they can recommend to the family, a free market in funeral celebrants in which the local vicar is asked only if he is known to do good funerals. This would also enable life-centred celebrants to compete fairly. As one funeral director commented to me wryly, he wants to return full-circle to clergy who specialise in funerals – though with the important difference that they would now specialise because they are good at funerals, not because they are hopeless at everything else!

Years ago, the family would in the first instance go to the vicar, who might advise them which funeral director to use, but those days are long past and nowadays most people go to the funeral director first and look to him for advice as to which clergy to use. Some clergy feel peeved about this, and resist giving the funeral director any choice over who should conduct the religious ceremony, but it is ultimately the family to whom they are denying choice. The result is that there are no controls on the bad vicar.

25

FUNERALS FOR BABIES

We will continue to argue about when life begins. But the end of a foetus is never a nothing.

Hospital chaplain, London, 1988

On Friday 26 August 1983, in a large city hospital, Sue Lyon gave birth to twins, her fourth and fifth children – Miriam and Miguel. This is her account of Miguel's birth:

A midwife sucked mucus out of Miriam's mouth and muted baby yells spoke life. Nothing stopped. There was no delay. As I sat up I felt something else coming out with the movement. It felt soft. I didn't have to push. I wondered if it was the first placenta. But suddenly expressions changed. The Sister quickly dragged a small sheet over my legs, preventing me seeing what I so badly wanted to see. 'Please leave the room, Mr Lyon.' Panic. What did she mean? David refused. 'Leave the room! It could be unpleasant.' She was shouting. She had lost her cool. David hesitated for a moment, being unused to being curtly commanded, and told her he would stay. 'Sue wants me here just now. I'm sorry, I'm not going to leave.' He was at the foot of the bed and saw that I had delivered the second twin. I felt the tension as the Sister continued to tell David to leave. So I asked 'Why should he go?' 'There's something wrong with the second baby,' she said. 'Well, we will have to accept that,' I replied.

David was at my side again. He'd seen the boy-baby and thought his head looked a little strange. He asked why they didn't try to resuscitate him. 'He's been gone a few days,' they said. The truth dawned. Our twin boy, eagerly anticipated for eight months, was dead. We asked straight-away to see him but were told, 'It isn't a pleasant sight. Are you sure you want to?' 'Yes.' Of course we were sure. We had to see our baby. 'We'll show you when we've cleaned him up.'

They hustled the baby out. Someone else thrust Miriam in front of me, as if to say, 'Here is the baby you were expecting.' After I was cleaned up, someone else brought Miguel back in. He was well-wrapped with just his poor little face showing, and lying in a cot. He looked very like Miriam. I said I wanted to see more of his body. I was just assured that he was all there. I didn't *see*.

From then on, I was treated as if I had *only* had *one* baby, but we knew we had had twins – a boy and a girl. Of course we were thrilled with Miriam and very grateful. But we had been given a boy, Miguel we called him, who was born dead.

Revolution

For a generation now, a revolution has been in progress. The revolutionaries are parents like Sue and David. They are challenging the age-old belief that babies who die before, at, or soon after birth are a nothing, an embarrassment, too hideous to contemplate. They are insisting these are human beings, to be loved, held . . . and given a decent burial.

Until just a generation ago little had changed since the middle ages. Foetuses were flushed down the hospital sluice just as in earlier years they had been taken off by the midwife and disposed of, without ceremony. Stillbirths were secretly placed by the undertaker at the foot of an adult woman's coffin, unknown to either the woman's or the baby's grieving relatives. Those who died shortly after birth were typically given a pauper's funeral, in the absence of the parents, in an unmarked grave. Such creatures were not yet human; they were disposed of like animals. In some parts of Britain today this continues; in other parts theirs are among the most personal and moving of all funerals.

An earlier revolutionary was the mother of Sian. Sian died

in 1967, after thirty-six hours of life. Her mother wrote twenty years afterwards:

> At the time of our daughter's death and since, I have been made to feel by people around that, as she was so young, grief would quickly pass. Our desire to have a proper funeral and cremation was regarded as very odd by the funeral director and others. His comment, 'We usually put them in someone else's coffin – why do you want to bother?', still bugs me enormously. I certainly needed the funeral and memorial to help me through that time. Both gave Sian a very definite identity, not just to me but to others, and this was very important for me to come to terms with her death.

Parents are beginning to insist that they have not produced a nothing, an embarrassment, but a child who has died. For the first time in recorded history some of those who die during or before birth are being given a decent burial.

It is now quite common in the babies' corner of a cemetery to see a little gathering: a vicar or hospital chaplain, two parents, perhaps one or two little children, a grandparent or a friend. The husband may carry the tiny coffin, or in the case of an early termination maybe a cardboard shoe-box; the priest says a prayer as the father and a friend lower the box into the ground. The funeral director, if there at all, may stand a step back, with little or nothing to do.

At a time when funerals are becoming ever more impersonal, we find a totally new and utterly personal form of funeral emerging. At a time when death is being taken over more and more by medics, funeral directors and other professionals, we find the most vulnerable group of bereaved parents insisting on, and getting, what *they* want. In a country where only ethnic minorities themselves dress their adult dead, and where white people find this rather macabre, white parents now frequently ask to dress their dead baby or child themselves, in its own clothes. Maura Page's study in the early 1980s found funeral directors in the North of England often reluctant to allow this; if this is now changing, it is only because of pressure from parents. Clergy who until recently refused Christian burial to even full-term babes that had not been baptised, are now conducting funerals for foetuses of only sixteen weeks.

Funerals for those who have died within nine months of conception have, in a generation, leap-frogged from being non-existent to precisely the kind of funeral that this book is advocating and that is otherwise so rare. With little or no help – at least in the early days – from hospitals or funeral directors, some of the most vulnerable bereaved parents have somehow by-passed all the problems described in this book, and shown that funerals can be personal, emotional, healing, participatory, and conducted with integrity. Something significant, something totally against the trend, is happening. But what, and why, and how?

Social birth, physical birth

According to the medics of the middle ages, life equalled breath. It started when you started breathing, and ended when you stopped breathing. Ever since, male academics have split hairs in order to arrive at clear definitions of life and death, definitions that make life easy for lawyers – ecclesiastical or civil.

Unfortunately, things are not that clear cut, as any woman knows who has felt her baby inside her womb. Physical definitions do not do justice to something as rich as human life, and throughout human history, social definitions have been more important.

In the middle ages it was not until baptism, when society welcomed the new human being into its midst, that the baby was considered human. Before then, it was a dangerous object: wild nature, not yet a part of society, and not entitled to Christian burial. Society could not say goodbye to something to which it had not yet said hello.

At the other end, life did not really finish until burial, when the living had done all they could to ensure the departed soul's passage to heaven. Baptism – the arrival of the baby into society – marked its entry from natural to human status; burial – seeing it on its way to heaven – marked its exit from human to spiritual status.

Today we have shifted the boundaries. In the view of many, the beginning of life has moved closer and closer to conception. The end of life, too, comes earlier for many, for old people forgotten in institutions have died socially, if not physically; is it any wonder their funerals have little to mark? We value the old less, and the very young more.

Even as recently as the Victorian period the aged still received more respect, and left a greater gap, than the very young. At the turn of the century *The Lady* advised nine months' mourning for a woman who had lost a grandparent, but only three if she had lost a child. In the advice of today's experts, those figures are reversed.

But even then things were changing. Magazines disagreed over the length of mourning for each category of person. Throughout the nineteenth century, tombs and epitaphs expressed more and more grief over the death of children. The Romantic movement allowed people to invest emotionally rather than economically in their children, and to display grief rather than resignation when they died. By the twentieth century, greatly increased life chances for little children were confirming romantic hope with statistical probability.

It used to be thought that the longer someone lives, the greater the gap when they die. But the death of hopes for the future can cause an enormous gap, as painful as the loss of an actual relationship. Unrequited love can be as painful as divorce. When a baby dies, it is not just an individual that has gone: there is a loss of purpose, of expectation, of hope. Our whole understanding of the meaning of life, of marriage, of our love for one another, disintegrates. I married you in order to raise a family, and now there is no family. When a mother bonds with her baby there is an intense falling in love – and then the object of her love is torn from her.

So, when a baby dies before, during or soon after birth, whatever the scientific definition of what has happened, there can be the most massive loss. Here is Sue Lyon again:

The shock of Miguel's death didn't hit us for a while. The next day, Saturday, I woke feeling a bit upset. On Sunday, David broke down in church, while I had a terrible nightmare review of the birth and woke up in hysterical sobs – it was just as it had all happened until Miriam was born, and then after that I delivered a heavy and solid . . . STONE!

Saying hello, saying goodbye

As a result of pressure from the parents of babies such as Sian and Miguel, hospitals and funeral directors are beginning to take infant deaths more seriously. Maternity wards in many hospitals in Britain now not only take great care over bereaved parents, but have routines to ensure that this care is taken.

My own local maternity unit has a checklist that staff have to fill in following an infant death. This includes ensuring that both mother and father are given the opportunity to see and cuddle the infant (for as long and as often as they like); that a photo is taken and given to them in an envelope which they are free to open if and when they choose; that a booklet on coping with the loss of a baby is given them; and that staff discuss with the parents some or all of the following:

1. The feelings they have experienced.
2. The feelings they are likely to have.
3. How long grieving can take.
4. The possible effects on them of other babies heard or seen in the hospital, encountered after discharge, or yet to be born.
5. Meeting people, both those who know of the loss and those who don't.
6. The options for the funeral.

One of the babies born in this unit was Rosalind, technically defined as a twenty-six-week miscarriage. Her mother told me that before the birth, 'they asked me if I'd like to hold the baby, but I thought, no, it'd probably be deformed. But after the birth, they asked me again, and I said yes, and was glad I did.' She also appreciated being visited by a social worker, the chaplain and by various other concerned professionals. Though hospitals have to offer to pay for funerals only for babies born after twenty-eight weeks[1] (before that they are defined as miscarriages and therefore not in need of a funeral), this hospital offered to arrange and pay for a funeral,

[1] Presumably, this will change to twenty-four weeks as a result of new abortion legislation currently going through Parliament.

which Rosalind's parents accepted. They asked for it to be conducted by the clergyman who had conducted their wedding, and very much appreciated his driving them to the cemetery; they were also pleased that there then arrived a real hearse containing a real coffin. The 'system' – a routinely managed follow-up to an infant death, a contract funeral paid for by the state, and rules slightly bent by caring officials – had served them well.

Clergy are beginning to see that baptism can express the 'hello' that is necessary before the funeral's 'goodbye'. They are responding to the requests from parents that their dead baby be baptised, recognising the pastoral value of this even if it means stretching their theology a little. Steve Webster, an Anglican clergyman whose own daughter Cherry died shortly after being born, writes:

> Traditionally, baptism is seen as an offering to God and a welcoming into the Church of a child or adult who is living. In practice, many chaplains have reached different conclusions . . . Parents need to be sensitively made aware that baptism is not a pre-condition for their child's acceptance by God. Chaplains, on the other hand, need to recognise the therapeutic value of baptism or service of blessing, as a means of affirming the child as a real person, loved by his or her parents and loved and valued by God. Even though my child was not baptised (but prayed for after she had died by my pastor who held her in his arms and blessed her), I believe the parents' wish must sensitively be respected.

When it comes to the funeral, Steve Webster writes:

> It is especially important to parents that their child's name be used and that they be allowed, if they wish, to contribute to the service by choosing a reading, poem or song. A printed service sheet with the child's name on it is a wonderful way to achieve all this.

Soon after Cherry's funeral, Steve and Linda Webster held a memorial service for their friends, recognising that their friends both grieved and wanted to share that grief publicly. A life had ended, and had to be marked.

And the future?

Although the death and subsequent funeral of a young baby is still too often handled impersonally and badly, the trend is away from this. The kind of funeral that is emerging is radical in almost every conceivable way.

The bereaved couple are at the moment of their child's death surrounded by an active group of medical staff who either were expecting a live birth, or are fighting for the life of the baby. They too are shocked and distressed by the sight of a dead infant; they too are bereaved. In the old days, as at Miguel's birth, they may protect themselves from their own grief by banishing the grief of the parents. But increasingly they are being trained to share openly in the shock and grief of the parents. The chaplain is soon called – he too may be a young father, she too may be a mother, and may feel deeply for the parents. Discussion about the funeral is begun with these people in the hospital, and options discussed; only then is a funeral director contacted, if at all.

This is very different from most adult deaths, where almost the first port of call is the funeral director. He does not share the shock and the grief; he can only be sympathetic, professional.

With infant deaths the funeral director is often reduced back down to the role of an undertaker. He does not direct the whole show. The parents have already worked out, along with medical staff and the hospital chaplain or their local vicar, what they want to do; they then contract the funeral director to perform certain specific services.

There are still complaints about impersonal infant funeral services, but things are getting better fast. The service is often conducted by the hospital chaplain, who unlike clergy who conduct the funerals of non-churchgoing adults is likely to have talked with the parents at length. A hospital chaplain is more likely than one of the parish clergy to be a woman, herself capable of bearing children. Nor will someone who has held in her arms the dead child as she baptised it give it a production-line funeral.

One Anglican hospital chaplain told me that he frequently conducts non-religious funerals for babies. He has shared in the grief of the parents, got to know and respect their beliefs and values, and can do no other than mark the death of this child in whatever way respects those beliefs. At a time when religious funerals seem to have a stranglehold on the British public, in the unpublicised infants' corner of the cemetery we find Christian ministers conducting personalised, non-religious funerals. (This particular chaplain tells me he is currently preparing for confirmation a woman at whose request he had conducted a non-religious funeral; she said it was the first time a clergyman had respected her and taken her seriously.)

The baby's older brothers and sisters will be eagerly, jealously, awaiting its arrival. The death can hardly be hidden from them. Too often we stupidly try to protect children from awareness of death, but increasingly they are joining their parents at the new-born baby's funeral. They should be given the choice. If they want to come, it can be a good idea for them to be in the charge of a friend or relative who can attend to them, freeing the parents to attend to their own grief.

Death is fearful for us adults because it is something over which we have no control, no authority; but it is not fearful for children whose lives are already under the authority of adults. Children are continually having to make sense of new experiences; they are continually having to readjust their mental spectacles as some strange new thing appears over the horizon that they have not encountered before. Death is nothing terrible, just another new experience to be adjusted to. But to tell children that this thing, uniquely, cannot be explored – that for this thing there are no spectacles – is to frighten them to the core of their being. As one South African funeral director has wisely written:

> In the face of death, we suddenly have no authority; we have no power to change things . . . But children have not reached such zeniths of authority. The only thing they have some authority over is either the dog or the cat, so for them death is not an abdication of power, it is a learning-experience where they are looking for meaning and truthfulness.

When today a little baby dies the funeral is increasingly likely – against all the historical odds – to have been freely chosen from a range of options, actively to involve the bereaved (including their children), to reduce the funeral director to a spectator, to be non-religious, and to be conducted by a cleric who knows and feels for the bereaved. In short, such a funeral marks the passing of a life in a way that makes sense to those present even at a time when nothing makes sense.

Fortunately, hospitals are getting the message, and many are taking care to train their staff to deal with infant death as a human tragedy, not as an embarrassing medical failure. And many funeral directors are getting the message too, and are now providing what bereaved parents want.

But the question for the future is this: Will this radical new form of funeral, created by pressure 'from below' – from bereaved people – become a model for the general run of adult funerals? Or will it get taken over by the well-meaning professionalism of medics, counsellors and funeral directors? Will they take the baby's funeral away from the people to whom it truly belongs? Will it follow the historical pattern of community-organised death and community-organised funerals being stolen by high-tech hospitals and Cadillac-operating funeral directors? Or is it the first-fruits of a consumer-led alternative to the impersonal, hypocritical, professional funeral that has so tragically become the norm in the modern world?[1]

---

[1] Chapter 19 describes some examples of memorials for young children. In the United Kingdom there are several self-help groups of bereaved parents. The national offices will be able to tell you about local groups in your area. Their addresses are listed in Appendix II.

CONCLUSION

Funerals too often fail to do their job of marking the death of a human being. They fail to give public significance both to a life and to the mysteries of death. Too often we exit from this world with a whimper, in a funeral that is a pathetic surrender to the imbecile rules of petty bureaucracy – for a society that believes in individual human dignity, a truly tragic last statement. A life lived in search of individuality and integrity is finally marked by a public surrender to hypocrisy, impersonality and bureaucracy, and in some places to status and profit.

The roots of this go to the heart of modernity. In Part Two I identified these – a pretended domination over nature which cannot cope with the physical inevitability of death; a self-control which cannot face the uncontrollable fact of death; a deference to the 'reason' and 'science' of males; an obsession with the individual and a cutting off of ourselves from the support of community even at the time when we most need its help; an immersion in a cash culture where everything – even someone to carry our coffin – has to be bought and sold, impersonally; a secularism which prevents us doing anything for the dead. No wonder funerals are lonely and pathetic, plastic and impersonal, with nothing left for us to do.

Funeral directors say that modern people have great difficulty coping with death; and in this they are right. They say that therefore the bereaved, in a state of shock at what they have not been prepared for, need professional people to do things for them; but in this they are wrong. Or at least partly wrong. It is precisely because we all too willingly hand the funeral over to the professionals that it means so little. The funeral will be reformed only when it is reclaimed.

But ordinary people are already reclaiming it. In the streets of Liverpool after the Hillsborough disaster, in London's gay community, among the distraught parents of stillborn children, in the suburbs of Melbourne, we find utterly modern people reclaiming the funeral for themselves. They are rediscovering the strength of community, they are participating creatively even while grieving deeply, they are reducing all-knowing funeral directors back to servant undertakers, they are doing their own thing if they find the church hypocritical.

The tide is turning. It is turning because the history of the modern world is turning. The women's movement is challenging male domination, the green movement is challenging our technological hubris and our isolating individualism, religious faith is by no means on the way out, the consumer movement is challenging know-it-all professionalism, and an increasingly educated public is beginning to demand what it actually wants. Such currents are transforming modernity, and empowering those who reject the technological, impersonal, isolated, bureaucratic, male-dominated funeral.

These new funerals are many and various. How you mark a death, like how you live a life, is largely governed by your ultimate faith; and since we live in a multifaith society, so we must have multifaith funerals. Faith in family life; faith in reason, technology and practicality; faith in the God of various official religions; faith in ethnic or other group identity (whether Jewish, gay, or Welsh); faith in self-actualisation as the human project – explicitly or implicitly, these faiths profoundly affect what goes on in the modern funeral.

In practice most funerals will be a mishmash of two or more such faiths – Christianity and family-worship, Islam and practical reason, military ethos and self-fulfilment. I myself am sceptical of the absolute faith some of us moderns place in the family, in self-fulfilment, in secularism, and in technological man; however, I cannot but be profoundly influenced by these faiths. They are a part of me, and will affect my own funeral. But I hope my funeral will challenge these faiths too, for death and the funeral both complete and challenge what we as a society live for.

So I am not recommending any one model. It depends on

your own values and commitments, your own beliefs about life and death. In a plural society these must be respected if funerals are to be conducted with integrity. What is certain is that the standardised product too often offered today by the local funeral director, the local church and the local authority is to many an offence.

Over to you

In my experience, on those rare occasions when someone requests a different kind of funeral, the funeral trade is more than willing to co-operate. The real block is not the funeral trade but our own unwillingness to contemplate the funeral, to work out what we want, and to organise it.

During a recent training session at a hospice, staff were asked to brainstorm on the word 'funeral'. They came up with negative images – black, death, coffin. Then they each had to devise their own funeral, which everyone did with surprising enthusiasm. Most wanted some input into their own funeral, if only by choosing a hymn; one woman wanted to go out in style in a Norse longboat that was covered in candles, floating out to sea! Then they brainstormed again on the word 'funeral' and this time positive images came pouring out.

One reason the funeral is stuck in the sterility of modernity is that people do not know of any alternatives. Time and again I have met people – whether it be Jane in Chapter 23, or the gay community in Chapter 13, or suburban Australians in Chapter 20 – who have needed to see a different model in practice before they could see how to arrange a more meaningful funeral themselves. Very few of us will launch out into something that seems to us totally original, least of all at a time of grief; we need to know someone else has tried it, and that it works. That is why in this book I have described lots of different models that are currently being tried, so that many more than those who attended those particular funerals will have their eyes opened to wider horizons.

My hope is that, by unearthing what makes a good funeral and by giving examples of people who are in the vanguard of change, this book will help you mark the death of those you care for – with integrity.

APPENDICES

Appendix I

PLANNING A FUNERAL:
A CHECKLIST OF OPTIONS

This checklist covers the issues raised in this book.

Ordinary people will only reclaim the funeral if they think about it in advance, in good health, and with family and friends.

Leaving a written statement of your preferences can be helpful to your survivors, though it is not legally binding.

Try to arrive at some consensus between what you want and what they want – when you are writing your will is a good time.

Please note that this is not a technical or legal 'What to do when someone dies' checklist (which in any case would vary from country to country). Some useful publications are listed under the heading 'Practical' in Appendix III, 'Further Reading'.

Disposing of the body

☐ Cremation. If so, where and how to dispose of the ashes? (see Chapter 17)

☐ Burial. If so, where? (see Chapter 18)

☐ Donation of the entire body to medicine. If so, you will not have to organise a funeral, but consider holding a memorial service.

☐ Donation of specified organs to medicine, with the body returned immediately for burial or cremation.

The funeral ceremony

☐ Religious, secular, or life-centred? (see Chapters 8 and 20)

☐ Anyone in particular to conduct the funeral? (see Chapter 12)

☐ Think about different ceremonies, perhaps one for close family and another for the wider circle of friends. (see Chapters 14 and 15)

☐ Where to hold the ceremony (or ceremonies), especially if cremation is envisaged? (see Chapter 17)

☐ What kinds of personal participation in the ceremony would mourners value? (see Chapter 13)

Who is to organise the funeral? (see Chapters 11 and 23)

☐ Would your family like to organise the funeral themselves?

☐ Do you belong to a religious or other community that organises funerals itself?

☐ If neither of the above, is there a particular funeral director you prefer?

Paying for the funeral (see Chapters 7 and 24)

☐ How much will the survivors be willing to pay?

☐ Methods of payment:
  ☐ Pay at the time of the funeral
  ☐ Pre-need contract with a funeral director
  ☐ Insurance scheme

Memorial (see Chapter 19)

☐ Would you like a specific memorial?

☐ What kind?
  ☐ Physical (e.g., a stone)
  ☐ Social (e.g., a party)
  ☐ Financial (e.g., endowing or giving to a charity or a local organisation)

Appendix II

NATIONAL OFFICES OF
SELF-HELP GROUPS

The following will be able to tell you about local groups in your area:

Age Concern, Pitcairn Road, Mitcham CR4 3LL (Tel. 081-640 5431)

The Compassionate Friends, 6 Denmark Street, Bristol BS1 5DQ (Tel. 0272 292778) – an international organisation of bereaved parents whose child (of any age, including adult) has died from any cause

Cot Death Support Group, 148 Hoppers Road, London N21 (Tel. 081-882 4363)

Cruse, 126 Sheen Road, Richmond, Surrey TW9 1UR (Tel. 081-940 4818) – a national organisation for widows and their children

Gay Bereavement, Unitarian Rooms, Hoop Lane, London NW11 8BS (Tel. 071-837 7324)

Help the Aged, St James Walk, London EC1R 0BE. (Tel. 071-253 0253)

Miscarriage Association, PO Box 24, Ossett, West Yorkshire WF5 9XG (Tel. 0924 264579)

Stillbirth and Neo-Natal Death Society (SANDS), 28 Portland Place, London W1 (Tel. 071-436 5881)

Support After Termination For Abnormality (SATFA), 29 Soho Square, London W1 (Tel. 071-439 6124)

FURTHER READING

There is a vast literature on death: attitudes, philosophy, bereavement, etc. With a few exceptions such as the very first section, the following selection concentrates on the much smaller literature on funerals.

Practical

Care of the dying

Shirley du Boulay, *Cicely Saunders* (Hodder & Stoughton, 1984). A biography of the founder of the modern hospice movement.

Robert Buckman, *I Don't Know What to Say* (Macmillan, 1988).

Harriet Copperman, *Dying at Home* (Wiley, 1983).

Derek Doyle, *Coping with a Dying Relative* (MacDonald, 1983). A practical manual on home care, but stops short at the moment of death.

Deborah Duda, *Coming Home: A Guide to Dying at Home* (Aurora, 1987). American, explores legal and spiritual aspects, and has a section on funerals.

Elisabeth Kübler-Ross, *On Death and Dying* (Tavistock, 1970). The classic work on the psychological stages of coming to terms with one's own death. (See also the section entitled 'Psychology', below.)

Arranging a funeral

Age Concern England, *Arranging a Funeral Factsheet*. Free

from Pitcairn Road, Mitcham CR4 3LL (Tel. 081-640 5431).

Church Information Office, *Funerals and Ministry to the Bereaved* (1989). A useful handbook, mainly for clergy, but also for funeral directors, cemetery and crematoria staff.

Consumers' Association, *What to do When Someone Dies* (Hodder & Stoughton, 1986).

DSS, *Help When Someone Dies*. Leaflet on social security benefits.

DSS, *What to do After a Death*. Leaflet.

Marion Wright, *A Death in the Family* (Optima, 1987).

Funeral ceremonies

Ian Ainsworth-Smith and Peter Speck, *Letting Go: Caring for the Dying and Bereaved* (SPCK, 1982). A helpful book, written mainly for clergy. Chapter 5 is on funerals and other rites around the time of death.

Ian Bunting, *Preaching at Funerals* (Grove Booklets, 1978).

Wesley Carr, *Brief Encounters* (SPCK, 1985).

David Durston, 'The Funeral Service in the Process of Grieving', *Bereavement Care* (Summer 1990). Explores the role of regression in the funeral, and how the funeral relates to the stages of grieving. Author conducts in-service training courses for clergy on funerals (write to The Vicarage, Sheriffhales, Shifnal, Salop, TF11 8RA).

Dally Messenger, *Ceremonies for Today* (Armadale, Victoria: Brian Zouch Publications, 1979). A useful source-book of readings and examples of Australian life-centred funerals.

Jane Wynne Willson, *Funerals Without God: A Practical Guide to Non-Religious Funerals* (British Humanist Association, 1989). Invaluable, not only for professional secular celebrants, but also for anyone who wishes to conduct a life-centred funeral.

The cost of funerals

Two recent British reports are:

Manchester Unity Friendly Society, *1989 Odd Fellows Survey of Funeral Costs*, 4 pages, free from 40 Fountain Street, Manchester M2.

Office of Fair Trading, *Funerals*, January 1989, 46 pages. (A critical response to this report is available from the National Association of Funeral Directors, 618 Warwick Road, Solihull B91 1AA.)

Bereavement

There is now a large number of popular books on bereavement (too many to list here), often written from personal experience. Your local bookshop will stock several. (See also Appendix II, above, and Colin Murray Parkes, *Bereavement*, in the section entitled 'Psychology', below.)

Children and death

E. Grollman, *Talking About Death* (Boston: Beacon Press, 1970). Explains death through the parent and child reading the book together.

J. Krementz, *How it Feels when a Parent Dies* (Gollancz, 1986). Eighteen children tell it like it is.

Stillbirth and Neo-Natal Death Society (SANDS), *The Loss of Your Baby*. A booklet for bereaved parents.

Academic

The following publications are listed:

1. As a brief guide for those who want to read deeper.
2. In place of detailed references, to acknowledge those authors on whom I have drawn, directly or indirectly, and to whom I am indebted.

The academic literature on twentieth-century funerals can be easily summarised. There is something on the funeral ritual of virtually every traditional society studied by anthropologists; a flurry of publications in the late 1950s and early 1960s on American funerals; and virtually nothing on modern funerals elsewhere. Psychological studies typically deal only with personal grief in the modern world, and ignore funeral rites. The result of all this is that little is known about the private face of death in traditional societies, or the public face of death in modern societies.

The most illuminating books on the public face of death in the West are by historians who, against the trend, seem to have taken this subject to their hearts. Philippe Ariès and Clare Gittings, who explore the transition from traditional to modern Europe, are among the very few authors who try to bring together the views of psychologists and anthropologists, which otherwise have no point of contact (for their works, see the section entitled 'History – Europe', below).

The United Kingdom

There are no up-to-date books on the British funeral. The following sociological and anthropological studies are helpful in giving an idea of where we have just been, rather than where we are now:

David Clark, *Between Pulpit and Pew* (Cambridge University Press, 1982). A study of folk religion in the Yorkshire fishing village of Staithes. Chapter 7 is on birth and death.

Judith Ennew, *The Western Isles Today* (Cambridge University Press, 1980), pp. 92–6.

Geoffrey Gorer, *Death, Grief and Mourning in Contemporary Britain* (Cresset, 1965). A classic study, this includes Gorer's seminal article, 'The Pornography of Death' (first published in *Encounter*, October 1955), which introduced the idea of death as the taboo of this century.

F. G. Vallee, 'Burial and mourning customs in a Hebridean community', *Journal of the Royal Anthropological Institute* 85 (1955), pp. 119–30.

W. M. Williams, *The Sociology of an English Village: Gosforth* (Routledge, 1958).

There is also the following up-to-date material:

Shirley Firth, 'The Good Death: Approaches to death, dying and bereavement among British Hindus' in A. Berger (ed.), *Perspectives on Death and Dying* (Philadelphia: Charles Press, 1989).

Lindsay Prior, *The Social Organisation of Death* (Macmillan, 1989). Highlights how modern death is bureaucratised.

Bernard Smale, *Deathwork* (Surrey University PhD, 1985).

An excellent but unpublished sociological study of English and North American funeral directing.

Rory Williams, *A Protestant Legacy: Attitudes to Death Among Older Aberdonians* (Oxford University Press, 1990). Good background reading to my Chapter 8.

The United States of America

This section includes not only material on funerals, but also a few examples of the vast North American literature on attitudes to death.

Robert Blauner, 'Death and Social Structure', *Psychiatry* 29 (1966), pp. 378–94. An important and influential article.

LeRoy Bowman, *The American Funeral: A Study in Guilt, Extravagance, and Sublimity* (Greenwood Press, 1959).

Richard G. Dumont and Dennis C. Foss, *The American View of Death: Acceptance or Denial?* (Schenkman, 1972). An excellent exploration of the thorny issue of whether Americans accept or deny death; essential for anyone wanting to ask the same question in another country.

Robert L. Fulton, *The Sacred and the Secular: Attitudes of the American Public Toward Death* (Milwaukee, WI: Bulfin, 1963).

Richard Huntingdon and Peter Metcalf, *Celebrations of Death* (Cambridge University Press, 1979). The final pages analyse the modern American funeral. (See also the section entitled 'Anthropology', below.)

Jessica Mitford, *The American Way of Death* (Hutchinson, 1963). The classic exposé of profiteering by the American funeral trade. Weak on why Americans want expensive funerals, but gave a big boost to the memorial society movement.

W. Lloyd Warner, *The Living and the Dead* (Yale University Press, 1959).

Evelyn Waugh, *The Loved One* (Chapman & Hall, 1948). A hilarious novel, mocking Americans for their belief in the funeral trade. Waugh, like Mitford, is a British author who sees dignity in simplicity.

Glenn M. Vernon, *Sociology of Death* (New York: Ronald Press, 1970).

Other modern countries

Graeme M. Griffin and Des Tobin, *In the Midst of Life: The Australian Response to Death* (Melbourne University Press, 1982).

R. W. Habenstein and W. M. Lamers, *Funeral Customs the World Over* (Milwaukee, WI: Bulfin, 1963). An encyclopaedic world survey, commissioned by the American Funeral Directors Association and justifying their own practices by highlighting the expense and elaborateness of funerals around the world.

Christel Lane, *The Rites of Rulers* (Cambridge University Press, 1981). On Soviet ritual; contains short but useful sections on funerals.

History – Europe

Philippe Ariès, *The Hour of Our Death* (Allen Lane, 1981) – first published in France as *L'Homme Devant la Mort* (1977). A vast and dazzling survey of European attitudes and practices from the middle ages to the present; it has been severely and justifiably criticised, but we are nevertheless in Ariès' debt for having opened up the subject.

Philippe Ariès, *Western Attitudes to Death: From the Middle Ages to the Present* (Johns Hopkins University Press, 1974). An early summary of Ariès' work, worth reading first.

Clare Gittings, *Death, Burial and the Individual in Early Modern England* (Croom Helm, 1984). Highly recommended.

Ralph Houlbrooke (ed.), *Death, Ritual, and Bereavement* (Routledge, 1989). A collection of essays covering the period 1500–1930, about half on the Victorian period.

John Morley, *Death, Heaven and the Victorians* (Studio Vista, 1971). Highlights the commercialism and status-seeking of the Victorian funeral. Contains a fascinating chapter on mourning dress (the source for my quotations from Victorian fashion magazines).

Ruth Richardson, *Death, Dissection and the Destitute* (Pelican, 1989). A history of the 1832 Anatomy Act, exposing the origins of the British fear of the pauper burial. A gripping read.

Joachim Whaley (ed.), *Mirrors of Mortality* (Europa, 1981). A useful collection of essays. Includes David Cannadine's 'War and Death, Grief and Mourning in Modern Britain', which attacks the conventional Gorer/Ariès adulation of Victorian mourning rituals; Cannadine argues that Victorian funerals were like twentieth-century American funerals, exploiting status-conscious people in a mobile, insecure society (see also V. Gordon Childe, *Man* 45 (1945), in the section entitled 'Anthropology', below). Cannadine's essay contains a fascinating account of war memorials and spiritualism, 1918–39.

History – United States of America

James J. Farrell, *Inventing the American Way of Death, 1830–1920* (Temple University Press, 1980).

R. W. Habenstein and W. M. Lamers, *The History of American Funeral Directing* (Milwaukee, WO: Bulfin, 1962).

David Stannard, *The Puritan Way of Death* (Oxford University Press, 1977).

Literature

Many novels include funeral scenes, providing good insights into funeral traditions. There are too many to list here, but see:

D. J. Enright, *The Oxford Book of Death* (Oxford University Press, 1983). A useful anthology of readings on death from novels, plays, poems and philosophy – though unfortunately containing only a short chapter on funerals.

Two short stories specifically about funerals (both of which raise the question of who the funeral belongs to) are:

Thomas Hardy, 'The Grave by the Handpost' in *The Distracted Preacher and Other Tales*, ed. Susan Hill (Penguin Books, 1979), pp. 331–42. The story highlights the importance of a proper burial.

Alifa Rifaat, 'At the Time of the Jasmine' in *Distant View of a*

Minaret, and Other Stories (Heinemann, 1983), pp. 77–87.
A delightful Egyptian story.

Anthropology

Helpful summaries of the anthropological literature on death rituals are to be found in Danforth and in Huntingdon and Metcalf.

Maurice Bloch and Jonathan Parry (eds), *Death and the Regeneration of Life* (Cambridge University Press, 1982). Analyses the frequent presence of fertility symbols in death rituals.

V. Gordon Childe, 'Directional Changes in Funerary Practices During 50,000 Years', *Man* 45 (1945). Argues that funerals become more elaborate at times of social instability.

Loring Danforth, *The Death Rituals of Rural Greece* (Princeton University Press, 1982). Intriguing analysis, drawing on Hertz and Lévi-Strauss; superb black-and-white photographs.

Jack Goody, *Death, Property and the Ancestors* (Tavistock, 1962).

R. Hertz, *Death and the Right Hand* (New York: Free Press, 1960). This key essay by a student of Durkheim lay untranslated for half a century. It shows how funeral rites – through affirming social solidarity – enable society, as much as the individual, to recover after the loss of a member. Hertz introduced the idea that the fate of the body models the fate of the soul.

Richard Huntingdon and Peter Metcalf, *Celebrations of Death* (Cambridge University Press, 1979). A good introduction to anthropological approaches to funeral rites.

John O'Shea, *Mortuary Variability: An Archaeological Investigation* (Orlando, FL: Academic Press, 1984).

Arnold Van Gennep, *The Rites of Passage* (Chicago University Press, 1960). First published in French in 1909, the book abandons the Victorian notion of ritual as 'primitive'; it contains the seminal idea that rites of passage contain three stages, developed later by Victor Turner, *The Ritual Process* (see the section entitled 'Ritual', below).

Psychology

Ernest Becker, *The Denial of Death* (New York: Free Press, 1973). A stimulating, maverick book, drawing critically on Freud and Kierkegaard: the human personality is based on repression of our physical nature, epitomised in sex and death. The denial of death is therefore not a peculiarly modern thing, but *the* fundamental human condition.

Elisabeth Kübler-Ross, *On Death and Dying* (Tavistock, 1970) – see also the section 'Care of the Dying', above. Trail-blazing, sensitive studies, based mainly on those dying of cancer – not necessarily generalisable. More recently Kübler-Ross has worked with people with AIDS.

Colin Murray Parkes, *Bereavement: Studies of Grief in Adult Life* (Tavistock, 1972). By a leading British expert; based largely on studies of widows whose husbands died before their 'three score years and ten'.

Lily Pincus, *Death and the Family* (Faber & Faber, 1976). How a widow grieves depends largely on the kind of marriage that has been lost. Helpful in pinpointing why people grieve in different ways.

Paul C. Rosenblatt, *et al.*, *Grief and Mourning in Cross-Cultural Perspective* (Washington: Human Relations Area Files Press, 1976). Secondary analysis of seventy-eight cultures, representing human culture around the world. Attempts to discover which mourning patterns, if any, are universal (finds little evidence that Christianity significantly affects funeral behaviour). Unusually, this study is based on learning theory, and is a stimulating antidote to the neo-Freudian theories of grief that are popular today (e.g., it disagrees that modern people deny death).

Architecture and design

The Churchyards Handbook (Church House Publishing, 1988). Includes photos of the best of English gravestone design.

Gilbert Cope (ed.), *Dying, Death and Disposal* (SPCK, 1970). Chapters 6 and 7 on crematorium design.

James Stevens Curl, *A Celebration of Death* (Constable, 1980). Encyclopaedic and fully illustrated introduction to the buildings, monuments and settings of funerary architecture in the Western European tradition.

Landscape Design 184 (October 1989). A special issue of this monthly journal, on cemetery design, including an article by Frances Clegg (see also my Chapters 18 and 19).

Theology

Gilbert Cope (ed.), *Dying, Death and Disposal* (SPCK, 1970). A very helpful collection of articles.

Geoffrey Rowell, *The Liturgy of Christian Burial* (SPCK, 1977). An introduction to the historical development of Christian burial rites.

Although not specifically about funerals, there is a large amount of literature on resurrection. For example:

S. G. F. Brandon, *The Judgement of the Dead* (Weidenfeld & Nicolson, 1967). A historical and comparative study of the idea of a post-mortem judgement in the major religions.

Hans Küng, *Eternal Life?* (Collins, 1984).

H. A. Williams, *True Resurrection* (Mitchell Beazley, 1972)

Rowan Williams, *Resurrection* (Darton, Longman & Todd, 1982).

Ritual

Roger Grainger, *The Unburied* (Churchman Publishing, 1988). Drawing on literature, social science, and the author's experience as a hospital chaplain. Excellent on the funeral as drama.

David Martin, *The Breaking of the Image* (Blackwell, 1980). A sensitive analysis of the nature of symbols, not specifically about funerals.

Bruce Reed, *The Dynamics of Religion* (Darton, Longman & Todd, 1978). A classic on the relation between congregation and priest, focusing on dependence and regression. Reed, like Turner (below), sees an oscillation between everyday life and religious ritual.

Victor Turner, *The Ritual Process* (Penguin Books, 1974). Draws on Van Gennep's (see the section entitled 'Anthropology', above) notion of liminality – the 'betwixt and between' experience dramatised in rites of passage.

INDEX

Numbers in italic refer to pages in the Bibliography.

THE C. S. LEWIS CENTRE

The C. S. Lewis Centre for the Study of Religion and Modernity is a Christian research organisation working in partnership with Hodder & Stoughton to publish thought-provoking material concerning the relationship between the Christian faith and the modern world. Following C. S. Lewis' example, it is the Centre's policy to reach a broad market, speaking to the ordinary person in an intelligent and informed way, and responding to the challenge presented to orthodox belief by the secular culture of our contemporary society.

For further information about membership, or about the Centre's publications, tapes, seminars, workshops, etc., please write to: The C. S. Lewis Centre, 47 Bedford Square, London WC1B 3DP.